THE CONCEPT OF MEANING

THE CONCEPT OF MEANING

by

THOMAS E. HILL
Bloedel Professor of Philosophy
Macalester College
Saint Paul, Minnesota

HUMANITIES PRESS

NEW YORK　　1971

SBN 391-00121-3

Library of Congress Catalog No.: 72-135982

Printed in the United States of America

TABLE OF CONTENTS

PREFACE

Most significant studies of meaning are rightly focused upon restricted ranges of meanings, but occasional attempts to see the subject in larger perspective are also required. The present inquiry is concerned with meanings of words in languages and of spoken and written sentences, but it is also concerned with a wider spectrum including meanings of spoken and written sentences, of signs and symbols, of physical and historical events, of material objects and mental images, of poems and paintings, of sculptures and symphonies, and even of life and of the universe. Its principal problem is that of formulating one or more concepts of meaning that does justice to the diversity of meanings and helps to illuminate the relations among the varieties of meanings.

By examining in some detail the main factors that enter into meaning situations, this inquiry attempts to formulate conditions requisite to an adequate conceptual characterization of meaning. In introducing discussion of each main factor, it sketches the thought of one or more advocates of a theory that tends to equate meanings with that factor, but discussion of each factor is focused primarily, not upon specific criticism of the theory through which that factor is introduced, but upon the relation of that factor to meanings themselves. In the ninth chapter, the inquiry arrives at a concept that appears significantly to characterize all varieties of meaning, but without in itself constituting an adequate concept either of meaning in general or of any particular variety of meaning. The final chapter attempts to support an account of the major varieties of meanings as distinct functions satisfied by the common concept developed in the previous chapter. The account of meaning that emerges is offered, however, not as a substitute for other accounts, but as a preliminary characterization of certain basic features of meaning concepts in which more useful operational accounts may well be grounded.

Although the parts of the book are intricately interwoven, readers who are primarily interested in review of current theories may wish to focus attention on chapters four through eight. Readers who are primarily interested in a systematic study of problems of meaning may wish to emphasize chapters one through three and chapters nine and ten.

The present inquiry grew out of the research involved in the preparation of my *Contemporary Theories of Knowledge;* it became a fascinating enterprise in its own right; and it leads into investigations preliminary to a subsequent book on *Value Concepts.* The philosophers to whom I am indebted are too numerous to name here. Professor Alan Donagan and Mr. David Lantz have read parts of the manuscript. Professor Keith Gunderson and Mr. Martin Gunderson have read the entire manuscript. I gratefully acknowledge helpful suggestions from each but hold none accountable for my errors. For the inspiration of my wife and her gracious assistance, I am, as always, thankful.

Macalester College
Saint Paul, Minnesota, 1970   Thomas E. Hill

INTRODUCTION

"Inferior to many of his animal competitors in strength and instinctive endowment, man owes his own superior accomplishments to an intelligence that can be construed in part as a capacity to create, apprehend, and be guided by meanings." Although the functioning of this capacity does not require reflection upon itself, it is often improved by such reflection; and while such reflection is usually directed to particular meanings, it inevitably rests upon more general assumptions about the character of meaning. Such assumptions themselves are often confused and in need of a criticism that, if well done, may yield clarifications all along the line of cultural advance. Contemporary linguists, anthropologists, sociologists, psychologists, theologians, and philosophers seem not unmindful of this consideration and are converging upon problems concerning meaning from a variety of different perspectives.

The majority of recent inquiries concerning meaning, instead of attempting to take into account the whole range of what is meaningful, have been focused upon language; and even among language-oriented studies, the center of attention has often been not meaning as such but linguistic expressions. Most writers who have been directly concerned with meaning of linguistic expressions have been mainly concerned with meanings of particular expressions. Thus despite current appreciation of the importance of meaning, direct and inclusive inquiries concerning meaning remain relatively rare.

In the endeavor to focus sufficiently upon the concept of meaning to bring to light the principal features of that concept and at the same time to achieve enough breadth of perspective to permit each aspect of the inquiry to be informed by what can be learned from the others, the present inquiry will attempt to take account of all of the main varieties of meanings of all of the main kinds of things that are properly said to have meanings. It will not, however, attempt either to establish meanings of particular signs or symbols, or to formulate a scientific theory of meaning in the sense of a conceptual scheme in the application of which meanings can be predicted, or to achieve an operational definition of any mode of meaning. Its main purpose will rather be to contribute to the sort of initial clarification of the concept of meaning that constitutes a prior condition to the formulation of any adequate scientific theory or of any operational definition of any mode of meaning.

The principal term indicative of the concept of meaning is the noun "meaning" as ordinarily used in such expressions as "a meaning," "the meaning," "my meaning," "his meaning," etc. Various forms of the verb "to mean" are also linked with the concept of meaning in that objects of the verb "to mean" are often properly referred to as meanings as, for example, what "book" means is often properly referred to as the meaning of "book", and what my statement means is sometimes properly referred to as the meaning of my statement. However, objects of the verb "to mean" are not always properly referred to as meanings. For example, when someone is said to mean John, John is not properly said to be his meaning; and when my gesture means Fred, Fred is not properly said to be the meaning of my gesture. Only when what is meant is appropriately called a "meaning" is the concept of meaning directly applicable to it.

The terms indicative of the other concepts that are closely associated with that of meaning and require consideration in any adequate account of meaning, such as "word," "sentence," "context," "response," "reference," and "use" are, like the term "meaning", all nouns in common use. Insofar as possible, all of these and other terms employed in the inquiry are to be employed in their ordinary senses. When for clarity special senses must be stipulated, these will be selected, as far as possible, from among ordinary ones and they will be specifically defined.

Inquiry concerning the concept of meaning appears to be confronted at the outset with at least two difficulties that require initial comment. One concerns the possibility that there are no meanings, and the other, the possibility that there is no single concept of meaning.

W. V. Quine, while by no means denying that "words and statements are meaningful," refuses "to admit meanings" lest he "invite hypostasis of meanings as entities."[1] In a similar vein, Max Black declares that "although words and gestures have meanings, there are no meanings that can be designated, and hence no philosophical problems of assigning such supposedly designated entities to the appropriate categories."[2] A good many other distinguished philosophers agree with Quine and Black on this point. But whether or not these philosophers are correct in holding that there are no meanings, examination of concepts, including that of meaning, fortunately requires no prior commitment concerning the existence of that to which these concepts are supposed to apply. To be sure one would not ordinarily wish to carry inquiry concerning a concept very far without some prospect that in some sense it made sense to talk about there being instances of the applicability of that concept; but the applicability of a concept can only be adequately determined as understanding of the concept itself advances. Eventually, in the course of the inquiry concerning the concept of meaning, the concept of meaning may become sufficiently clarified and sustained by acceptable examples to dissolve serious doubts concerning its applicability. Meanwhile, lest inquiry concerning the concept of meaning appear less interesting, on account of such doubts, than it need appear, a few initial remarks concerning the applicability of the concept of meaning may be in order.

If talk about meanings implies that meanings are things or events or ideal entities having causal properties, and if every use of a word is supposed to be a reference to a meaning, then talk about meanings may indeed be misleading and erroneous. But talk about meanings need not, and does not ordinarily, carry any such implications. We repeatedly talk about masses, fields of force, biological functions, social trends, diseases, virtues, properties, concepts and much else that does not in the strictest sense exist, without being unduly tempted to think that we are referring to particular things, events, or ideal causal entities; and there is no more reason why we must be so tempted in the case

---

[1]W. V. Quine, *From a Logical Point of View* (Cambridge: Harvard University Press, 1953), p. 11.

[2]Max Black, *Models and Metaphors* (Ithaca: Cornell University Press, 1962), p. 24.

of talk about meanings than in these other cases. Moreover, as in our ordinary discourse we speak and write, while we are quite ready to recognize that we are referring to the things or events that we are talking about, we do not suppose that we are referring to our meanings. To say that John's utterance had a significant meaning need not suggest that any thing or event was tied to that utterance as its meaning or that what it meant caused anything to happen, nor does the ascription of meaning to John's utterance imply that John was referring to his meaning. Ordinarily, meanings are meant but not referred to though they may be involved in referring to other things; and when they are referred to, it is usually not by their own bearers but by other terms. In any case, whatever may be the risks involved in talk about meanings, people continue, not only to speak, write, and respond as though words, things, and events had meanings, but also to talk about meanings with full assurance that they are neither talking nonsense nor speaking in deviant ways; and no way whatever has yet been suggested for talking about what people seem to be talking about when they talk about meaning save by way of using such terms as "meaning." Accordingly, the most promising procedure in the matter in hand is presumably to begin, not by abandoning such terms as "meaning," but by endeavoring to discover what people are getting at in using these terms.

 Whether or not there are any meanings, some philosophers have grave doubts concerning whether or not there is any single concept of meaning. They are disposed to think that there is a whole family of concepts of meaning. If, in fact, what is referred to as the concept of meaning is a whole family of concepts, this would of course block the path of an inquiry based on the assumption of the unity of the concept of meaning; but it need be no serious obstacle to the sort of inquiry undertaken here. Indeed, if the manner in which meaning phenomena are conceived involves the sort of diversity indicated, a primary purpose of the sort of inquiry undertaken here is to disclose this fact. Actually, the existence of a family of concepts of meaning would not even require the modification of the title of the inquiry; for the title need imply no more than the consideration of whatever conceptual factors are connected with the term "meaning" in the indicated sense. The inquiry is an endeavor, not to achieve a monistic interpretation of meaning, but to represent the conceptual factors involved in meaning as having no more and no less unity than is indicated by the kinds of instances in which we do, or would be prepared to, use the common noun "meaning."

Responsible inquiry concerning any concept, requires careful examination of situations in which the terms to which a concept answers occur. Apart from such examination, there can scarcely be any adequate determination of criteria for the use of these terms, the properties which anything must have for these terms to apply to it, or any other features of the functioning of the terms that are pertinent to the character of a concept. Inquiries that endeavor to clarify the concept of meaning usually begin by laying down initial definitions of meaning and subsequently attempting to show that other features of meaning situations and other concepts related to that of meaning can be brought into conformity with these initial definitions. The concept of meaning is, however, notoriously complex, and this sort of direct approach to it has yielded an embarrassing diversity of irreconcilable views each focusing attention upon certain aspects of meaning to the neglect of others. Accordingly, I shall reverse the usual procedure and attempt initially to examine in some detail other features of meaning situations and other concepts related to that of meaning that are both interesting and in their own right and significantly suggestive with respect to the character of meaning. I shall then come directly to consideration of the concept of meaning only after prior examination of these related matters has brought to light some major requirements of an adequate account of the concept of meaning and some significant suggestions concerning the character of such an account.

A meaning situation can be thought of initially as a situation of some feature of which someone says, or could plausibly say, that it has a meaning. The principal mark of such a situation is the use or usability, with reference to some central feature of the situation, of some such expression as: "The meaning of '....' is ----" "A meaning of '....' is ----." " '....' has the meaning ----." " '....' has the meaning that ----," " '....' has a meaning." Meaning situations are also often indicated by the verb "to mean" used, or usable, in such expressions as

" 'Square' means ----" or "Your coming means ----." However, this clue to meaning situations must be employed with caution; for the verb "to mean" is often preceded by a reference to a person or persons, and followed by a reference to an object or an intended action without, as has been noted, referring to anything that can be called a meaning. For example, if John means that apple as he points his finger, that apple is nevertheless not John's meaning; and if John means to go, going is not John's meaning. Meaning situations are sometimes distinguished by use of such nouns as "significance," "signification," and "import" and by corresponding verbs. But such expressions clearly indicate meaning situations when, and only when, they apply to situations in which something can be said to have a meaning, and when they can be appropriately rephrased in terms of the sorts of expressions previously indicated.

The principal factors in meaning situations are suggested by the following considerations: Every meaning is a meaning of something, is meant or eventually determined in some way or through some function, and within some setting. Thus every meaning situation may be said to include, in addition to a meaning: a bearer of meaning, a meaning function or way of meaning, and a context. However, in addition to these factors that are plainly common to all meaning situations, many, and perhaps all, meaning situations also involve other factors that are often thought of as constituting either crucial aspects or the contexts of meanings or meanings themselves. Such factors include stimuli that prompt the production of bearers of meaning, responses to such bearers, referents of these bearers, uses of these bearers, and the confirming conditions of statements.

In the first three chapters of the present inquiry, I shall examine the roles in meaning situations of factors that are both common to all such situations and so sufficiently distinct from meanings as to be unlikely, upon reflection, to be identified with, or substituted for, meanings. Since the matters to be considered in these chapters have not usually been matters of primary concern in inquiries concerning meaning, and since they are less controversial than some matters subsequently to be considered, I shall, in discussing them, look directly to the data of meaning situations referring only incidentally to the views of other writers. In chapters four through eight, I shall consider the roles in meaning situations of some other factors so intimately related to meanings that in discussions of meaning they are sometimes identified with meanings and sometimes substituted for meanings. Since the matters discussed in these chapters have been crucially important in recent accounts of the concept of meaning, I shall in each chapter begin with some suggestions offered by writers who have emphasized the factor under consideration in that chapter, and then go on to evaluate and build upon these suggestions, not so much in order to confirm or to reject them, as in order to use them as points of departure in clarifying the relation of the factor under consideration to the concept of meaning. In the ninth chapter, I shall, in the light of whatever requirements and suggestions for a satisfactory account of the concept of meanings may have been disclosed in the earlier chapters, endeavor to work out an account of the concept of meaning that, insofar as possible, meets these requirements and embodies these suggestions. In the final chapter, I shall undertake to develop and support this account by showing how meanings of each of the principal varieties can be satisfactorily represented only by some such account as the one indicated, and how the insights involved in each of the main sorts of other accounts are suitably recognized in this account.

CHAPTER I

BEARERS OF MEANING

Among the various factors that enter into a meaning situation, one, that of which the meaning is a meaning, may be regarded as a kind of focus around which the other factors fall into perspective. Not only is this factor that of which the meaning is a meaning, it is also that of which the meaning context is a context, that which the agent is stimulated to produce, and that to which the respondent is disposed to respond. It is also that in a meaning situation which refers, when anything does, and that which has, or may have, any of a variety of specific uses.

That every meaning is a meaning of something or other is evident alike in the character of meaning situations and in the logic of ascriptions of meaning. No situation is encountered or can be thought of in which something is a meaning without being a meaning of anything. Most ascriptions of meaning include a specific reference to that of which the meaning is a meaning, and those that do not remain open to the question, "Meaning of what?" Instances in which one asks himself "How shall I put my meaning?" are only apparent exceptions; for in such cases one is in search of a sharable outward bearer for a meaning that already has, within his own experience, a bearer apart from which it would not be a meaning at all.

It would be convenient to have a single simple term for that of which a meaning is a meaning, and various attempts have been made to provide such a term; but all such attempts put excessive strains upon common usage and tend to become misleading. C. S. Peirce and, following his lead, Charles Morris and Max Black are disposed to refer to everything of which a meaning is a meaning as a sign. Ernst Cassirer prefers the word "symbol," and Susanne Langer takes all the factors in questions to be either signs or symbols. But in ordinary language, not

1

everything which has a meaning is properly said to be a sign, and not every such thing is correctly said to be a symbol. Indeed, it is not even the case that everything of which a meaning is a meaning is properly said to be either a sign or a symbol. Even the most common of things that have meanings, namely words, are not ordinarily said to be either signs or symbols, and a good many other things said to have meanings fall outside the domains of these terms. Accordingly, in order to avoid the confusion likely to be engendered by employing a term that already has an established meaning to convey a related but different meaning, I forego further search for a single term suitable to the purpose in hand and refer to anything of which a meaning is a meaning by the cumbersome, but not unduly misleading, expression "bearer of meaning."

Every important factor in meaning situations has, at some time or other, been identified by someone with meaning itself. In this, bearers of meaning are no exception; and that this should have been so, at any rate in unreflective thought, need not be surprising. Bearers of meaning are deeply embedded in the situations to which they belong and hence are initially not easily pried loose from other factors in these situations. Thus, a bearer of meaning tends to take on the aura of the thoughts, feelings, volitions, and valuations appropriate to its referents and its meaning. For this reason, children and primitive people often feel that in learning names, they gain power over persons and things, and even highly cultured people often react to words in ways more appropriate to referents of words. The type of thought known as "general semantics" takes as an essential part of its mission the task of warning against the sort of identification of bearer and meaning involved in this kind of reaction, and that such identification should by all means be avoided is clear. However, most mature adults, at any rate when they reflect upon the matter, can distinguish fairly well between what has a meaning or referent and the meaning or referent itself; and, as far as I know, no responsible theory of meaning has attempted specifically to identify the two. Hence, while granting some practical significance to warnings against the identification of bearers of meaning and meanings, I shall focus upon other matters concerning bearers of meaning. I shall endeavor first to indicate some principal varieties of bearers of meaning, and then comment very briefly upon changes in bearers of meaning and their impacts upon meanings.

The purpose of this account of varieties of bearers of meaning is not to draw up at the outset definitive lists of what can and what cannot have meaning. Such lists would not, for reasons that will subsequently appear, have much point; and, in any case, they could not be achieved without prior definition of other factors in meaning situations including meanings themselves. The purpose is rather, by taking note of some main varieties of bearers of meaning, to suggest at the outset something of the scope and character of the data that have to be taken into account in an inquiry concerning the concept of meaning. Since no definition of meaning is as yet available, the initial method of identifying varieties of bearers of meaning must consist for the most part in noticing the kinds of things and events to which people actually do, or show themselves ready to, ascribe meanings. Such a procedure—imperfect as it is — is scarcely likely to lead one very far astray; for while an individual may easily be mistaken about the meaning of a particular thing or event, or even about whether that thing or event has a meaning, persistent tendencies of substantial groups of people to treat instances or classes of things or events as meaningful in some way or other are likely to be for the most part well-founded.

Although nothing substantive is to be hinged upon an initial broad classification of bearers of meaning, such classifications can be useful instruments for a more detailed survey of the varieties of such bearers. Among the broad classifications that have been thus far developed, two appear to be especially useful for present purposes. The first is a traditional classification according to sources of signs and based on the distinction between what have been called "natural" and "conventional" signs. The underlying distinction was delineated by Augustine when he remarked that "natural signs are those which, apart from any intention or desire of using them as signs, do yet lead to the knowledge of something else, as, for example, smoke when it indicates fire; [and] .... conventional signs .... are those which living beings mutually exchange for the purpose of showing, as well as they can, the feelings of their minds, or their perceptions, or their thoughts."[1] The second classification distinguishes bearers of meaning on the basis of their logical status as particulars or as kinds: Extending a terminology commonly limited to linguistic expressions to other bearers of meaning as well, one may refer to the factors distinguished in this second classification as tokens and types.

In the pages that follow I shall initially group bearers of meaning according to a distinction similar to the first of the two just mentioned and then go on to subdivide those that fall under each of the resulting groups according to the second of the two distinctions mentioned. However, while the first of the two distinctions to be used is similar to the one described by Augustine, I shall alter the traditional terminology, which, indeed, is not quite suited to the distinction that Augustine's remark delineated. The term "natural" as applied to bearers of meaning not produced to be such bearers, suggests that such bearers are of nonhuman origin whereas in fact many of them, such as houses, tools, and many other artifacts, are of human origin; and the term "conventional," as applied to bearers of meaning produced to convey meanings, tends to ascribe to language, an artificiality and formality that are by no means always characteristic of it. I shall, accordingly, refer to bearers of meaning which are produced, either consciously or unconsciously and either momentarily or over extended periods of time, to be bearers of meanings, as "designed bearers of meaning"; and bearers of meaning which are not produced to bear meanings, I shall call "undesigned bearers of meaning." Since undesigned bearers of meaning are likely to be more primitive than designed ones I begin with them.

1. Undesigned Bearers of Meaning

Of things commonly said to have meanings but not produced to that end, the most obvious are physical objects and events, and of these objects and events, a very substantial proportion consists of natural objects and events not produced by human actions at all. Thus, we say of a flash of lightning

---

[1]St. Augustine, *On Christian Doctrine,* in *Great Books of the Western World* (Chicago and London: Encyclopedia Britannica, Inc., 1952), p. 637.

that it means imminent thunder and of lowering clouds that they mean rain. We say that cool breezes mean that autumn is approaching, and that the returning robins mean that spring is coming. The crouching tiger is said to mean that the antelope is in danger; and the trumpeting elephant, that a stampede is impending. The first streaks of dawn are said to mean that daylight is approaching; and darkness at noon, that the sun is eclipsed. A spontaneous cry, a contorted face, or a writhing body may mean that a man is in great pain; and a flood of tears, that a woman's pride has been deeply wounded.

Other things commonly said to have meanings but not produced to that end are objects and events produced by human beings but produced for purposes other than bearing meaning or even for no particular purposes at all. Thus, a well-built house is said to mean that its inhabitants will be warm in winter; and a tight-fitting shoe, that the wearer will suffer. A wide highway is sometimes said to mean that it will carry a heavy flow of traffic; and a vacant office building, that the management is inefficient. An abandoned windmill may mean that times are changing; and a boy's operating a handpump, that the economy of his area is retarded. We may intelligibly say that a laborer's leaning upon his shovel means that he is weary, that a student's nodding over his book means that he find the book dull, and that a farmer's diligently harrowing his black earth means that his crop will probably be good. Fingerprints of a certain sort may mean that Jones alone could have been the murderer; and tool marks of a certain sort on a violin may mean that only Stradivarius could have been the maker of the instrument.

Not all undesigned bearers of meaning are, however, physical objects. Many such bearers of meaning are mental states or events. Dreams have long been said to have meanings, and some psychologists now claim to have established a science of disclosing these meanings. Daydreams are often considered just as meaningful, and analysts undertake with painstaking care to trace out their significance. Physicians and laymen alike find meaning in all manner of twinges and twitches. The throbbing in my head may be said to mean that I have undergone excessive strain; the spots before my eyes, that my retinas have been damaged; and the aching in my fingers, that my arthritis has returned. Isolated sensory experiences grounded in environmental objects are also often said to have meanings, especially when the significance of these experiences is not immediately apparent. Thus, I may at first be uncertain of the significance of the light flashing across my field of vision and subsequently be ready to say that its meaning was that a meteor had come into the earth's atmosphere. With regard to a fully developed percept, such as my present percept of the tree in front of me, it is ordinarily more appropriate to speak simply of seeing the object than to bring the language of meaning into play. But if anyone has occasion, e.g., in a philosophical discussion, to ask himself what his present immediate experience as he looks at a tree means, he may reply just that it means that a tree is in front of him.

Things and events that have meanings without having been produced to that end may be of any degree of comprehensiveness, and some of them are wholes including as parts things and events that have been produced to have meanings. Thus one may ascribe a meaning to a quarrel between a man and his wife, the arranging of a business contact, or the initiation of a campaign. In similar fashion, people often ascribe meanings to even larger wholes such as the French Revolution, the First World War, or the Cuban crisis. People also ascribe meanings to their own and other people's lives, to whole civilizations, to life itself, and even to the universe.

That which is said to have meaning without being produced to that end is usually a *particular object* or event such as *this* cloud, *my* headache, or *that* transaction. However, as the examples already given show, people also sometimes say of certain *kinds* of things and events that they mean this or that. Thus, one says, not just that this cloud means that it will rain soon or that this thunder means that lightning has occurred, but also that clouds (generally) mean that rain is likely and thunder that lightning has occurred. One also says that returning robins (generally) mean that spring is about to return, that recurring headaches mean that organic disorders are likely, that cold weather means snow may fall, and that repeated sneezing means that one may be catching cold.

Since in common usage a sign is a thing or event that gives evidence of another thing or event, and since such a thing or event is just what most undesigned bearers of meaning are, most undesigned bearers of meaning can be regarded as signs. But not all undesigned bearers of meaning can be so regarded. An event resulting from an earlier event can be regarded as a meaning of the earlier event without the earlier event's being a sign of the resulting one. My presently seeing a spot of light in the sky may be said to be among the meanings of certain light waves having been transmitted from a certain star centuries ago, but the transmitting of these light waves can scarcely be properly spoken of as a sign of my seeing the spot of light. Moreover, by no means everything properly regarded as a sign in the ordinary sense of the term is an undesigned bearer of meaning. Signs in this sense include deliberate gestures, algebraic symbols, billboards, and many other things that are specifically designed to have meanings and hence are not undesigned bearers of meaning.

2. *Designed Bearers of Meaning*

Unlike undesigned bearers of meaning, designed ones are produced in order to bear meanings. Thus whereas undesigned bearers of meaning can be put to use for the expression of thoughts and feelings only as suitable events occur and can be successfully designated for that purpose, the availability of designed bearers of meaning is as ample as man's ability to produce sounds, inscriptions, and other objects and events to which eventually apprehensible meanings can be given. This feature of designed bearers of meaning gives to those able to produce them an enormous advantage over all competitors and has permitted man to achieve cognitive, emotional and practical capacities altogether beyond the reach of creatures that can only take their bearers of meaning as they come.

Ernst Cassirer, Susanne Langer and others are inclined to use the term "symbol" to apply to all purposely produced bearers of meaning, and the domain of the term so interpreted is roughly the same as that of "designed bearers of meaning." However, the range of designed bearers of meaning is far wider than that of symbols as the term "symbols" is ordinarily used. Designed bearers of meaning include not only mythological, aesthetic, religious, and scientific symbols, but also ordinary words, gestures, books, musical and literary compositions, and many other things that cannot be called symbols in any common use of the term.

A great many designed bearers of meaning are non-linguistic physical objects and events, and with these I begin.

Although facial expressions and body movements and attitudes are originally in some degree spontaneous and retain something of that character through the course of life, the human individual learns very early that these responses are taken by other people as expressions of his feelings and intentions, and so he cultivates and employs them to make his feelings and desires known. Insofar as facial expressions and body movements and attitudes are so employed, they are designed bearers of meaning. Thus the grimacing face may be not merely a product of pain but the intended expression of it. The child's withdrawing from the bad-tasting medicine may be not merely a result of a previous experience but a way of conveying an intention to resist in the present. A fist deliberately clenched or a chin pugnaciously thrust forward is likely to mean aggression; and an intentionally outstretched hand or a gracious smile may well mean friendliness.

In contrast to facial expressions and body movements and attitudes, some designed nonlinguistic bearers of meaning have little or no natural connections with what they mean and must be wholly learned within the community that employs them. Such bearers of meaning include prearranged and commonly understood signals. Among these are primitive signals indicating the presense of quarry, the imminence of danger, the approach of friends, or the withdrawal of enemies. The signals of more developed societies include the colored lights and shaped signs by which highway and railroad traffic is regulated; the bugle, whistle, and flare signals used to direct the movements of troops under fire; and the radar signals controlling air traffic. Every cohesive group, whether large or small, develops its own signals, and in general, the more cohesive the group the richer is the fund of signals which members use to express accepted meanings.

Institutional emblems are symbols, often of long standing, representing more or less distinctive occupations, ancestries, or ideas of distinguishable groups of people. Their origins are frequently obscure, but their present emotional significance may be very strong, and their cognitive meaning reasonably clear. Thus the cross, the crescent, the swastika, and the hammer and sickle carry widely known and deeply felt meanings. Less widely recognized but conveying ample meanings within their circles are the flags of small nations, the serpentine emblem of the medical profession, the barber's pole, and the pawn broker's balls. Among primitive peoples the totem animal has great symbolic significance, and in contemporary Western civilization, the American eagle, the British lion, the Democratic donkey, and the Republican elephant continue to carry meanings commonly recognized and felt. So also do the colors of colleges and the coats of arms of proud families. Medals may be significant of notable events or persons. Insignia and uniforms are official marks of groups entitled to use them. Among the best known and most effective of symbolically significant materials is currency; and even where money in the usual sense does not exist some goods in trade take on symbolic significance all out of proportion to their intrinsic utility.

Rituals are sequences of actions performed in prescribed ways by authorized persons for ends other than the consequences normally to be expected from such actions. The origins of existing rituals have often been forgotten and the present meanings of such rituals are often far from clear. But that these rituals were initially in some measure designed to express meanings and continue to express meanings (however remote the current meanings may be from the original ones) no one can very well doubt. Frequently, words constitute a part of a ritual, but generally the major significance of the ritual is carried by the actions involved. Thus, widely recognized meanings are found in such formal rituals as the sacraments of baptism and the Lord's Supper, military salutes, inaugurations of public officials, courtroom procedures, and in wedding and funeral ceremonies. Multitudes of less formal rituals play substantial roles in the lives of families, schools, clubs and unions; and it may well be doubted that any sort of community can exist without some rituals. Rituals often say in silence as much as many words, and however some of their more obscure and primitive aspects may be deplored, they supply a large part of the cohesive structure by which individuals fit into societies and are able to get along with one another.

Among the freest and most creative of material non-linguistic designed bearers of meaning are non-linguistic works of art. Whereas signals, emblems, and rituals are often held within rigid bounds, and even gestures and facial expressions include a restricted repertoire, the range of expression open to the artist is almost without limit. To be sure, he must often work with recalcitrant materials and he can scarcely avoid the use of some conventional patterns. But advancing sciences give him increasing mastery over his materials; and through and beyond the conventional patterns, he is able to create forms with range, depth and power far beyond the capacity of the unaided human body or of standard symbols to express. Thus, the composer puts his thoughts and feelings into fresh patterns of sound; the sculptor, his into shapes of stone and bronze; and the architect, his into enduring forms in concrete and steel. To be sure, some artists deplore quests for meanings of their work; but what they reject seems to be not so much meanings as extraneous meanings such as are often ascribed to music designed to represent rustling trees and babbling brooks or buildings designed to represent stories or social movements. They deny that their works are representations, but they scarcely wish to say that their works are altogether without meanings.

Non-linguistic designed bearers of meaning, such as those so far considered, may be particulars or kinds and so may be referred to as either tokens or types. Thus, a certain blood-stained American flag may have meant courage and determination at Iwo Jima, or the American flag may mean courage and determination. Similarly, that baptismal service may have meant the dedication of that infant, or baptism may mean dedication. Statements ascribing meaning to the non-linguistic material bearers of meaning in question may, moreover, be ambiguous as to the token-type status of the bearer to which the meaning is ascribed. For example, a statement that the cross or the swastika or baptism or the saluting of the flag or the twelve o'clock whistle means this or that may be an ascription of meaning either to a particular cross or to any cross, either to a particular instance or baptism or to any instance; and similarly for the other examples. Sometimes the context clarifies the issue but not always. Failure to make the distinction between instance and kind, or token and type, has produced special confusions with reference to works of art. It seems, for example, to be one of the roots of the prolonged controversy concerning whether the meaningful work of art is the physical object or event produced by the artist or the recurring pattern initiated by that object or event. Due attention to it might yield at least some initial agreement to the effect that, in some instances, either the particular or the kind could appropriately be called a work of art; and that whereas with reference to the visual arts, it is the particular that seems to be focal, with reference to other arts, it is the kind.

The most significant of all designed bearers of meaning are linguistic expressions. This class of bearers of meaning is distinguished from all others by being made up of repeatable units, each having its own meaning and capable of being linked with other such units in composite structures, according to accepted rules, so as to yield other, and often quite new, meanings. Such bearers of meaning are of the highest importance in the life of man in that, apart from them, most of man's industry, commerce, communication and thought would be impossible. For this reason, in many inquiries into meaning, these linguistic bearers preoccupy almost the entire field, nearly all others being treated as either of little importance or derivative from these.

Whatever is to constitute a repeatable unit capable of having its own meaning and of becoming a part of larger meaningful structures must be not only producible but readily producible. The available material for this purpose is basically of three kinds: vocal, graphic and manipulative. Vocal linguistic expressions make up by far the most common kind, and they are usually thought to be the earliest. They have the advantages over the others of being more readily produced, and with greater facility for reliable elaboration than any other kind of bearer of meaning.

For many centuries, the resources and techniques of vocal linguistic expression have been explored, and during the past century and a half—especially during the present century—they have been subjected by students of scientific linguists to minute scrutiny.[2] The inquiries of linguists have disclosed, among other things, that while possible variations of sounds producible by varying positions of tongue and lips, tensions of vocal cords and flow of breath are virtually infinite, only within certain limits are these variations distinguishable, that even of distinguishable vari-

---

[2]Cf. for example: Ferdinand de Saussure, *Course in General Linguistics*, Tr. by Wade Baskin (New York Philosophical Library, 1959); Edward Sapir, *Language* (New York: Harcourt, Brace and Company, 1921); Leonard Bloomfield, *Language* (New York: Henry Holt and Company, Inc., 1933); and Zellig S. Harris, *Methods in Structural Linguistics* (Chicago, University of Chicago Press, 1951). See especially the summary in Roger Brown, *Words and Things* (Glencoe: The Free Press, 1958 Chapter I.

ants only a fraction is used in all known languages, that in any given language a much smaller fraction is used, that within any language only certain orders of sounds are permissible, and that changes in the sound patterns of a language tend to follow certain formulatable laws. Linguists undertake to describe a language as objectively as possible by recording all detectable sound differences as phones of the language; combining those that are structurally similar and disclose no functional difference as the phonemes of the language, and distinguishing the basic meaningful units as the morphemes of the language. They then endeavor to search out the rules by which the morphemes are brought together to form larger meaningful units and so to set forth the grammar of the language. Sometimes they also become specifically concerned with meanings but for the most part they leave this inquiry to others. As a result of all these labors, our current knowledge of the descriptive character of vocal bearers of meaning has reached a rather remarkable degree of refinement though a great deal remains to be done.

Partly because graphic language is commonly supposed to depend upon spoken language, graphic bearers of meaning have not been studied with quite the same minute care that oral ones have. However, the historical data are much easier to get at, and the essential facts are well-known.[3] While some sorts of graphic expressions may be very ancient indeed, it seems likely that even these were influenced in some degree by already well-developed speech habits; and most written languages are largely representations of the speech of people who use them. However, the particular conventions by which the transcription occurs vary considerably. The earliest graphic bearers of meaning were probably pictograms or pictures representing objects and events. These came to be accompanied by ideograms or pictures representing ideas that could not be literally depicted; and the pictographs and ideographs were often placed in orders corresponding to those which were used in speech, thus constituting logograms. In time, the pictures used in picture language became largely conventionalized. Subsequently, owing to the inconvenience of learning enough symbols to cover the range of objects, events, and ideas needed, conventionalized picture symbols came to represent syllables;

---

[3]Cf. Roger Brown, *Words and Things*.

and from these symbols, there eventually emerged alphabets and punctuation marks capable of representing, though by no means always definitely, most of the functionally significant sounds of spoken languages. In the interest of economy, most systems of writing make no attempt to represent refinements of intonation and vocal quality that give to speech much of its flexibility and richness; and no usable system of writing could in the nature of the case fully represent all aspects of speech. Although graphic bearers of meaning have, accordingly, less flexibility than vocal ones do, they have the significant advantages over vocal ones that they can be repeatedly revised before production and that they can be made to endure almost indefinitely. This latter advantage has been somewhat offset in recent years by the improvements of methods of oral transcription.

The third group of bearers of linguistic meaning, somewhat loosely gathered under the heading manipulative, is almost entirely dependent upon the other two in that instances of it almost always represent vocal or graphic bearers of meaning. This representation is characteristic of standard sign languages used by the deaf and dumb and of semaphore and telegraphic codes. In principle, manipulative bearers of meaning need not, however, always be thus derivative. It is quite possible that rudimentary sign languages developed among some primitive peoples as early as vocal ones; and some primitive peoples as well as certain monks sworn to silence are said to communicate in signs that are not altogether representative of sounds. Moreover, all manipulative codes develop at least some symbols that represent no spoken or written word; and it is quite conceivable that within new electronic techniques, some quite new linguistic systems may be shown to be feasible. Radio and television are, of course, basically ways of extending the range of auditory and visual bearers of meaning rather than manipulative bearers of meaning as such; but they are like some manipulative bearers in depending upon manufactured devices. Advocates of the relatively new discipline known as "information theory" have developed an elaborate mathematical and physical science designed to determine the capacities and limits of various communication media, especially electronic ones.[4]

---

[4]Cf. Claude E. Shannon and Warren Weaver, *The Mathematical Theory of Communication* (Urbana, Illinois: The University of Illinois Press, 1964).

While this new science can, as Yekoshua Bar-Hillel has pointed out in his *Language and Information Theory*,[5] scarcely be expected to make any substantial change in our understanding of meaning, it throws significant light on the potentialities of certain kinds of bearers of meaning; and while the scientific devices with which it is preoccupied have as yet supplied no basically new kinds of bearers of meaning, they give to those we have a range that was scarcely conceivable in earlier years.

With reference to linguistic bearers of meaning in general, considerable controversy has centered in recent years upon questions concerning whether words or sentences are more basic. The answer presumably depends upon the particular character of the question asked. If the question is, What are the meaningful building blocks in terms of which thoughts are expressed? the answer will be one thing; but if the question is, Against what modes of expression must our accounts of the meaning be tested? the answer will be another. In any case it will be convenient to begin here with words (singly or in standard compounds) and their graphic or manipulative counterparts.

Words are classified by traditional grammarians in line with their meanings as nouns, verbs, adjectives, adverbs, pronouns, and prepositions. Some modern grammarians have undertaken to work out more scientific classifications in terms of the formal contexts into which words fit without reference to what they refer to or mean. That most words have meanings, if not alone at least in context, will generally be recognized without question, though some inquirers have been disposed to regard some familiar words as dubious because of their lack of referents or of the impossibility of verifying their applications. However, such words continue to be a part of the stock of words commonly used with every appearance of being intended to express meanings; and the best procedure with reference to them has generally been thought of late to be rather to ask how and what they mean than to attempt to reject them out of hand on the basis of prior commitment to a theory of meaning.

Nearly all of the linguistic bearers of meaning actually produced are in the form of sentences. A sentence is not merely a

---

[5]Yekoshua Bar-Hillel, *Language and Information Theory* (London and Jerusalem: Addison Wesley Publishing Company and The Jerusalem Academic Press Ltd., 1964), p. 296.

string of words but one or more words presented in general accord with a system of rules of grammar in some degree mastered and internalized by competent users of a language. Such rules have been made explicit by traditional grammarians by reference to patterns of meaningful words. Recent grammarians have attempted to work out the rules of grammar in a more objective manner, by formulating, with minimal reference to meaning, the structures necessary to explain the syntactical competence of a user of a language. Not all sentences are fully grammatical, but virtually all sentences actually uttered or inscribed are designed to express meanings. Such sentences are often declarative but they may be interrogative, exclamatory, imperative, or of one of many other kinds. The sentences with which inquirers concerning meaning have been usually been most concerned have been the declarative ones.

A few decades ago, advocates of operational and verification theories of meaningfulness were disposed to call in question the meaningfulness of all sentences save grammatical declarative ones indicating specific modes of verification. However, in recent years it has become more evident than ever that only a fraction of meaningful sentences are declarative, and that even the attempt to distinguish between meaningful declarative sentences and non-meaningful ones can be extremely difficult. Accordingly, with reference to sentences actually uttered or inscribed, as with reference to words in common use, the soundest procedure would seem to be to inquire what and in what ways they may mean, and to consider them meaningless altogether only if no meaning can be found for them.

Linguistic bearers of meaning containing sentences as parts include prose paragraphs, poems, speeches, essays, books, and libraries. They may also be united with bearers of meaning of other sorts to form dramas, operas, legislative and judicial declarations, and many other kinds of expressions. While extensive linguistic bearers of meanings are made up of sentences, somewhat as sentences are made up of words, and while the former type of composition involves rules as well as the latter, the modes of assembly and the rules of composition of sentences, on the one hand, and more extensive linguistic expressions, on the other, are quite different from one another. The rules governing the composition of paragraphs and speeches are far less rigid than those governing the composition of sentences and for the most part these latter rules concern not so much how the composition in question can be achieved as how it can be made clear and forceful. Moreover, much of the secret of the composition of effective sequences of sentences lies in subtleties that have never been analyzed and perhaps never can be.

The distinction between tokens and types, though capable of application to other bearers of meaning, applies most specifically to linguistic expressions. Those linguistic expressions that are actually uttered or inscribed to express meanings are always tokens while linguistic expressions thought of as classes of expressions available for use on appropriate occasions are types. Thus if, looking at the cover of a book, I say, somewhat surprised, "The book is red," the expression is a token sentence and each of its verbal parts is a token word. But the word "red" and each of the other words thought of as an available part of the English language is a type; so also is the sentence insofar as it is thought of as a part of the language though sentences are not usually thought of in this way. A confusing feature of the token-type distinction as applied to linguistic expressions is the fact that the very same words may be used to ascribe a meaning to a token and to ascribe a meaning to a type. At a critical point in his acceptance speech at the Republican National Convention in 1964, Mr. Barry Goldwater declared that "extremism in defence of liberty is no vice." Many people entered into the subsequent debate on what the statement meant. What was it of which the meaning was being discussed: Mr. Goldwater's utterance or the sentence in English that he used? The expression, "Goldwater's statement meant ----" could have referred to either. This sort of ambiguity is often encountered. While no rule can be laid down to determine in a given instance whether a token or a type is under consideration, the following would in general appear to hold. On the one hand, where single words are concerned, people are usually—though not always—more interested in the type than in the token. A word is not ordinarily uttered by itself and if it were, it would not say anything except in an instance of a one word sentence. While a person sometimes wants to know what a word means in someone's utterance or inscribed statement, what he is more likely to want to know about a word is how the word type is or could be used in the construction of meaningful sentences.

It is this sort of question that dictionaries, explanations of words to children, and some philosophical discourses undertake to answer. But, on the other hand, where sentences are concerned, the situation is different. There are few standard sentences, and most sentences that are uttered or inscribed are used actually to say something. What one usually—though not always—wants to know with regard to a sentence is not what its type could be used to say but what its token does say. When what is concerned is a statement of an important person on an important occasion, whether an inquiry about it is focused upon the token or the type will depend upon the context of the inquiry.

Not all designed bearers of meaning are physical objects or events, for the images and thoughts that men's minds create may quite as readily have significations beyond themselves as any painted picture or spoken word. To be sure one's mental images depend upon his experiences of physical objects; and, as Ludwig Wittgenstein has shown, it is difficult to see how a purely private language could even get started. Nevertheless, once one has gained some facility in the formation of images, he may create, almost without limit, new ones with meanings to suit his needs; and once he has attained, in interaction with the world and his fellows, some facility in the use of words, he may think as well as speak his words. One does not have to have images of his drawings before he draws them or of his sentences before he utters them, for he may produce images in the drawings or thoughts in the speaking. But one often does devise images before drawing and thoughts before speaking; and when he does, the images he imagines and the thoughts he thinks may be quite as pregnant with meaning as any sketch he puts on paper or any words he utters. Indeed, in meanings of the images and thoughts that men devise lie the roots of much of their most useful and creative achievement. If a man is lost in a city the mental map that he produces may yield the requisite clue to his way home; and if he is confronted with a dilemma, his envisagement of the problem often indicates the manner of its resolution. When a gifted architect forms a mental image of the chapel he hopes to build, the meaning of his image may include the plans of a masterpiece. When a brilliant mathematician makes a mental model for inquiry in a segment of his field, the meaning of the model may indicate a breakthrough in his discipline even though the proofs may require many months. In a simple melody in the mind of a composer may lie meanings that come to be more fully expressed in a great symphony; and in the present dreams of a statesman, there may be meanings that will yield the promise of a better world.

Do concepts have meanings? A concept differs from a word in that it is never uttered, and from an idea in mind in that it does not occur. Moreover, it seems to be, if not *the* meaning of a word, at any rate often *a* meaning of a word as, for example, the concept of a male human being is a meaning of "man." Accordingly, a concept can scarcely have a meaning in the way in which a word has a meaning or even in the way in which an idea has one. Nevertheless, it may have a meaning by virtue of what is implied by its being true of something as, for example, the concept male human being may include among its meanings the concept rational animal in that anything's being a male human being means or implies its being, among other things, a rational animal. Thus it should not be surprising that philosophers and ordinary men alike seriously inquire concerning meanings of concepts of friendship, courage, love, virtue, justice, mind, body, and death.

Do propositions have meanings? A proposition[6] may be construed as either a sentence, a sentence with its meaning, a meaning of one or more sentences, or an ideal sentence or a class of sentences all of which have the same meaning. Under the first and fourth interpretations, propositions have meanings either in the same way, or in ways similar to the ways in which any sentences have meanings. Under the second interpretation, the one in which a proposition is construed as a sentence with its meaning, a proposition does not strictly have a meaning but it does include distinguishable bearer and meaning factors. Under the third interpretation, the one in which a proposition is a meaning of a sentence, a proposition clearly does not have a meaning in the manner in which a sentence does, for by definition it is in this case, such a meaning. Nevertheless, even in this case it may have a meaning in the manner in which implications of propositions are properly said to be meanings of propositions as, for example, one meaning

---

[6]That a proposition cannot without risk of serious confusion ordinarily be referred to as a meaning of a sentence was called to my attention by Professor Alan Donagan.

of something's being square is its being rectangular. It is therefore in no sense odd that civil rights leaders and constitutional
lawyers debate concerning meanings of the proposition that all
men are created equal, that mathematicians undertake to draw out
meanings of propositions laid down in their postulates, or that
judges explain the meanings of propositions upon which juries
must base their decisions.

Among the kinds of things of which people are prepared to
say that they have meanings, is a kind of sentence which requires
special attention both because of its special importance for the
present inquiry and because of the danger of confusing it with
other kinds. I refer to sentences used to ascribe meanings to
things other than themselves including other sentences. If I say
"The book is boring," the bearer of meaning is the statement,
"The book is boring," and the truth of the statement depends
on the facts about the book. But if I say " 'The book is boring'
means that the book makes one weary," the bearer of my meaning is not the statement "The book is boring," though it includes
that, but the longer statement " 'The book is boring' means that
the book makes one weary." and the truth of this statement
depends, not on the facts about the book, but on the meaning of
the statement, "The book is boring."

3. Changes in Bearers of Meaning and the Impact of Bearers Upon Meanings

Particular non-recurrent events that have meanings are in an
important sense not subject to change, not indeed because any
particular force of theirs prevents change, but just because, as
events that occur only once, they are not the sorts of things
that could change. Their meanings also are not subject to change,
not again because of any peculiar merit of theirs, but just
because, either by the conventions operative at the time or
by laws of nature operative at all times, their meanings are
determined for all time at the times of their occurrence.[7]

Unlike events, physical objects that have meanings can change.

---

[7]See Jonathan Cohen, *The Diversity of Meaning* (London: Methuen and
Co., Ltd., 1962), pp. 3ff.

Indeed, as continuing through time, they are prime instances of that which does change; and no matter how permanent they seem, they remain subject to radical change. The most enduring mountains are eroded; the most ancient rivers alter their courses; dry lands are covered with water; the seas are drained; the stars become cold; planetary systems decay; and each stage of each changing natural object has causal meanings that differ from those of each other stage. Artifacts are, as a rule, even more subject to change as bearers of meaning. The pyramids in their present rough state are no longer quite the bearers of meaning they were in the days of their polished splendor; and the Parthenon and the statuary that once adorned its pediments have passed through many changes of state and meaning since their beginning. Much more quickly the houses that we live in and the scores of artifacts that we daily use change their character and meanings as they grow older. Pictures come to have different meanings as they begin to fade, and manuscripts and even inscriptions in stone come to be altered bearers of meaning as they are torn, erased, written over or chipped or marred.

If word types that have meanings are narrowly construed so that for every change of pattern there is a different type, then there can scarcely be any change of word type; for then everything that would otherwise be thought of as change in a word type would become simply an exchange of one word type for another. However, if words are to be usefully thought of as types, the types in question must be more broadly conceived; so that, for example, the utterance of "blue," in Oxford English, in the cockney speech of London slums, or in the speech of Charleston or New York, may all be regarded as utterances of a single type, and inscriptions ranging from elegant engravings to miserable scrawls with gross misspellings may be taken to be instances of inscriptions of the same type. If word types are thus broadly construed, then word types can be taken to endure through time and, accordingly, to be alterable in time. Thus, such words as "man," "love," "April," and "father" have undergone progressive changes in form, in sound and appearance from early, to middle, to present-day English. Linguists have traced out the character of many such changes in word types in minute and often fascinating detail for many languages; and they have even laid down rules governing the characters of these changes.

Details of these findings are, however, beyond the scope of the present account of bearers of meaning, which must now be focused briefly upon the impact of changing bearers upon meanings.

When bearers of meaning are objects whose meanings are rooted in their causes and effects, every considerable variation in the bearer carries with it a correlated variation in meaning, for causes and effects to go together. Thus the gently sloping valley we now see has very different causal meanings from the rugged canyon that once was here, and the scarlet leaves of autumn have a meaning different from the green buds of spring. The newly built cathedral bears the marks of past and future very different from that of its ruined shell of centuries later, and a well worn coat has readily determinable meanings very different from the equally determinable ones of a coat fresh from the factory.

When bearers of meaning are symbols and word types, their impact upon the conventional meanings that they have is likely to be much less reliable or marked than is that of physical objects upon the causal meanings that they have; for symbols and word types need not be similar to, or causally linked with, or related to their meanings in any other way save by the dispositions of persons who use and understand them. Nevertheless, even symbols and word types may themselves have some powerful impact upon meanings and the concepts their users employ.

Presumably in the early stages of the development of language, words and symbols are very closely linked with objects and events indicated by their uses. Indeed, as Ernst Cassirer points out in his monumental *Philosophy of Symbolic Forms*, primitive modes of communication are marked by the prominence of indicative and imitative gestures, and onomatopetic expressions; and primitive concepts of spacial, temporal, and numerical relations are deeply dependent upon the use of the body and its parts in mimetic and analogical representations. Cassirer has convincingly shown how the notions of being inside and outside are linked with being inside or outside the body, how rigidly, among some primitive peoples, counting is tied to the use of fingers and toes,[8] and how tenuous

---

[8]Ernst Cassirer, *The Philosophy of Symbolic Forms* (New Haven: Yale University Press, 1953), Chapters 2 and 3.

in primitive thought is the boundary between symbols and what is symbolized.

Although, as the development of language progresses, there seems to be, as Cassirer endeavors in great detail to show, a progressive liberation of the uses of symbols and words from the objects and events to which they tend at first to be tied, powerful impacts of word types and symbols upon their own meanings are by no means confined to primitive stages of language. Upon this fact poets and orators depend for much of the effectiveness of their art; and some psychological studies, such as that of Heinz Werner and Bernard Kaplan in their book, *Symbol Formation,* supply considerable experimental evidence to show the meanings of many words are deeply colored by the character of the word types of which they are meanings.

In the course of the development of languages to be sure, not only do many forms of expression become sufficiently conventionalized to free their uses from narrow restraints imposed by incidental features of word types, but new forms of expression are evolved to meet the growing conceptual needs. Even with reference to these new expressions, however, the character of expressions themselves continues to have a considerable impact upon the meaning both by facilitating and by restraining the development of the relevant conceptual systems. Galileo's formulations of the laws of falling bodies would scarcely have been conceived in the way they were apart from some such system of algebraic notation as was available to Galileo, and the account he eventually produced might have been quite different both in form and thought had he been obliged to work with another system. Newton was able to give adequate expression to his principles of mechanics only when he had worked out the notation of his calculus, and current quantum mechanics is both facilitated and restrained by the character of the notations it employs.

What can be readily thought at any stage of any culture inevitably depends in no small part upon what systems of bearers of meaning are available in the primary language of that culture. In this connection, Benjamin Whorf cogently argues, with reference to the Hopi Indians, that the linguistic modes of the indication of plurals, quantities, times and intensities tend to yield ways of seeing things and events quite different from those likely to occur among users of "Standard Average European" languages,[9] and that in the use of relating expressions, such as "that," following sensation words, "English compared to Hopi is like a bludgeon compared to a rapier."[10] Whorf goes on to argue, with some pardonable exaggeration, that "every language system is a vast pattern system, different from others, in which are ultimately ordained the forms and categories by which the personality not only communicates, but also analyzes nature, notices or neglects types of relationships and phenomena, channels his reasoning, and builds the house of his consciousness."[11] While a language system contains more than the word forms and syntax that constitute its bearers of meaning, and while one's experience is not wholly contained in the available linguistic forms or incapable of using those forms to build new concepts; there can be little doubt that the patterns of words and syntax of some languages make refined thoughts and analyses in some areas more readily possible than in others, and that the most highly developed language patterns for some areas of experience lie outside those of the Western World.

---

[9]Paul Henle, *Language, Thought and Culture* (Ann Arbor: The University of Michigan Press, 1959), pp. 12 ff.

[10]Benjamin Whorf, *Language, Thought and Reality,* J. B. Carroll, ed. (Cambridge, Mass. and New York: Technology Press and John Wiley and Sons, Inc., 1956), p. 85.

[11]*Ibid.,* p. 753.

CHAPTER II

WAYS OF MEANING

The foregoing account of bearers of meaning discloses that while a given object, event, fact, or situation may not have a meaning in the way that one initially has in mind in inquiring concerning its meaningfulness, virtually anything that can be mentioned at all has a meaning in some way or other. Hence, much more revealing with reference to a possible bearer of meaning than the question whether or not it has a meaning is the question in what way or ways it has or can have a meaning. Accordingly, the ways of meaning, or meaning functions, which were mentioned earlier as important in meaning situations, must now be examined in some detail.

As will presently become apparent, many factors converge in the eventual determination of a meaning. The eventual determination of meanings have sometimes been thought of as all of a single kind. However, examination of actual meaning situations discloses that the eventual determination of meanings takes place in several different ways. The major ways of the eventual determination of meanings are relatively few in number, but the differences between them run so deep that to ascribe to something a meaning as determined in one way is to say something radically different from what would be said in ascribing to it a meaning as determined in another way. Each major way of eventual determination of meanings yields meanings quite different from that produced by any other; and each is grounded in a function such that, given appropriate bearers of meaning, whatever satisfies that function may be said to be a meaning of a kind which that function distinguishes. Thus, a way of meaning is a manner of eventual determination of a meaning that justifies one in calling the meaning so determined a meaning of a certain kind.

While inquiries concerning meaning are seldom preceded by

systematic delineation of major ways of meaning and while they
sometimes become confused through failure to keep the distinctions between the ways clear, these distinctions themselves have
often been noticed and apparently require only to be pointed out
to be acknowledged. Whatever the details may be, the general
character of what appear to be the major ways of meaning would
seem to be suggested by the following considerations. Apparently
the meaning of a bearer of meaning is eventually determined either
by the intentions of an agent in using a bearer, the intentional
dispositions of one or more agents relative to the use of a bearer,
the causal connections of a bearer, or the implications of a bearer.
The ways of meaning and meaning functions involved in these
manners of determination of meanings may be referred to respectively as intentional, dispositional, causal, and implicative.

In the succeeding sections of the present chapter, I shall
attempt, with respect to each major way of meaning and meaning
function, to delineate its character, indicate the sorts of bearers
of meaning to which it is applicable, and confirm its frequent
occurrence by reference to examples. I shall then go on to discuss
some complexities of the ways of meanings. In a later chapter I
shall attempt to show that the suggested list of major meaning
functions and ways of meaning is essentially complete.

1. The Intentional Way of Meaning

A bearer of meaning has a certain meaning in the intentional
way, relative to a given agent, if and only if that agent intends,
in producing that bearer, to lead a respondent to apprehend that
meaning as his meaning.[1] The function in which this way of meaning is grounded may be formulated as follows: X is a meaning
of a given bearer in the intentional way, relative to a given agent,
if and only if that agent, in producing that bearer, intends to

---

[1]The character of intentional meaning has been carefully worked out
by H. P. Grice. Especially illuminating is Grice's clear recognition that
what the utterer intends his hearer to understand is not only his meaning
but that this meaning is intended. See H. P. Grice, "Meaning," *Philosophical
Review*, LXII (1957), pp. 377-388; P. F. Strawson, "Intention and Convention in Speech Arts," *Ibid.*, LXXVIII (1964), pp. 439-460; and H. P.
Grice "Utterer's Meaning and Intentions," *Ibid.* LXXXVII (1969), pp.
144-177.

lead a respondent to apprehend X as what he intends his respondent to apprehend.

The very special interest that attaches to meanings in the intentional way is rooted in the fact that when someone says something, or in some other manner undertakes to convey a meaning; what people most commonly want to know is, not what the expression that he uses could be used to lead a respondent to apprehend, or even what it is commonly used to leads respondents to apprehend, but what the agent in fact intends to lead a respondent to apprehend. Even when courts of law seek to determine how an expression used by an agent is commonly used, they often do so because so to do is to come as near as they can come to ascertaining what the agent probably did intend to lead his respondent to apprehend.

Most instances of the intentional way of meaning simply occur without being remarked upon, as when one makes a statement or waves a flag intending thereby to express a meaning that requires no further comment. But sometimes, for example, when one's language is not clear or when his meaning needs special emphasis, one may explicitly ascribe a meaning in the intentional way to his own or someone else's words or deeds. When one does ascribe a meaning in the international way to any bearer of meaning, he is likely to do so by means of some such form of statement as the following: "I (you, he we, they) mean (means) ------ by '.....'." "My (your, his, our, their) meaning in saying '.....' is ------." "What I (you, he, we, they) meant by '.....' is ------." The occasions on which one would be likely to say to another person anything like "You mean ------ by '.....' " are relatively rare, for normally—though not always—a speaker may be expected to know his own meaning better than his audience does.

The basic ingredients of an instance of the intentional way of meaning are a context, an initial intimation of meaning or "proto meaning," prior connection linking possible bearers with possible meanings, prospective apprehension by a respondent, an intention of an agent, a bearer of meaning, and an eventuating meaning. Each of these ingredients requires some comment.

a. Since a bearer of meaning in the intentional way occurs at a particular time and place and under a particular set of circumstances, its *context* consists in each case of an enormously complex, and in some respects, unique pattern of physical, social, and psychological factors—subsequently to be further discussed—each of which contributes in its own way to the making of the intention on which the meaning eventually depends.

b. Any of those specific occasions on which a meaning in the intentional way emerges presumably involves some intimation of an initial experiential content which the agent is to seek to lead his respondent(s) to apprehend. This initial content cannot quite be identified with the meaning itself, for as yet it has no bearer and it may be altered in acquiring a bearer. It is rather a sort of "*proto-meaning*" consisting of ideas, thoughts, feelings, and impulses, sometimes quite incompletely focused, that the agent seeks to make apprehensive to himself or others and that may be substantially sharpened and modified before they emerge as what the agent intends to make apprehensible.

c. Apart from connections prior to the occasion of the production of a bearer of intentional meaning, linking the prospective bearer with the eventuating meaning, the agent would have nothing to work with in the effort to make his meaning apprehensible to a respondent. Sometimes the requisite *prior connections* are similarities between a bearer and instances of what it means. Thus one may express his meaning by making drawings, showing pictures, imitating actions and sounds, and producing words and symbols that retain something of the "dynamic structure" of what they mean.[2] Sometimes requisite links are psychological continuities linking bearers and meanings, as when one points with his finger or draws an arrow pointing toward an object that exemplifies what he means. Sometimes they are accidental associations that have taken hold in the dispositional patterns of individuals, as when one refers to the tools or clothes that belonged to a departed friend to suggest the thought of the friend himself. Often prior connection that facilitate the use of an object or event as a bearer of meaning are causal, as when one refers to clouds to signify rain, to a fire to signify warmth, or to a barometer reading to signify air pressure. Sometimes the relevant prior connections are implicative relations, as when one seeks to express the fact that someone is rational by pointing out that he is human. The most common of the prior connections on which

---

[2]Cf. Heinz Werner and Bernard Kaplan, *Symbol Formation* (New York: John Wiley and Sons, 1963).

people's expressions of their intended meanings depend are cultural patterns, and among these the most important are those constituting language. The most obvious of the links between bearers and meanings involved in a language are those of its vocabulary; but equally important, and quite as indispensable, are the principles of its grammar, which permit a competent user to say things that he has never specifically learned to say.

Neither linguistic devices nor any other ready-made connections between bearers and meanings are, to be sure, likely to be adequate by mere mechanical application to render a meaning apprehensible in a specific situation; for since every situation has unique features, some ingenuity is always needed to this end. Moreover, on many occasions real creativity is required, and some of the finest expressions of genius have been expressions to which no current types of bearers were adequate. Nevertheless, even creative expressions of meaning must have some rootage in prior connections, else they would have no means of taking hold upon the experience of respondents.

d. Bearers of meaning in the intentional way are always directed toward *respondents*. The intended respondent may be another person or group of persons or any person or group that may happen to attend. The respondent may also be the agent himself; for some bearers of meaning are designed for the clarification or intensification of one's own experience, and when no other respondent is involved the agent always is. Bearers of meaning in the intentional way are intended to lead respondents to apprehend the agent's meaning as his meaning in using the bearer. While what the respondent actually apprehends may affect the agent's future modes of expression, it has no bearing upon the agent's present intended meaning. But what the agent expects the respondent to apprehend has a significant effect both upon the agent's choice of a bearer and upon the specific character of his intended meaning. The meaning one intends always approximates the meaning he expects his respondent to apprehend, and no one can intend by a certain bearer to make a given meaning apprehensible to a respondent unless he takes that bearer to be likely to lead the respondent to apprehend that meaning.

e. The focal factor in any instance of meaning in the intentional way is the intention itself. Contexts, prior connections,

anticipated responses, and structure of selected bearers all enter
into the making of the intentions on which meanings in the intentional way hinge; but however such intentions themselves are
determined, it is they alone that in the end determine meaning in
this way. What is referred to here as the intention on which a
meaning hinges is to be broadly conceived as a setting oneself
to do something that one takes to be possible. It is much like
the intention to open a window, to go to a city, or to make a good
marriage. It differs from such intentions as these not so much in
its structure as an intention as in its objective. It is setting oneself, not to do an overt non-semantic act, but to produce a bearer
of meaning that will enable a respondent to apprehend one's
meaning. Its objective includes both the production of a suitable
bearer and the respondent's apprehension of the agent's meaning
as his meaning; but its existence as an intention does not depend
upon the successful achievement of either objective. All that is
required is that the bearer that is produced be intended to
express the relevant meaning. Although only a being capable of
consciousness can intend anything, one must not unduly stress
the element of conscious cognition or volition in the intending
that determines intentional meanings. Indeed, at this point one
must stretch the common notion of intention somewhat to allow
for quasi-conscious efforts to express meanings. Intentions to
express meanings are, indeed, often quite deliberate and
involve specific awareness of just what is intended; but a genuine
intention can also exist without deliberation and with no more
in consciousness than an indefinite feeling of just what is intended.
Quite without forethought, I intend to keep my car in the road;
and in an intention to make a good marriage or to create a
significant art object, much of what is intended may be scarcely
more than hinted at in conscious thought. All that is required is
that subsequently one be able, without self-deception, to acknowledge meanings presently pointed out as meanings previously intended.

    f. Being produced at particular times and places in particular
circumstances, *bearers of meaning* in the intentional way are
always particulars, tokens rather than types. Many—though not
all—of these bearers of meaning are, indeed, instances of previously
established culture types, e.g. words and symbols; but every one
of them is itself a particular, an utterance, inscription, or some

other particular thing or event. Being produced to express meanings, the bearers of meanings in the intentional way are also
always designed bearers of meaning. To be sure, they may involve
in their contexts, or even as parts of themselves, things not
produced to bear meanings; but as whole bearers of intentional
meaning, they cannot but be productions of agents. In expressing
the belief that it's going to rain, one may point to a dark cloud,
and in expressing his anger, one may shake a stick at his antagonist;
but the bearers of meaning involved are not the cloud and the
stick only but the pointing to the cloud and the shaking of the
stick. Thus representative bearers of meaning in the intentional
way include uttered and written sequences of words, gestures,
facial expressions, rituals, noddings, drawings, paintings, sculptures,
and references to all manner of things and events. They vary in
quantity from the softest tones and the smallest markings to the
most heroic symphonies and the most voluminous documents,
and, in complexity from the simplest points to the most involved
configurations and the most sophisticated discourses. When they
are verbal they are always at least sentences that constitute
bearers of meaning by virtue not only of the words that compose
them but also of the syntax that structures them.

      g. The *meaning* that eventuates in an intentional meaning
situation is often the same as the "proto-meaning" with which
the agent began. But often the limited range of bearers suggested
by prior connections and expectations concerning apprehensions,
together with a subtle impact of the bearer itself, modifies the
proto-meaning, so that the eventuating intended meaning is
just the meaning intended by the agent in producing the bearer.
What the specific character of this eventuating meaning may be
is a question that must await consideration in a subsequent
chapter.

      A bearer's having a certain meaning in the intentional way
is not a subjective matter in the manner in which an agent's own
or someone else's thinking that he intends to express a certain
meaning is; and an agent's report of his own intentional meaning
is not incorrigible just because he believes it. A bearer's having a
meaning in the intentional way depends upon an intention to
lead a respondent to apprehend a meaning not upon a belief,
either on the part of the agent or on the part of a respondent,
that such an intention exists. The existence of the intention is

subject to many other tests in addition to the report of the agent. However, a bearer's having a certain meaning in the intentional way remains subjective in at least these respects: that the meaning is eventually determined by the agent's own intention; that whatever other valid tests may be applied to the agent's report, the agent retains a mode of access to the determining intention that no one else has; and that insofar as the agent understands his own intentions, is honest, and knows the language in which he reports, his report is entitled to preferential treatment.

A bearer's having a certain meaning in the intentional way is not either timeless in the manner in which necessary truths are timeless or subject to change in the manner in which things and institutions are subject to change. It is rather an occurrence at a particular time and place and, like most occurrences, takes place once and for all without having the sort of endurance that things subject to change must have. Like any other occurrence, it can be subsequently recalled and either correctly or incorrectly described; but it cannot either, on the one hand, be made permanent or, on the other hand, be caused to change. What I meant yesterday by saying that all was well, or what the framers of the Constitution in 1787 meant by the language of the "Preamble," is whatever at the time the respective words were intended to express; and while the meanings of the words in English may change, no interpretation now offered and no change even in the meanings of the words in any way alters the initial meaning in the intentional way.[3]

2. The Dispositional Way of Meaning

The dispositional way of meaning is closely related to the intentional one in that instances of meaning in the intentional way are manifestations of meanings in the dispositional way and in that the dispositional way is defined partly in terms of the intentional way. A bearer of meaning has a certain meaning in the dispositional way, relative to an agent, if and only if, were

[3]Cf. L. Jonathan Cohen, *The Diversity of Meaning* (London: Methuen and Co., Ltd., 1962), pp. 3ff.

that agent to use that bearer in a certain kind of context to lead a respondent to apprehend a meaning as his meaning, he would in all probability intend, in using that bearer, to lead the respondent to apprehend that meaning as his meaning. The function in which this way of meaning is grounded may be formulated as follows: X is a meaning of a certain bearer, relative to a given agent, if and only if, were that agent to produce that bearer to lead a respondent to apprehend something as what he intended that respondent to apprehend, he would in all probability intend that respondent to apprehend X as what he intended that respondent to apprehend.

For a bearer to have a certain meaning in the dispositional way is not for someone actually to use that bearer to lead someone to apprehend that meaning as his meaning but for someone to be ready in certain situations so to use that bearer. The readiness in question is not a momentary urge but a set or established tendency relative to situations and likely to be sufficiently manifested in such situations. Its psychological structure and physiological base may be interesting in their own right and subject to investigation in various ways; but for purposes of initial definition of the dispositional way of meaning, the relevant kind of readiness is sufficiently defined by reference to the situations in which it operates and the responses it yields. Since for a bearer of meaning to have a certain meaning in the dispositional way is not for someone to be ready to express that meaning by it in just any circumstances but rather for someone to be ready to do so in certain specifiable types of circumstances, any satisfactory formulation of the dispositional meaning of a bearer must include a specification of the kind of circumstances in which one is disposed to use that bearer to lead to the apprehension of that meaning. The relevant circumstances may be of any kind the agent is able to distinguish; but for purposes of practicable definitions of dispositional meanings, the distinctions between kinds need not be too finely drawn.

Since bearers of meaning in the dispositional way must be ready for use in any instance of a context of a certain kind, they can scarcely be the sort of momentary particulars (i.e., particular utterances, gestures, etc.) that the bearers of meaning in the intentional way usually are. The bearers of meaning in the dispositional way are most often types, such as words and culturally established symbols; but not infrequently they are quasi-permanent particulars, such as statues, monuments, rivers, and mountains. For bearers of meaning in the dispositional way to be ready for use in the manner that manifests their meanings as dispositional meanings is for agents to be ready in suitable circumstances to use instances of them to lead respondents to apprehend meanings. In most cases bearers of meaning in the dispositional way are designed bearers of meaning. Insofar as they are types they are for the most part not designed by momentary action or decree but by being evolved in cultures through months, years, and even centuries. Some enduring particulars that have meanings in the dispositional way are produced by artists and artisans to bear the dispositional meanings they have, but the meanings that they acquire may require long periods to mature. Some natural objects and types not made or chosen by man have dispositional meanings, but even these are rarely altogether free from the impact of cultural forces.

Resting as they do upon readinesses of individuals or groups to use bearers to lead respondents to apprehend meanings in specifiable contexts, dispositional meanings include a variety of modes depending upon what readinesses are involved. When the readiness is common to all or nearly all human beings, the mode of the dispositional way of meaning may be appropriately referred to as the *natural* mode. When the readiness is rooted in membership in a social group, the mode may be appropriately referred to as the cultural mode. And when the readiness is that of a person or an individual who, though belonging to a group, is disposed to use bearers of meaning in ways that diverge from those of the group, the mode may be referred to as a *personal* one.

a. The natural mode of the dispositional way of meaning is one in which the meaning of a bearer depends in the end on dispositions natural to man and likely to be operative in any human being. Thus a bearer has a certain meaning in the natural mode of the dispositional way of meaning if and only if were any human being to use that bearer to lead a respondent to apprehend a meaning as his meaning in certain circumstances, in all probability he would intend to lead that respondent so to apprehend that meaning.

Most instances of meaning in the natural mode of the dispositional way, like most instances of meaning in the intentional

way, occur without anyone's having any occasion to remark that
they have occurred. When one does have such an occasion and
ascribes a meaning to a bearer in the natural mode, one is likely
to use some such form of expression as the following: " '......' is
always used to mean -----." "All human beings mean by '.....'
-----." "People always mean by '.....' -----." Sometimes the form of
expression used is such that the words alone fail to distinguish an
instance of ascription in other related modes and ways. For
example, an ascription in the form "They always mean ----- by '....' "
could easily be an ascription of meaning in the cultural way,
and "It always means -----" could be an ascription either in the
cultural mode or in the causal way. In most such instances the
character of the context of the ascription will be adequate, if the
question arises, to determine whether or not the intent of the
ascription is to represent the meaning as sustained by a common
human disposition or by a culturally oriented disposition.

The dispositions on which instances of the natural mode of
the dispositional way of meaning depend are dispositions common
to all or most human beings to use certain types and certain
enduring things to express certain meanings. Included in these
dispositions are expectations that respondents will take the bearers
used to have the meanings usually intended. The respondent is
very often the same as the agent, for natural meanings are as
often evoked to clarify and reinforce a meaning for one's self
as to do so for another. Natural dispositions to use a bearer to
express a meaning always rest upon prior affinities between the
bearer and the meaning. Such affinities are often the long-recognized
ones of similarity, spatio-temporal contiguity, and causal connection. They seem also to include some of the affinities more recently
insisted upon by Gestalt psychologists, such as symmetry, simplic-
ity, closure, and completion. Often several of these affinities operate
in conjunction with one another.

Things and events that have meanings by virtue of dispositions common to all or most human beings are of many
varieties. In some instances a bearer of meaning in the natural
mode is a sample of the kind of thing meant. Thus, the table on
the floor of the department store tells the story of the store's
tables of that kind far better than the clerk can do, and the
traveling salesman's most persuasive arguments are in his sample
case. Sometimes bearers of meaning in the natural mode are

iconic representations, for example in drawings, statues, miniatures, models, and words that resemble instances of what they mean. Much more often bearers of meaning in the natural way are mental signs of instances of what they mean. Within this class fall many auditory, tactile, and other sensations and images as well as some more abstract ideas that men commonly use to facilitate their recognition and manipulation of objects and events. Many bearers of meaning in the natural mode are things and events having significant structural features isomorphic with those of instances of what is meant. Phonographic records, computer punch cards, musical scores and pictorial scripts may be bearers of this sort.

Among the most interesting bearers of meaning which most human beings are disposed to use are some that are connected with what they mean, not by close resemblances or specific structural connections, but by looser and at the same time highly suggestive analogies. Among these bearers of meaning are metaphors, which, though dependent to be sure on the cultural forms of language, derive their main thrust and principal interest from similarities that most human beings in suitable circumstances can recognize and would find appropriate. Another variety of the same general sort consists of symbols naturally suggestive of various emotions which artists weave into their works to achieve desired effects. More controversial are the symbols that psychologists and psychoanalysts insist are repeatedly to be found in dreams, fantasies, poems, and unguarded conversations. For example, Sigmund Freud contended that "The Emperor and the Empress ... represent the dreamer's parents; ... the dreamer himself or herself is the prince or princess; ... all sharp and elongated weapons, knives, daggers, and pikes represent the male member; and ... small boxes, chests, cupboards, and ovens correspond to the female organ."[4] Carl Jung adopted the even bolder thesis that primordial archetypes, deeply rooted in brain structures and racial memories, are constituents of a collective unconscious that dispose men to use certain symbols repeatedly with the same meanings. Such archetypes include those of God, representing

---

[4]Cf. Sigmund Freud, *The Interpretation of Dreams,* in *Great Books of the Western World* (Chicago: Encyclopedia Britannica Inc., 1953), Vol. 54, p. 283.

psychic energy; the Old Wise Man, personifying past experience; and the child hero, symbolizing the emergence of the self.[5] A much more modest claim for natural symbols is made by Mrs. Suzanne Langer, who tells us that "the image of a rose symbolizes feminine beauty so readily that it is actually harder to associate roses with vegetables than with girls," and that fire is a natural symbol of life and passion, ... of all that is living, feeling, and active."[6]

Not all bearers of meaning in the natural mode of the dispositional way are the kind that get their meanings through resemblances; some of them are the kind that get their meanings from causal connections and some, from casual associations. All men are disposed to refer to what is regularly or strikingly connected to a given kind of event to express a meaning associated with that event. Thus, in suitable circumstances, one is disposed to refer to or to simulate a sharp blow or a wound in order to indicate that someone is in pain, to point to the declining sun to warn of impending darkness, or to refer to fallen trees to remind someone of a tornado that has touched down.

The main point of inquiry into the natural mode of the dispositional way of meaning is not, however, to uncover and analyze instances of meaning in that mode for their own sake. Pure instances of meaning in this mode are, if they exist, difficult to discover, and more difficult to be sure of, and most of the instances of meaning with which people are likely to be concerned belong largely to other ways and modes. The main point of inquiry into this mode is rather to gain such insight as can be gained through it into the substantial natural element involved in many instances of other modes and ways and modes of meaning. To be sure most instances of the natural mode occur in situations already deeply grooved with learned responses, but all human responses rest in part upon foundations of natural dispositions whose impact is disclosed in some degree by inquiry into the natural mode. Natural dispositions have already been seen to constitute prior conditions for many instances of inten-

---

[5]Benjamin B. Wolman, *Contemporary Theories and Systems in Psychology* (New York: Harper and Brothers, 1960), p. 309.

[6]Suzanne K. Langer, *Philosophy in a New Key* (New York: New American Library, Twelfth Printing, 1962. Cambridge: Harvard University Press, 1942 and 1951), p. 128.

tional meaning; and when words are not readily available for
what one wishes to say, one is likely to look to such dispositions
as a foundation for natural signs that will do the job. Cultural
meanings of words are also, as will presently be seen, deeply
rooted in natural dispositions; for the conceptual schemes implicit
in our vocabularies tend to follow natural cleavages in things.
The formal structures of language are by no means altogether
conventional, for the grammatical patterns which enable competent speakers of any language to compose and understand new
sentences seem clearly to contain universal elements.[7] And even
the personalized dispositions of eccentrics and geniuses to use
bearers in their own special ways are often, as will presently
appear, firmly grounded in dispositional factors common to all or
most human beings.

b. The mode of the dispositional way of meaning next to
be considered differs from the natural mode in that in every
instance of it, the meaning, however deeply rooted in natural
dispositions, is eventually determined by the dispositional patterns
of a social group. One might be inclined to refer to this mode of
meaning as conventional, but the term "conventional" suggests
an artificiality that cannot properly be ascribed either to language
or to some other varieties of the mode in question. Hence I
refer to the mode of meaning to be considered as the cultural
mode. A bearer of meaning has a certain meaning, relative to a
given cultural group, if and only if, were a member of that group
to use that bearer in certain conditions to lead a respondent to
apprehend a meaning as his meaning, he would in all probability
intend to use that bearer to lead that respondent to apprehend
that meaning as his meaning.

The cultural mode of meaning is the one with which dictionary makers, teachers of English, and instructors in other languages
are primarily concerned. It is the way of meaning in which parents
bring up their children in the effort to impart to them the
common instrument of expression. It is the way of meaning in
which communicants in religious groups and initiates in fraternal
organizations are instructed. This is the way of meaning with
which rival philosophical claimants for the right use of cherished

---

[7]See Noam Chomsky, *Aspects of the Theory of Syntax* (Cambridge:
The M.I.T. Press, 1965), pp. 47 ff.

words and symbols are concerned. It is also a way of meaning with which critics of art and literature are in considerable part pre-occupied.

Ascriptions of meaning in the cultural mode are often—though not always—formulated in a manner rather different from that in which ascriptions of meaning in the intentional way are formulated. Ascriptions of meaning in the intentional way characteristically begin with references to agents and proceed to point out what these agents mean by a given bearer of meaning: "I mean ---- by '......'," or "James meant ---- when he said '......'" Ascriptions of meaning in the cultural mode, however, character-istically begin by references to bearers of meaning and go on to say what those bearers of meaning mean. The agents involved are mentioned, if at all, only parenthetically. Thus one may say: " 'Square' means rectangular and equal sided"; " 'Procrastination,' in English, means putting off"; or "The cross means, for Christians, redemption." Sometimes, in order to emphasize the contrast be-tween the modes of expression of one group and those of another, an ascription of cultural meaning may begin with a reference to the group, e.g., "We in the West mean by 'democracy' government for and by the people"; but ordinarily both expressions of meaning in the cultural mode and explanations of such expressions are oriented to a single cultural group, so that no explicit reference to the group is required. All that is needed in such cases is to mention the relevant bearer of meaning and to say what it means.

The social groups whose dispositions determine meanings in the cultural mode and to which such meanings are relative may vary in size from families and other small groups of associates among whom meanings of bearers are well established to whole collections of nations and races having common languages or sharing symbolisms. It is not essential to a bearer's having a certain cultural meaning that any member of the relevant group be using that bearer to express that meaning at any given time or even that each of the members thus use it at any time at all. Some members of the group may not yet have acquired the use of the bearer of meaning in question; others may never acquire it; some who have, may never use the bearer; and some who use it may use it to express a different meaning. It is essential to a bearer's having a certain meaning in the cultural mode that most of the mature members of the relevant group be so disposed with reference to that bearer that, if any such member were to use it, there would be a substantial probability that he would be using it to lead a respondent to apprehend that meaning. It is not necessary that the bearer of meaning in question be usually used in every context to have the meaning in question; it is necessary that that bearer be usually so used when it is used within contexts of certain specifiable kinds. It is also necessary that these contexts be mentioned in any full account of the meanings in question.

The dispositions on which meanings in the cultural mode of the dispositional way depend, like the intentions on which meanings in the intentional way depend, are in considerable degree shaped by the expectations of agents with respect to the responses of respondents, and these expectations in turn are constantly being molded by actual responses. No group of people would ever develop a language or any system of symbols apart from the responses of members of the group, and how any given word or symbol is used is constantly being influenced by what the user has learned to expect the respondent to take the word or symbol to mean. In an instance of the intentional way of meaning, the bearer's response is often widely at variance with the meaning that the speaker expects to convey; for in such an instance, an intentional act that allows little opportunity for corrective processes is determinative. However, in instances of the cultural mode of the dispositional way, the determinative factors are enduring dispositions of whole groups of people which can be, and are being, constantly adjusted by reference to responses actually produced. Thus, differences between meanings that agents are usually disposed to intend and those that respondents usually apprehend are, on this level, not likely to be very great.

Like intentional meanings, meanings in the cultural mode of the dispositional way (i.e., cultural meanings) nearly always involve prior connections with the sorts of things that become their bearers. In instances of cultural meanings, the connections in question are primarily those initiated, confirmed, manifested, and altered by repetitions of bearers of intentional meanings with their meanings; for basically cultural meanings are just those meanings which members of cultural groups have learned by repetition to intend and understand certain bearers to mean in suitable circumstances. However, the prior connections that enter into the links between intentional meanings and their bearers operate upon cultural meanings on a much larger social scale and through far longer periods of time than they do upon intentional meanings alone. Thus, likeness between objects or events and what they mean, similarities linking sounds meant and words spoken, naturalness of gestures, recognized causal links, and various other prior connections may be refined and transcended in the learning of groups to an extent to which they seldom are in the learning of the individual as such. Moreover, even initially arbitrary connections of bearers and meanings are likely to pass through many phases before they yield culturally established words and symbols. Most current words and symbols are clearly derivative from words and symbols of earlier cultural eras; and while many words are linked with their meanings by ties that appear in the end to be quite arbitrary, or can at any rate no longer be traced, all current connections between established symbolic forms and their meanings have come to be established in communicative interaction and many of them have very long histories.

Whatever may be the prior connections of a bearer of meaning in the cultural way and whatever the previous histories of such bearers, the current meanings of bearers of meaning in the cultural mode are always directly determined by the dispositions of the members of cultural groups whose members use them. The dispositions in question are readinesses of individuals conditioned by social interaction to use bearers to express certain meanings under certain circumstances. To be sure they rest in the end upon dispositions of individuals; for groups as such do not have dispositions in a literal sense, and it is basically individuals who can be ready to use bearers to lead respondents to apprehend meanings. Nevertheless individuals are for the most part carriers rather than makers of the main dispositional ties by way of which they are ready to use bearers of cultural meanings. With reference to verbal bearers of cultural meanings, dispositions to use them as they are now used are likely to have existed long before the emergence of a given individual, to endure long after his departure, and to change in predictable ways over which he has little control. The basic meaning dispositions prevalent in the group are inculcated in the individual from the earliest years by training, example, observation, and experience; and the process of learning within the group goes on continuously throughout the life of the individual. A given individual is likely to contribute little beyond the transmission of what has been learned. For such reasons as these, despite their actual individual bases, the dispositions on which cultural meanings depend behave as if they had a sort of life of their own beyond that of the individuals who are their carriers and sustainers.

Most bearers of meaning in the cultural way are types. Of these the most conspicuous are words and standard phrases, i.e., utterance and inscription patterns which the members of groups are disposed to use in appropriate circumstances in endeavoring to lead respondents to apprehend their meanings. Since sentences are for the most part particular utterances or inscriptions framed for specific occasions, sentences are likely to be thought of mainly as bearers of meaning in the intentional way rather than in the dispositional one. But some short sentences become standard tools of a language and may be said to have cultural meanings somewhat as words do. Moreover, any intelligible sentence can be said to have cultural meaning to the extent that competent users of the language in which it occurs would be ready to use it if just the right circumstances should occur. The possibility of building culturally meaningful sentences out of the words and phrases of a language depends, of course, on the syntax of the language. Other important type bearers of meaning in the cultural mode include rituals, myths, social stereotypes, commercial, political, religious, scientific and aesthetic symbols, and all manner of emblems and insignia. All of these type bearers of meaning are designed not indeed for the most part by decisions of individuals or particular occasions, but by social interaction across the years, centuries, and millenia.

Some bearers of meaning in the cultural mode are, however, not types but more or less durable particulars through reference to which members of a group are disposed to express certain meanings under certain circumstances. Among the most prominent bearers of meaning of this kind are works of art. Works of art have meanings in other ways; but their meanings both in the intentional way and in the natural mode of the dispositional one are notoriously difficult to get at, and their meanings in the cultural mode are for many purposes the more interesting. A meaning of a work of art for a given culture in a given period may be taken to be a meaning that sensitive persons in that culture and in that period, would, in specifiable circumstances, be disposed to intend to lead respondents to apprehend if they were to produce or refer to that work of art to lead respondents to apprehend any meaning. Thus, meanings of Leonardo's Mona List and Michelangelo's Moses in our cultural era are meanings that sensitive persons in this era would, in suitable circumstances, intend to lead respondents to apprehend if they were to produce or to refer to these works of art to lead us to apprehend meaning at all. Important examples of the kinds of bearers of cultural meaning under consideration other than works of art are well known geographical features, public buildings, commemorative statues, and historic objects by reference to which members of nations and religious groups are disposed to express ideas and ideals held in common. A Japanese manifests the relevant kind of disposition when he declares that he is returning to the land of Fujiyama; and so does a loyal American when, looking at the Statue of Liberty, he says that this is the spirit of his native land. The meaning situation is similar as a patriot bids us remember Bunker Hill or a minister reminds us to look to Calvary.

c. The mode of dispositional meaning now to be considered, to which I refer as the personal mode, has not heretofore been much discussed and may be less important than the ones discussed in the preceeding pages; but many instances of it represent preliminary steps in the learning of cultural meanings, and other instances of it involve meanings that eventually add new richness to cultural meanings. A bearer of meaning has a certain meaning in the personal mode of the dispositional way of meaning if and only if, were an individual to intend in using that bearer, in at least partial independence of natural and cultural dispositions, to lead a respondent to apprehend a meaning as his meaning, he would in all probability intend in using that bearer to lead the respondent to apprehend that meaning as his meaning. This is the mode of meaning primarily manifested in the dispositional patterns of a child who is in process of learning the words and symbols of his language and culture. It is also the mode of meaning primarily manifested in expressions of creative persons whose quest for adequate expression leads them beyond cultural matters.

Since most sentences of the personal mode of dispositional

meaning are of little public interest, occasions specifically to remark upon them are relatively less frequent than occasions for remarking upon meanings in the cultural mode. An expression by means of which one ascribes a meaning in the personal mode to a bearer is likely to give a prominent place to reference to the person who uses the bearer in his own special way and to suggest that a disposition to use the bearer, rather than an instance of its use, is in question. Such an expression may take one of the following forms: "I (you, he) (always or usually) mean(s) ---- by '.....'." "I (you, he) use(s) '.....' to mean ----," "When I, (you, he) say(s) '.....,' I (you, he) mean(s) ----." " '.....', as he (always) uses it, means '-----'."

The prior connections of possible bearers and meanings on which the dispositions involved in meanings in the personal mode are built include all those kinds of prior connections on which dispositions in any of the modes of the dispositional way are built as well as such dispositions themselves. Thus the personal dispositions of the child, the eccentric, and the genius may all be influenced by natural tendencies, current cultural dispositions, and of all that goes into the making of any of these factors. These dispositions themselves, insofar as they eventually determine meanings in the personal way, always include, however, aspects that, even when influenced by factors common to accepted meanings, deviate significantly from accepted meanings.

Bearers of meaning in the personal mode may include instances of all those kinds of bearers that have meanings in the other modes and many more besides; for an individual may be reliably disposed to use any widely used bearer of meaning to express a meaning somewhat different from accepted ones and he may also invent bearers of his own which he is disposed to use in his own way. Actually, children who have not yet mastered the vocabularies, syntax, and symbols of their own cultures are constantly using standard bearers to express their own special meanings, and creative persons, fully cognizant of standard meanings, often adopt new uses of old bearers and invent new bearers with new meanings. It is in such ways as these that languages change and that some of the most fruitful of man's works are achieved. Wittgenstein's repudiation of private languages because of the lack of clear criteria may or may not be sound; but regardless of whether or not it be called language, the development of quasi-private patterns of bearers and meanings has been and will continue to be an inexhaustible source of both of nonsense and of cultural advance.

Instances of bearers' having meanings in various modes of the dispositional way of meaning differ from one another in their degrees of objectivity, but all of them have a greater degree of objectivity than do instances of bearers' having meanings in the intentional way. Although instances of meaning in the dispositional way depend upon dispositions of individuals, such dispositions have of necessity some temporal spread, cannot be reliably ascertained directly by introspection, and are subject to objective tests that are scarcely applicable in the same manner to instances of meaning in the intentional way. Instances of meaning in the cultural mode are not dependent upon the thoughts, intentions or dispositions of any particular individual. They are phenomena that precede and outlast any given individual and with reference to which the usage of an individual may well be deviant. Nevertheless, even instances of the cultural mode of meaning remain relative to the particular cultures to which they belong and to specific periods of that culture.

Just because meanings in the dispositional way depend upon dispositions that have some temporal spread, they are subject to change as meanings in the intentional way are not. Obviously the dispositions of the child with reference to word types, change drastically from his earliest attempts to use them to the time of his mastery of his language. The peculiar aspects of the personal dispositions of adults with reference to word types and other bearers of meaning alter less rapidly than do those of children, but nonetheless they too change in the course of each individual's life. Bearers of meaning in the cultural mode evolve much more slowly than do those in the personal mode, but evolve they inevitably do. Indeed, over long periods, older languages become unintelligible to users of newer ones and once dominant symbolisms come to be unrecognizable. Because meanings in the natural mode are at the outset difficult to identify, it is not easy to say to what extent they change; but it would be, to say the least, very surprising to find that even these did not, in the course of evolution, also change.

3. *The Causal Way of Meaning*

All instances of the intentional and dispositional ways of
meaning depend directly or indirectly upon the intentions of
agents to lead respondents to apprehend meanings; they could
accordingly all be grouped together by reference to this basic
intentional orientation. Instances of meaning in the causal and
implicative ways, now to be considered, need involve no agent,
no respondent, and no intention. What they have in common is
rather just an inferability of meanings from bearers by virtue of
which they could be grouped together and referred to as inferen-
tial ways of meaning. Instances of the causal and implicative
ways of meaning nevertheless have a good deal in common with
instances of meaning in the intentional and dispositional ways,
and they ought not to be treated, as they often are, as though
they represented no more than unimportant derivative ways of
meaning. They frequently constitute the prior connections on
which meanings in the intentional and dispositional ways depend;
they involve something's pointing beyond itself, much as do
instances of meaning in other ways, and they are quite as readily
ascribed to their own bearers as meanings in the intentional and
dispositional ways are to theirs.

The factors eventually determining meanings in the causal
way are causal relations through which these meanings can be
correctly inferred from their bearers. Thus a bearer has a certain
meaning in the causal way if and only if that meaning can be
correctly inferred from it through a causal relation of that
bearer. The function in which this way of meaning is grounded
may be formulated as follows: X is a meaning of a given bearer
in the causal way if and only if X can be correctly inferred from
that bearer by way of causal connections of that bearer.

The causal way of meaning is the one in terms of which we
speak of meanings of common events in our daily lives when we
wish to explain them or to indicate their probable consequences.
"His repeated failure to show up for his appointments meant
that his memory was already slipping." "This promotion means
that I shall have to put in many more hours of hard work." It is
also the way of meaning in which certain characteristic claims in

the natural and social sciences are formulated. "This precipitate can only mean that nitrogen was present and that to complete the analysis we must test for the presence of carbon." "This distribution of votes means that the people of this area are dissatisfied with the policies of the present administration, and that no candidate who is too closely linked with that administration is likely to be elected for many years." The causal way of meaning is the one in which most historical claims when stated as meaning claims are meant. "The rise of Napoleon meant that people were not then ready for democracy, and the rise of recent dictatorships means that a predominantly demoractic world is a long way off yet." Even the meaning claims that manufacturers and salesmen press upon customers are likely to be formulated as ascriptions of meaning in the causal way. "This automatic device means that the oven needs no watching." "This inner tire means that you always have blow-out protection."

Ascriptions of meaning in the causal way make no explicit or implicit reference to anyone who means anything by the bearer or infers anything from the bearer. Instead, without mentioning either agent or respondent, they ascribe to things and events, meanings inferable from them through causal links. "That thunder means distant lightning." "Lowering clouds mean imminent rain." "That grey light means that the sun will soon be rising." "That click of the door means that our guest has come in." "The tone of his speech meant that his nation was determined to fight." "The recent deterioration in our relations with our allies means that we are losing the cold war." "An inevitable meaning of war is that innocent people suffer."

As the foregoing examples suggest, the range of possible bearers of meaning in the causal way is very great. Such bearers are very often particulars or tokens. "That cloud means rain." "That footprint means that a man has been here." "The Cuban crisis meant danger of nuclear war." Bearers of meaning in the causal way may equally well be classes or types. "Clouds mean rain." "Footprints of a certain kind can only mean human footsteps." "Arms accumulations always mean danger of war." For the most part, bearers of meaning in the causal way are undesigned. They are often natural objects and events, and when they are man-made, they are usually made for ends other than producing meanings. However, from a certain point of view, the

work of a manufacturer or an artist may sometimes be thought
of as having been designed to have the causal meaning it has. A
mattress maker may produce his goods to mean good sleep; a
shoemaker, his to mean foot comfort; and a painter, his to mean
a certain aesthetic experience. Even bearers of meaning in the
intentional way can be construed as in a broad sense bearers of
causal meanings. Such bearers are in an inclusive sense caused,
and their results are in such a sense effects though for most
purposes interest is likely to center more upon the roles of such
bearers in intention and disposition than upon their roles as
effects or causes. Similar considerations apply to responses
elicited by bearers of meaning in the dispositional way. Complex
events including both designed and undesigned elements often
have important meanings in the causal way. "Thus, the inaugural
ball meant a beginning of rift in the party." "The life of John
Bright meant a new beginning in social legislation." "Life on this
earth will always mean achievement." Indeed, as must by now
be readily apparent, no limit can be placed on the things and
events that have meanings in the causal way. Literally everything
in the world must be supposed to have at least some meaning in
the causal way, for everything in the world presumably has
causes and effects. On this ground alone, even if on no other,
the previously offered suggestions that although not everything
has a meaning in every way, everything has a meaning in some
way or other, would seem to be amply justified.

    While adequate description of the causal way of meaning
does not require any particular theory of causality, it does
require that the causal connections on which instances of
meaning in the causal way are based be distinguished from mere
beliefs as to the existence of causal connections even when such
beliefs are grounded upon the best available scientific evidence.
That something means something in the causal way entails not
just that someone believes, even on excellent grounds, that the
two are causally conected but that they actually are so connected.
Thus, if I say that those clouds mean rain and rain fails to
come, I subsequently say, not that the clouds meant rain, but
that I thought that the clouds meant rain when, in fact, they
really didn't. And if I say, in full accord with current scientific
theory, that the presence of a certain precipitate means the
presence of radioactive material, but, in fact, the expected material

fails to accompany the precipitate, I say that I thought that the presence of the precipitate meant the presence of radioactive material but that it really didn't.

The causality on which meanings in the causal way depend must be broadly conceived, and the range of causal connections giving rise to causal meanings must be wide if it is to conform at all to actual ascriptions of meanings in the causal way. The relevant causes may be proximate: "The murder of the archduke meant war." They may be intermediate: "The encirclement of Germany meant war." Or they may be remote: "The rise of nationalism meant a long succession of wars." The relevant causes may be sufficient causes: "The destruction of the brain means death;" or necessary ones: "The existence of life means the presence of oxygen." They may be of the one-many type, the many-one type, or the one-one type. Where animal behavior is involved, the causes may be natural: "The presence of the meat meant salivation;" or they may be conditioned: "The ringing of the bell meant salivation." The relevant causal connections may link physical objects or events with one another, or they may link physical and mental objects or events with one another: "The high fever meant that I could no longer think clearly, but the thought of you quieted my nerves and quickened the pace of my recovery."

The causal relations on which meanings in the causal way depend need not necessarily be rigid in the sense that the effect either could not have been other than it was or could have been predicted categorically or absolutely. A substantial tendency is often sufficient to ground a causal meaning. While ascriptions of causal meanings presupposing high degrees of causal regularity are justified only if corresponding degrees of regularity exist, ascriptions presupposing lesser degrees of regularity may be quite as fully justified by lesser degrees of existing regularity. Thus, if I say categorically that arctic winds always means cold weather, only invariable sequences of events of that order can justify my statement. But if I say more casually that frequent exposure often means colds, my statement may equally well be justified by a modest level of correlation between exposures and colds.

Although the link by virtue of which bearers have meanings in the causal way is grounded in real causal connections, it can scarcely be simply identified with such connections. If this cloud means rain, and these insults mean hurt feelings, one can still not simply point out the rain caused by the cloud or the hurt feelings caused by insults and say that this rain is the meaning of this cloud, and that these hurt feelings are the meaning of these insults. The links between bearers and meanings in the causal way are more complex than any such account would suggest. Actually what these links between bearers and meanings are can scarcely be adequately seen apart from a well-developed account of what meanings are. Since no such account is as yet forthcoming, what for the present needs emphasis is just the consideration suggested in the initial definition of the causal way, that for a meaning to be meant in this way is for it to be *inferable* through a causal connection. If those clouds mean rain or those insults, hurt feelings, the links between the bearers and the meanings consist not simply in the causal connection involved, but in the more complex facts that from those clouds it can be validly inferred through real causal connections that it's going to rain, and that from those insults it can be validly inferred through real causal connections that hurt feelings are very likely to follow.

The inferability of meanings in the causal way from their bearers may, as examples already cited amply indicate, be either from cause to effect or from effect to cause. Thus, by way of their effects, clouds mean rain; and by way of their causes, they mean the condensing of water vapor. In terms of causes, wet pavements mean recent rain; but in terms of effects, they mean hazardous walking. The Cuban missile crisis meant, as to its causes, the determination of Russia to expand its power; and as to its effects, a limitation upon that expansion. This sort of two-directional link between bearer and meaning is peculiar to the causal way of meaning and is not paralleled in any of the other ways of meaning.

Because of this two-directional inferability, the variety of kinds of causal relations, and the possibility of multiple causes even of the same kind, every bearer of meaning in the causal way has not one but many meanings. Thus, the outbreak of World War II may properly be said to mean any of the many things that from different points of view are correctly said to be its causes and any of the many things that may correctly be said to be its effects. An astronomical event may be said to mean any of the events leading up to it and any of the events that follow upon it. For this reason, while one may say of a given event that it means this or that, what an event means in the causal way is much better spoken of as *a* meaning of the event than as *the* meaning of the event.

Since the number of near and remote causes and effects of any event is virtually infinite, we can scarcely ascribe to an event all the causal meanings it has, and the causal meanings that we do ascribe to events are often selected by way of our interests. Such interests are initially those that most obviously affect our destinies and the satisfaction of our desires. "The election of that candidate means the continuation of peace and prosperity." Sometimes these selective interests enter into and give an evaluative character to our ascriptions of meaning, as when a lover says of his beloved that her every act is full of meaning or when a despondent man declares that life is "full of sound and fury, signifying nothing." However, whatever may be the subsidiary role of interest in our ascriptions of causal meanings, such ascriptions remain essentially ascriptions of what is causally inferable. This essential grounding of causal meaning in causal inferability as such is clear when the interest by which an ascription is prompted is a scientific interest, for scientific interest is basically interest in causal connections as such. It is also apparent in those instances in which people ascribe causal meanings on the basis of no apparent interest at all; for here while interest recedes into the background, causal inference remains. If someone says that the breaking of the dam means the washing of some leaves downstream or that the election of the candidate means that the population of that man's home town is reduced by one, a hearer may indeed wonder why anyone should say such a thing, but he will not for that reason want to deny that the causally inferred consequences are meanings of the breaking of the dam and the election of the candidate. Even in those ascriptions of causal meaning in which an evaluative component comes prominently into play, the causal factor remains crucial. When the lover says that his beloved's acts are meaningful, he suggests that these acts have inferable causes in her affection, which, moreover, are precious to him. When someone says that life is meaningful, he says in effect that the events that make up life have inferable causes and consequences, which, moreover, are of real worth. When one says that life has no meaning, he is saying either that life has no inferable consequences or that those that it has are worthless. In all such cases inferable causes and/or effects constitute the essential base upon which whatever evaluative component is present is built. When the ascriber includes in his ascription an evaluative component as well as a causally inferable one, he is understandably adding a factor which he nevertheless does not take to be essential to causal meaning as such; for even one who says that life is meaningless will, when pressed, acknowledge that to the extent that life has consequences and causes, it may have causal meaning though it has no meaning that is of any value to him.

Something's having a certain meaning in the causal way is not, like something's having a certain meaning in the dispositional way, subject to significant change. When the bearer of a meaning in the causal way is a particular, the causal root of the meaning is an event that lacks the sort of duration required for the applicability of the concept of change. When the bearer is a type, the inferred cause or effect is linked with the bearer by a law of nature, and for all practical purposes laws of nature must be regarded as changeless. Thus, on the one hand, the causal meaning of Brutus's fatal thrust and of the dropping of the bomb on Hiroshima do not change because they occurred as they did and had the consequences they did, without being the sorts of things that could be said to change; and on the other hand, the causal meanings of falling bodies and colliding objects do not change, because the laws of mechanics remain unchanged.

4. The Implicative Way of Meaning

We often say that something has a certain meaning when the meaning is eventually determined neither by anyone's intention or disposition nor by any causal connection but by the logical implications of the bearer. In such situations the bearer has a meaning in what I have called the implicative way. Thus, a bearer of meaning has a certain meaning in the implicative way if and only if, in conjunction with contextual assumptions, it logically implies that meaning. The meaning function in which this way of meaning is grounded may be expressed by saying that X is a meaning of a certain bearer in the implicative way if and only if that bearer, in conjunction with contextual assumptions, logically implies X.

Ascriptions of meaning in the implicative way usually affirm of an appropriate bearer just that it means this or that or has this or that meaning. No reference to an agent is stated or implied. Phrases referring to bearers of meaning in such ascriptions do not carry the quotation marks that often enclose the corresponding phrases in ascriptions of meaning in the intentional and dispositional ways, and the meaning is usually formulatable, as a *that* clause. Thus, granted in each instance certain obvious contextual assumptions, one may say such things as the following: "This figure's being a triangle means that the sum of its angles is 180°." "That there is a thought means that there must be a thinker." "Your defending that man means your defending an alien against an American." When, as often happens, the form of the ascription is insufficient by itself to distinguish an ascription of meaning in the implicative way from an ascription of meaning in some other way, the character of the meaning situation referred to and of the context of the ascription are usually sufficient to show whether or not the meaning ascribed is supposed to depend upon an implicative relation.

The implicative relation that determines meanings in the implicative way is not an implying in the sense of suggesting or hinting as when, for example, one says that James's remark implies that Smith's project is useless. Meanings determined by this latter sort of relation may best be thought of as belonging to an indirect mode of intentional meaning, i.e., the words spoken are intended to carry directly a certain standard meaning but indirectly, and more pointedly, a further hinted meaning. The implicative relation in question is also not that sort of implying according to which the occurrence of one event suggests the likelihood of another as when a succession of storms is said to imply a prior disturbance on the surface of the sun or when a man's odd behavior is said to imply that he has been drinking. Meanings determined by that sort of relation may be best regarded as meanings in the causal way. However, the relation that determines meanings in the implicative way is not confined to formal logical relations. It is rather a kind of entailment, including not only formal logical entailments, but a great many other principles deeply rooted in our thought and language by virtue of which

given certain premises, certain conclusions follow no matter what
the facts of the world are. Thus, in terms of the relation in
question, not only does (A and B) imply B, but that John is a
bachelor implies that he has no legitimate children, and that
Minneapolis is north of Kansas City implies that Kansas City is
south of Minneapolis.

Bearers of meaning in the implicative way can be particular.
"That lot's being square means that a diagonal will cut it in
half." They may also be general, "Any square can be bisected
by a diagonal." The bearers of meaning in question may be
designed. "My wearing this badge, in the present circumstances,
means that I am acting in an official capacity." Or they may be
undesigned. "That gases are physical means that they have mass."
That to which meaning is commonly ascribed in the implicative
way includes words, concepts, facts, sentences and propositions.
When meanings are ascribed to words and concepts, the underlying thought seems to be that the applicability of these to
something has a certain meaning; for words and concepts as such
scarcely have implications in the relevant sense. Thus, it may
well be that when someone says that "squareness" means rec-
tangularity, what he is getting at is that anything's being square
means that it is rectangular; and that when someone says that
red means being colored, what he wants to express is that something's being red means that it is colored. It seems also to be the
case that to say that a fact has a certain implicative meaning is
basically to say that a proposition to which the fact answers has
a certain meaning, and that to say that a sentence has a certain
meaning in the implicative way is in the end to say that one or
more propositions expressed by that sentence has that meaning
in that way. That which is said to have meaning in the implicative
way seems basically, therefore, to be propositional in character.

Whereas meanings in the dispositional way can and do
change and those in the causal way, insofar as they represent
generalizations, could but do not change; meanings in the implicative way, insofar at any rate as they are basically propositional,
neither do nor could change. Thus if all men's being mortal and
Socrates's being a man once meant that Socrates was a man,
it must, in the way in question, always mean that; and if the
presence of two couples of objects once means the presence of
four objects, it must always mean that.

The implicative way of meaning should not be assimilated to the intentional way or the dispositional way, as is likely to be done when one remarks that the meaning of a sentence token is whatever the sentence implies or that the meaning of a word is whatever its applications imply. To be sure such remarks as the foregoing are basically correct, but to make them without qualification is to obscure the fundamentally different modes of eventual determination of intentional and dispositional meanings, on the one hand, and implicative ones, on the other. Uttered and written sentences and word types come to have their meanings by virtue of the intentions of the speakers and the dispositions of the members of language groups; but only when the intentional and dispositional meanings of sentences and words are determined can words and sentences have implicative meanings. Indeed, it seems to be what is intentionally or dispositionally meant by sentences, not just sentences, and what is meant by applications of words, not just words, that have implicative meanings. "Here is a cube" means (implicatively) that here is a figure with eight corners; but until intentional or dispositional meanings of "Here is a cube" are determined to the effect that here is a solid figure bounded by equal squares, the sentence does not have implicative meaning. To be sure, implicative meanings may overlap with some aspects of intentional or dispositional ones; for what a person actually intends in making a statement, or what members of a language group are disposed to intend when they use a word, may include some implications of the most literal intentional or dispositional meanings of the expressions in question. For example, a perceptive person, or conceivably most of the members of a language group, may actually intend, or be disposed to intend, in speaking of cubes, not merely the literal meaning of "cube", but the implied notion of having eight corners as well. However, there are surely limits to what a person or a group of people intend, or are disposed to lead their respondents to apprehend, of the implications of their expressions; and some of these implications are matters for further exploration that, far from being intended or disposed to be intended, may be quite surprising when discovered. For example, not many people, in speaking of cubes, intend to lead their respondents to apprehend the notion of being twelve-edged or being such that the area of each face can be doubled by using its diagonal as the side of a square, though these notions are implied in so speaking.

When the distinction between the intentional and dispositional ways of meaning, on the one hand, and the implicative way of meaning, on the other hand, is kept clearly in mind, it is not difficult to see why an objectivity attaches to implicative meanings and a corrigibility, to ascriptions of such meanings which do not attach to intentional or dispositional meanings and ascriptions of such meanings. The intentional meaning of an utterance is eventually determined by the intention of an agent, but once this meaning is determined, this intention has done its work; the implicative meanings of the utterance, or of the propositional meaning it expresses, hinge directly, not on this intention, but on the place of the resulting intentional meanings in a logical system. Similarly, while the dispositional meaning of a word depends upon the dispositions of users of the word concerning its use, once that meaning is determined, these dispositions have done their job, and other broader, logical factors that cannot be dug out of these dispositions alone come into play. Accordingly, while an ascription of an intentional meaning to a sentence is essentially incorrigible when the ascriber knows the intentions of the agent, and an ascription of dispositional meaning to a word is incorrigible so long as the ascriber knows the disposition of the relevant language group, ascriptions of implicative meanings remain corrigible even when the intentions of the agents and the dispositions of the language group concerning the sentence or word are well known.

5. Some Complexities of Ways of Meaning

Thus far four major ways of meaning have been presented, largely as distinct from one another. In actual meaning situations, these four ways of meaning are often so intricately interwoven with one another in complex patterns that to think of each only in isolation from others would be to fail to appreciate, and even to misconstrue, the relations of these ways to one another.

The complexities are in the main of two kinds. On the one hand, something may have meanings in each of several different ways. On the other hand, something's having a certain meaning

in one way may depend upon something's having another
meaning in the same or another way. I shall illustrate several
varieties of each of these main kinds of complexities, and comment briefly upon the effect of each upon the integrity and usefulness of the distinction between the major ways of meaning
themselves.

a. Many bearers of meaning have meanings in more than
one way. If someone says "It's cold" that means one thing by
his intention and quite possibly something very different by the
rules of English. If my book, which was on the desk a moment
ago, is now on the floor, that may mean causally that the book
has fallen and implicatively that the book is now on one part of
the interior of the building. If the lion roars in a certain manner
that means, under certain circumstances, in the natural mode of
the dispositional way, that the lion has made a kill; in the causal
way, it means, among other things, that other lions are likely
soon to appear on the scene. Many bearers of meaning may
indeed have meanings in all of the ways thus far discussed. Thus,
if I say "The telephone has just rung," this may mean
intentionally that the telephone has rung and I would like for
someone to answer it; dispositionally, just that the telephone has
rung; causally, that someone does answer it; and implicatively,
that there has been a sound. The situation is similar with reference
to most bearers of meaning in the intentional way, in that almost
all of them also have meaning in all the other ways.

Do such complications as these entail fusions or overlappings
that undermine the integrity of the ways of meaning or destroy
the usefulness of the distinction between them? I think the
answer is clearly in the negative. With reference to any given
meaning situation, one is likely to focus his attention at any
given moment upon a bearer's meaning in one way rather than
several. The fact that other people now, and he himself at other
moments, may focus on other ways in which the same bearer
has meaning need lead to no confusion. The way in which any
bearer has a given meaning is usually apparent in the character
of the relevant meaning situation. And the way in which a
meaning is on any given occasion being ascribed to a bearer is
usually evident in the form and content of the ascription and in

b. I come now to the second, and more involved, of the
the character of the meaning situation referred to.

two kinds of complexities among ways of meaning mentioned at
the outset. Not only may the same bearer have meanings in
several different ways and more than one meaning in the same
way, but a bearer's having a certain meaning in one way may
depend on something's having another meaning in the same or
another way. Two varieties of this complexity, which are
oriented in opposite directions, require consideration. One hinges
upon the manner in which the incidence of meanings depends
upon prior conditions and the other, upon the manner in which
one meaning may be built upon or give rise to others.

In previous discussion of each of the ways of meaning, it
had been noted that any given instance of that way of meaning
is likely to be dependent on prior connections. As may now be
seen, these prior connections are often instances of something's
having another meaning in the same or another way. Thus, every
statement or use of accepted symbols to express a meaning in
the intentional way depends upon the prior existence of
meanings in the cultural mode of the dispositional way; and
even when intentional expressions of meaning in some measure
transcend the cultural mode they must still in considerable
degree depend upon meanings in other modes and ways. Most
instances of meanings in the cultural way require as prior
conditions not only prior cultural connections and continued
repetitions of intentional meanings but also social causal
relations belonging to the fabric of the way of life in which they
emerge. All instances of the causal way of meaning depend on
meanings in terms of associated laws and boundary conditions,
and there could be no implicative meaning apart from a pattern
of meanings in which it is embedded.

The complexities that ways of meaning may take on by
building meanings on meanings are somewhat less obvious but
just as inevitable as those involved in the prior connections of
meanings. What someone directly intends to lead a respondent
to apprehend by a given bearer may itself acquire another
meaning in another way, and that meaning in turn may take on
still another meaning in the same or another way; but all of the
meanings involved may in one fashion or another belong to the
initial bearer in the intentional way. Thus, if a grief-stricken man
says, "My wife is critically ill," what he directly intends to lead
a respondent to apprehend is that the woman to whom he is

married is in a certain physical condition, but that condition causally means danger of death, which in turn means implicatively that he may be widowed, which in turn means causally that his children may be left without the care they need and that many of his fondest hopes may be disappointed; yet all these meanings may be included in one manner or another in what he intends to express. Dispositional meanings tend to expand in similar fashion. A bearer of meaning may have a certain primary meaning in the cultural mode, which by way of natural human dispositions yields another meaning, which by way of implications has other meanings; and yet all these meaning may belong to a broadly conceived dispositional meaning of the original bearer. Expansions of instances of causal and implicative ways of meaning are likely to be virtually infinite by reason of the fact that limits can scarcely be set to causal connections of an event or to the implications of a proposition despite the fact that people's interests are usually focused upon limited ranges of causes, effects, and implications.

Among the most striking kinds of compoundings of meanings are metaphors. Metaphors are produced by the bringing together of bearers that, though diverse, are capable of yielding together new meanings that could not be produced by any one of these bearers alone and perhaps not by any other combination of expressions. Thus, when the poet tells us that "life is but a stage," by linking elements belonging to different modes of discourse, he creates a fresh meaning that can scarcely be reproduced by any more literal mode of expression.

None of these complexities of ways of meaning need, however, compromise the integrity of the ways of meaning; for in principle, and often in practice, careful analysis can, once the ways of meaning are clear, disclose what subsidiary bearer has what meaning, in what way, and how far the range of the meaning of the original bearer reaches, from what points of view. Certainly the complexities of the ways should not be regarded as detrimental to the usefulness of the distinctions between these major ways of meaning; for such complexities tend to reinforce the need for the very sort of tools of analysis that are afforded by these distinctions for the tracing out of the main lines of the functioning of bearers of meaning.

In concluding this discussion of ways of meaning, I wish to comment upon two further matters. One concerns the comprehensiveness of the indicated ways of meaning, and the other concerns the relations of ways of meaning to the character of meanings.

Thus far, I have claimed concerning the four indicated ways only that there are such manners of eventual determination of meaning each yielding a distinct variety of meaning. However, although I have not specifically asserted that there were no other ways of meaning, and although the ways indicated can conceivably be differently defined or rearranged at some points, it seems initially unlikely that there are other major manners in which anything is so determined as to justify us in calling it a meaning. In the chapters that follow I shall examine with considerable care most of the main features of meaning situations; and if there are other ways of meaning they should emerge in such an examination. I shall also subsequently return specifically to the question of whether or not there are other ways of meaning. Meanwhile, on the basis of a preliminary scanning of the actual uses of the word "meaning" and of the scope of the ways indicated, it seems safe to assume, pending further inquiry, that at any rate most instances of meaning will lie within the range of one or more of the indicated ways.

To sketch the character of the major ways of meaning is to be sure, to imply some limitations upon the circumstances under which anything can, or can not, be a meaning and to suggest some restrictions concerning what a meaning can, or can not, be. However, to sketch the character of the main ways of meaning leaves the major issues concerning the other features of meaning situations, and even concerning the concept of meaning itself, for the most part, wide open. If all meanings are either intended, disposed to be intended, causally inferable, or implied, the question concerning just what can satisfy the functions involved remains unsettled, and in exploring other features of meaning situations in the chapters that follow, as well as in inquiring directly concerning meanings, I shall also be specifically exploring this question.

CHAPTER III

CONTEXTS OF MEANINGS

Every meaning situation includes, and depends upon, not only a bearer of meaning and an eventual determination of meaning but also a context in which the bearer occurs and the determination of the meaning comes to focus. That every bearer of meaning occurs within a context is evident both in the general fact that it occurs at all and in the particular facts concerning the setting of each bearer of meaning that any one has ever taken the trouble to examine. That eventual determinations of meanings are deeply molded by their contexts is indicated both by the manner of their emergence from these contexts and by the striking variations that occur in meanings when contexts are varied and bearers and ways of meaning are kept constant. If any bearer of meaning is context free, it is so only in that certain of its crucial contextual factors remain constant over considerable ranges of instances, not in that contextual changes would not alter it.

The context of any bearer of meaning includes all those factors in the setting of that bearer which significantly affect the eventual determination of the meaning. Its boundaries can accordingly scarcely be sharply drawn and they differ for different purposes. In its foreground are distinguishable factors whose bearing upon the eventual determination of the meaning are abundantly evident. These foreground factors fade gradually into background factors still affecting the eventual determination of the meaning but with diminishing directness and force. Within the context of a bearer are often included a variety of specific factors, such as stimuli to the production of the bearer, expected responses to the bearer, and referents of the bearer, all of which will require consideration later on. For the present, I shall forego discussion of these specific factors and direct attention to some more general features of the character of contexts and of their modes of impact upon meanings. In this connection the various ways of meaning require separate consideration.

1. Contexts of Bearers of Meaning in the Intentional Way

All intentions, including those which eventually determine meanings in the intentional way, depend upon and are shaped by environments out of which they emerge. They are in large measure products of natural, social, and personal histories. Apart from some such environments and histories their occurrence is scarcely conceivable or their character intelligible. Thus, by shaping the intentions that eventually determine meanings in the intentional way, contexts of bearers of meaning in this way mold the meanings themselves.

However, this shaping of intentions and of the meanings that depend on them need not be thought of as compulsive or rigid. Some interpreters of the relevant intentions are indeed disposed to think of them as involving, in some metaphysical sense, an element of genuine spontaneity or freedom. Without needing to go this far, one should recognize that such intentions are scarcely to be thought of as determined by their contexts in quite the same manner as many natural and social events are determined by their contexts. A stone falls by forces over which it has no control. A prisoner is confined by powers outside himself. A compulsive drinker acts by forces he can no longer resist. A person who intends to express a certain meaning acts by his own initiative and by no external compulsion. However strong the impact of the entire contextual situation, the intentional act is one's own act, and however certain it may in principal be that just this act will occur, ones does not act under the sort of constraint that requires the stone to fall, the prisoner to remain within bounds, or the alcoholic to seek another drink.

Although the intention on which an intentional meaning eventually depends is not rigidly determined by the context in which the bearer of the meaning occurs, the context itself is already fully determinate when the bearer occurs. Every bearer of meaning in the intentional way is a particular produced at a particular time and place. The factors that enter into the making of the relevant intention and the production of the bearer may have been in formation for a long time and remain in process of being shaped until the intentional act that produces the bearer occurs; but once that occurrence has taken place, the formation of the context is complete, the pattern of the context is fully achieved, and the contextual material has done its work. The eventuating meaning is relative to this context in having emerged in it, and in having been shaped, through the determinative intention, by it, but the meaning is not relative to this context, as some meanings are relative to contexts, in the sense that the meaning may be different depending on what the context is. The meaning of the bearer in question cannot vary according to contexts for the reason that one and only one fully determinate context is already given. This context may not be fully or adequately known, but it is just as it is and the bearer has its meaning in just this context and no other. Accordingly, in ascribing a meaning to a bearer in the intentional way, one need not say, as one must in some other instances, that the bearer has such and such a meaning relative to this context. Indeed, one need not necessarily mention the context at all, for while the context may for some purpose require searching out, it cannot now be varied or altered in any way.

Since meanings in the intentional way are eventually determined solely by the intentions of agents in producing bearers of meaning, one may be disposed to think that knowledge of contexts is not required for the apprehension of meanings in the intentional way. Moreover, if intentions could be fully known apart from contexts, meanings could indeed be known apart from contexts. In practice, however, intentions can scarcely be separated from contexts or known apart from them. Rarely, if ever, can one apprehend even his own intentional meaning altogether clearly apart from the context of its bearer; and even if one did thus know his own meaning, he could scarcely explain it to anyone else altogether apart from this context. Where the intentional meaning of another person is in question, the attempt to determine a meaning apart from context can at best be no more than a guess. Every expression is in itself at least potentially ambiguous and incapable of conveying a clear message except within a suitable setting. Thus not only are meanings in the intentional way shaped through relevant intentions by the contexts that come to focus in these intentions, but to apprehend these meanings requires ample apprehension of these contexts.

Although the various factors constituting the context of a

bearer of meaning in the intentional way converge upon the intention that determines the meaning, not as separate entities, but as an integrated contextual pattern, they can be separated in thought and, for expository purposes, presented as various kinds of contexts. Of such factors, four principal varieties may be appropriately referred to respectively as physical, social, semiotic, and psychological contexts. Each of these kinds of contexts of bearers of meaning in the intentional way is now briefly to be considered.

a. Every bearer of intentional meaning occurs in a physical context. Whatever else an intention is, it is interwoven with a physical environment that includes both the remotest galactic expansion and the nearest intracellular adjustment. Whether or not there would or could be any intentional meanings, or what such meanings could possibly be like, apart from a physical order, we have no way of being certain; but that in fact man's intentional meanings invariably occur in physical contexts and that the character of these meanings is contingent on the kind of physical order that there is, is an inescapable aspect of human existence. As will subsequently be seen, what all men tend to mean in using certain bearers of meaning depends upon certain common characters of man's relation to the physical world in general, and what groups tend to intend in using certain bearers depends on the relations of these groups to the characters of the parts of the physical world in which they live. What is more specifically pertinent for present purposes is that the intentional meanings of individuals as such depend upon, and are disclosed by particular physical contexts in which those intentional meanings are expressed at particular times and places.

If I say, "Now the sun is setting," in the evening when all is well, my meaning is concerned with a certain more or less observable fact; but if I say the same words in the middle of the day when a friend is dying my meaning may be something quite different. If I say, as I scan the sky, "A new star is now rising," what I say concerns an alleged astronomical fact; but if I say the same words as I watch the performance of a brilliant new actor, what I say is primarily concerned not with astronomy but with the theater. "It's cold" means one thing spoken in a laboratory in the course of a low temperature experiment, and another out of doors on an autumn day. "It's tall," means one thing when said of a giraffe and another when said of a robin. If a man wounded in battle says, "Water!" very likely he means that he wants water; but if a chemist in reporting the result of an analysis says, "Water," he does not mean that at all. A driver who turns on a blinking light on the left-hand side of his car shortly before coming to an intersection evidently intends to signal a left turn; but a driver who gives the same signal when there is no intersection and a slow vehicle is ahead of him usually intends to express another meaning. A man who wildly waves his arms evidently means one thing when he is confronting a giggling infant and quite another when he is sinking in quicksand.

In multitudes of instances like the foregoing, the impact of the physical context upon intentional meaning is so obvious that though apart from apprehension of the physical setting the meaning would remain obscure, no special attention to the physical setting is required. However, in some instances the bearing of the physical setting is less obvious and calls for special notice. Thus, for example, a puzzling passage in a letter may become clearer when one realizes that the writer was ill or in danger at the time of the writing; and many a passage in literature is illuminated by knowledge of the physical surroundings in which it was produced.

b. While the contexts of bearers of intentional meanings could conceivably be construed of as wholly physical, certain aspects of such contexts are most illuminatingly thought of not simply as physical events but as social interactions among human beings. Apart from contexts consisting of such interactions, there could probably be no intentional meanings, and most such meanings as there are could not be understood. The communicative use of signs and symbols is notably dependent upon social intercourse; and with reference to the use of language, it has become at least debatable whether or not the notion of a private language is even intelligible. As will subsequently be seen, what all human beings are disposed to mean by expressions in the use of which they agree depends upon general social conditions which all human beings share; and what groups of human beings are disposed to mean by expressions in the use of which their members agree depends upon the particular cultural conditions of these groups. But quite apart from the impact of these broader conditions on what all men or members of groups are disposed to intend to reference to particular social situations in which these expressions express by the expressions they use, what individual human beings do intend to express at particular times and places by the expressions they do use depends upon, and may be clarified by, occur.

Thus, for example, a move of the hand that would mean one thing from pulpit or rostrum may mean something quite different when executed by a pilot newly returned from a dangerout mission. A man's placing his hand over his heart may mean one thing in a doctor's office and another on the parade grounds as the flag passes. The blowing of a whistle means one thing at a traffic intersection, another on a football field, and still another on a battlefield. The sentence, "He wants the chair," is likely to mean one thing when uttered at a university board meeting and another when uttered at a furniture sale. The word sentence, "Strike!" means one thing at a baseball game and another at a union rally. "The jack is in the corner" means one thing in a garage and another in a stable. "The host is providing abundant food" is likely to have quite different meanings when said at a dinner party and at a conference on parasitology. And "The collection is ample" conveys one meaning in an art gallery and another in a church.

c. One part of the context of bearers of meaning in the intentional way that belongs mainly to the social context is nevertheless sufficiently distinct and important to require consideration as a "semoitic" context. This context consists of those culturally conditioned signs, symbols, word patterns, and systems of such factors among which a bearer of meaning in the intentional way occurs.

The impact of semiotic contexts upon a meaning in the intentional way involves two distinguishable aspects, one of which may be thought of as formal and the other as material. The formal aspect is concerned with the impact of the ordering of the bearers of meaning among which the bearer under consideration is placed upon the meaning of this bearer; it may be referred to as a syntactic aspect. The material aspect is concerned with the impact of the meanings of the other bearers upon the meaning of the bearer under consideration; it may be called a semantic aspect. The formal or syntactic aspect can be studied in partial independence of the material or semantic one, but the converse of this does not hold. Each aspect involves what might be called a horizontal dimension, which consists of culturally oriented standard structures into which a bearer or its meaning could be fitted, and a vertical dimension, which consists of an actual pattern in which a bearer is in fact set. Each dimension of each aspect also involves both immediate and more remote phases.

The immediate impact of the vertical or actual setting of a word upon the meaning of that word is is often readily apparent from the actual placing of the word and can be ascertained with a minimal knowledge of grammar. Thus, the sound or inscription "right" used in an adjectival position means one thing and the same sound or inscription used in a noun position means another. The situation is similar with respect to "kind," "good," "hand," "round," "ground" and multitudes of other sounds and inscriptions. In a verb position, such expressions as "bear," "saw," "lay," "pay," and many other expressions have one meaning; while in noun positions, their meanings may be radically different. Countless other less striking differences are indicated by actual simple syntactical patterns of words in sentences. Light is sometimes thrown upon the meanings of sentences by their syntactical relations to surrounding sentences, and sometimes the syntax of a sentence in a remote paragraph will help to illuminate that of a given sentence. Moreover, not only the meanings of verbal bearers, but also those of mathematical symbols, codes of many kinds, and even elements of ritual and works of art are often affected and illuminated by the patterns of symbolic factors in which they are actually placed.

However, the impact of syntactical contexts upon the meanings of bearers in the intentional way can scarcely be amply appreciated apart from substantial knowledge of and attention to a "horizontal" dimension of syntax consisting of alternative orders of bearers of meaning that are possible in the existing culture. The fact that a sentence is meaningful at all depends upon its being framed within some established syntax, and only as an individual has in some degree mastered such a syntax can he begin to formulate or express clear propositional meanings. Apart from syntactical patterns, strings of words could mean little or nothing unless meanings for them were memorized; and most sentences that are actually used are not memorized but newly made by the use of established vocabularies and well-known syntactical rules. Moreover, what is true in this respect of verbal expressions is also eminently true of mathematical systems and of some ritualistic and other symbolic systems. In order to be ready fully to appreciate what a bearer means in the situation in which it is placed, one must often know a good deal about what the bearer could mean in situations in which it could be placed.

The second of the two aspects of the impact of semiotic patterns upon the meanings of bearers in the intentional way, i.e., the material one, is much less often commented upon by linguists than is the first or formal one. It is, however, very important and is in fact often remarked upon in ordinary conversation. Quite obviously the meaning of any given word is very often dependent, not merely upon its formal relations to nearby words in its context, but also upon the meanings of such words. Thus "table" means one thing when the conversation is about data and another when it is about furniture. "Light" means one thing when associated words are concerned with illumination, another when they are concerned with colors, and still another when they are concerned with weights. Similar considerations apply to such common words as "man," "cause," "fair," "point," and countless others. The surrounding texts that by the character of their meanings help to determine and illuminate bearers in the intentional way are not always included in the same sentence or even the same paragraph. Indeed the whole character of the meanings involved in an entire essay, novel, or speech may throw light upon the meaning of a given bearer; and the meanings of the various bearers used may play upon one another in intricate fashion.

However, it is not only in the context of a particular discourse that contextual meanings affect the meaning of a bearer. The fact is that every bearer of meaning in the intentional way functions in relation to a whole system of meanings each of which is intricately interwoven with many others, and perhaps with all others. The language with respect to which an utterance operates is not merely a system of syntactic structures; it involves also a system of meanings, every part of which affects and is affected by every other, and no part of which can be fully understood apart from explicit or implicit involvement of other parts. What is true of languages in this matter is also true of all sorts of symbolic systems.

d. When someone produces a bearer intending to express a meaning, it is surely to be expected that his physical and social surroundings and the setting of what he says in actual and possible semiotic contexts will have a bearing on what he intends to express, but his intention is itself most distinctively psychological, rather than physical, social, or semiotic. Accordingly, it is to be expected that the context most intimately related to an intentional meaning will be a psychological one consisting of thoughts, feelings, wishes, hopes, desires and the like preceding, accompanying, and interwoven with the determinative intention. Since scientific psychology is often predominantly behavioristic and since the psychological accompaniments of meanings are quite varied and are evidently not meanings themselves, inquiries concerning meaning have for the most part in recent years been disposed to neglect the psychological contexts of bearers of meaning in the intentional way. However, that such bearers are deeply embedded in vastly complex contexts of this sort can scarcely be doubted, and that such contexts are varied should be all the more reason for noting them.

In the broad psychological background of every bearer of meaning in the intentional way, lie the essential features of the psychology of man as man, the culturally conditioned psychology of the group to which the agent belongs, and the psychological history of the agent himself. In the more specific context of a given bearer of meaning in the intentional way, are the thoughts, feelings, impulses, etc. that more or less immediately precede and accompany the intention that produces the bearer. It is directly in the milieu of these experiences that the intentions determining meanings in the intentional way are formed; and upon refined discernment of these experiences, whether by introspection, report, or inference from behavior, often depends the understanding of an intentional meaning.

If I say that the sun is setting on an evening when my friend is dying somewhere else, a hearer may be quite uncertain as to what I mean until he learns what I have been thinking of; and if I speak of my friend's "going west," whether I mean that he has died or that he has taken a trip to California may be unclear until the hearer knows what has been going through my mind. If the chairman at a conference calls for the tables, either physical tables or mathematical ones can be taken to be what he means until the responding officials know what he has been concerned about. Even at night under the stars, it may not be clear whether one who speaks of the birth of a new star is speaking the language of astronomy or that of the theater. At a meeting on parasitology, whether the speaker means by "the host" the entertaining institution or the victim of a parasite may, in some cases, not be clear until the speaker's train of thought can be disclosed. What is true of shorter expressions can also be true of sentential expressions in which the meanings of the separate words are clear enough. When the young man said to the young lady, "I wish we could go right on seeing one another," the young lady was uncertain whether to take his words as a proposal, an expression of intention to break the engagement, or a suggestion of perpetual courtship; and until she had some further clue as to what he had been thinking and feeling, she remained at a loss as to how to respond. Moreover, quite apart from such instances of gross ambiguity as the foregoing, many subtle shades of meaning involved in multitudes of expressions of intentional meaning cannot but be obscure until the psychological contexts from which they emerge become reasonably plain.

2. Contexts of Bearers of Meaning in the Dispositional Way

Since the bearers of meaning in the dispositional way are not particular tokens produced at particular times and places to express intended meanings then and there but either types or enduring particulars that people are disposed to use to express various meanings in certain kinds of circumstances, contexts of bearers of meaning in the dispositional way are often not given with the bearers. Indeed for any given bearer, the context may be any of many possible kinds, and the meaning may vary according to the kind of context. The meaning of bearers in the dispositional way are relative to contexts in a way that the bearers of meaning in the intentional way are not. The meanings of bearers in the intentional way are relative to their contexts only in the sense that they mean what they do in the specific contexts which they have, but the bearers of meaning in the dispositional way are relative to their contexts in the sense that they may be different depending on which of many possible kinds of contexts is chosen. If on a certain occasion I say, "This man is bright," my words mean what they do in just the circumstances in which I utter them; but the English word "bright" may mean a variety of different things depending on the kind of circumstances in which it is used.

Because a bearer of meaning in the dispositional way may have different meanings depending on which of various possible contexts are chosen, a statement ascribing a meaning to a bearer of meaning in this way (eg., a word in English) must, if it is to be complete, include an indication of the kind of circumstances for which the bearer is being said to have this meaning. Hence, a full definition of any bearer of meaning in the dispositional way must specify for each meaning the kinds of context for which that meaning is relevant. It won't do just to say "bright" means keenly intelligent. One must rather say that "bright" has this meaning, e.g., in the context of discourse about mental aptitude, another meaning in another kind of context, still another meaning in a third kind of context, etc.

Not only ascriptions of meaning in the dispositional way but even apprehensions of meaning in this way are dependent upon indications of contexts chosen. This is, moreover, not merely a matter of contingent fact, but is rather rooted in the character of meanings in the dispositional way themselves. If, as is clearly the case, every bearer of meaning in the dispositional way emerges from and is shaped by a context and if acquiring words and symbols is, as it is, largely learning in what situations words and symbols apply with what meanings, then that any dispositional meaning of a bearer of meaning could be apprehended apart from some indication of its context is implausible. But if, as has been suggested, every meaning in the dispositional way is relative to a context in the sense of varying according to which of various possible contexts is chosen, and if every complete ascription of definition of a meaning in this way must specify the contexts for which it is applicable, then that the dispositional meaning of a bearer could be apprehended apart from an indication of its context is not only implausible but impossible.

Many bearers of meaning in the intentional way are manifestations of dispositions that determine dispositional meanings with reference to the kinds of contexts in which bearers of meaning in the intentional way actually occur. Hence, it is to be expected that the major varieties of contexts in which bearers of meaning in the dispositional way are found will be of the same physical, social, semiotic and psychological varieties as those in which bearers of meaning in the intentional way are found. Examination of instances amply bears out this expectation. Indeed, since meaning-producing intentions are usually manifestations of meaning-producing dispositions relative to suitable contexts, almost all contexts of intentional meanings are illustrations of kinds of contexts to which dispositional meanings are relative. Accordingly, instead of attempting to say more about major kinds of contexts of meanings in the dispositional way, I shall simply assume that they are basically the same sorts of physical, social, semiotic, and psychological contexts encountered in connection with meanings in the intentional way and proceed to discuss the related matter of the ranges of contextual materials that characterize all kinds of contexts of bearers of meaning in the dispositional way. The ranges in question may be thought of as a series of concentric circles beginning with very broad conditions necessary to the existence of dispositional meanings but only loosely related to the particular character of such meanings and moving progressively toward conditions in which such meanings are directly rooted. Since meanings in the intentional way are manifestations of dispositional ones, such a procedure should throw some light upon the character of intentional meanings and their contexts as well as upon that of dispositional ones and their contexts.

The widest range of contextual backgrounds of any bearer of meaning in the dispositional way consists of those conditions that are required for the production of any sentient beings. Such conditions include cosmological and geological conditions suited to the production of sentient beings. Since these broad contextual conditions underlie all instances of dispositional meanings they are of no use in distinguishing one dispositional meaning from another. However, since things and events very similar to bearers of meaning in the dispositional way are sometimes produced by inanimate objects, attention to conditions essential to the production of sentient beings may be helpful in distinguishing bearers of dispositional meanings from these other things and events. For example, regarding radio signals received from another planet, one of the first requirement for determining whether or not the signals represent words in use on that planet is the clarification of the general contextual matter of whether or not, on other grounds, that planet can be said to be suited to sustain sentient beings.

A somewhat narrower but still wide circle of contextual conditions of dispositional meanings is that of the conditions that are common and peculiar to all human experience. Such conditions include much more restricted patterns of physical and chemical conditions than do those essential to the support of sentient existence as such; they include, for example, the development of enormously complex physiological and psychological structures and capacities, and the existence of at least rudimentary societies. Again, since most of the conditions in question are common to all bearers of dispositional meaning attention to them is of little use in distinguishing the meaning of one such bearer from that of another. However, since the kinds of things and events that human beings are disposed to produce to express their intended meanings may be produced in ways that involve no intentions at all, attention to physiological, psychological and sociological structures common to the contexts of bearers of dispositional meanings may help to distinguish dispositional bearers of meaning from these other things and events. For example, if a sound similar to the expression, "Look out!" should be produced by wind in the trees, we could assure ourselves by the mode of its production that it did not mean what that expression in English ordinarily means.

More restricted than contextual conditions common to human beings but still very broad are the geographical and historical contextual factors that largely determine the differences between one culture and another. Such factors include climate, terrain, soil conditions, floods, famines, migrations, cultural contacts, and conquests. The effect of such factors can be seen in the meanings of the words, symbols and symbolic patterns of any culture, and attention to them can be illuminating in searching out the dispositional meanings of these bearers of meaning. Thus, the vocabularies, developed by peoples living in polar regions, are found to be very different from those of peoples living in the tropics. Those of peoples living in the mountains are very different from those of peoples living on the plains; and those of peoples living by the sea, from those of peoples living on the desert. A

culture that has long existed in isolation is likely to attach
meanings to many of its symbols very different from those attached
by a culture that has existed in constant contact with other
cultures; and a people that has often conquered or been conquered
by other peoples is likely to have a different sort of symbolism
from that of a people that has lived at peace with its neighbors.

More directly illuminating with reference to bearers of
meaning in the dispositional way than the conditions that lead
to differences between cultures are the ways of life that in
considerable part constitute cultures. So deeply rooted are the
words and symbols of a culture in the ways of life of that
culture that few if any of these words or symbols can be
adequately understood apart from some insight into these ways.
The symbols of the Aztecs, the ancient Chinese, and modern
Europeans for their deities are almost unintelligible apart from
knowledge of the ways of life of their respective cultures. In the
Middle East, vocabularies relating to camels are highly developed,
and those relating to seals are hardly developed at all. Among the
Eskimos, the converse is true. Meanings of coins, bank checks,
postage stamps, and tax receipts vary greatly in their significance
depending on the ways of life to which they belong. Expressions
generally signifying democracy, justice, marital fidelity, chastity,
and friendship differ greatly in specific meaning depending on the
cultural patterns of those who use them. Among the ways of life
that enter into the making of a culture are included, along with
those that are common to the whole culture, some that are peculiar
to special sub-cultures. These also must be included in the contexts
that are relevant to dispositional meanings. The language and
symbolisms of farmers and merchants, fishermen and mechanics,
and industrialists and educators almost always differ in important
respects; and anyone who hopes to understand the modes of expression of members of these groups must take the relevant contextual differences into account.

Closer still to bearers of meaning in the dispositional way
than the ways of life that in part constitute cultures are the
culture-oriented symbolic systems to which these bearers belong.
Such systems include those of numbers, those of weights and
measures, those of laws and rituals, and above all those of language.
They consist of, not only dispositions to use well-established
word types repeatedly to express the same meanings but also dis-

positions to relate word types to one another in reliable patterns capable of producing new meanings. Such systems are usually highly integrated, so that each part depends in some measure upon every other. Apart from such systems, the expressions of meanings would be confined to very elementary levels; with the aid of such systems meanings appropriate to very complex situations can be achieved.

Such systems, insofar as they are linguistic, include, in addition to vocabulary, formal grammatical or syntactical parts consisting of rules concerning what forms of expressions can be put together in what ways. They also include important semantical relations. Words stand in revealing relations to coordinate and contrastive sets of words. Some patterns of words, such as "Slumber runs rapidly" and "The grass chews sadly," though quite in order grammatically, have to be regarded as not ordinarily making sense. Allowable sentences fall within certain orders of sense as well as within orders of form. To the syntactic and semantic systems to which words belong may be added the genetic patterns of their development. While the systemic context that is most important with reference to a word is its place in a living language, a word does in fact also have a history which tends to be carried forward in its meaning and may need exploring in order to facilitate full understanding.

When one has oriented a word or some other bearer of meaning in the dispositional way within the syntactic, semantic, and genetic patterns to which it belongs, he may not yet have arrived at the context to which the meaning of that bearer is most specifically relative. Most bearers of dispositional meanings involve dispositional sets with reference, not only to other parts of the cultures and systems to which they belong, but also to alternative possible specific contexts inside these systems. Often—though not always—the meaning of a bearer will vary according to such alternative specific kinds of possible contexts. Thus, for example, "square" has one meaning with reference to such contexts as those involving boxes and drawings, another with reference to those involving modes of dancing. A magazine is one thing where battleships are concerned and another where printed matter is under discussion; and a picture of an eagle means one thing in a periodical on nature study and another in a piece of nationalistic literature.

Three kinds of situations are encountered concerning the

relevance of specific possible contexts to the meanings of bearers of meaning in the dispositional way. One is the kind of situation in which it is possible to distinguish a few relatively clear-cut kinds of contexts each of which is connected with a distinguishable meaning. "Red," in the context of qualities, means a color of a certain sort; in the context of ideologies, it means having a certain sort of politics. The second kind of situations is one in which the variety of possible contexts is too great to be traced out, and in which the meaning of the bearer of meaning varies almost continuously with variations in contexts. Such terms as "lovely," that depend for their applicability on circumstances too complex and variable to mark out in clearcut classes, would seem to be of this sort. Actually, it seems likely that a substantial proportion of bearers of dispositional meaning fall within the kind of situation in which definitive contexts cannot be neatly laid out; for it may be doubted that the full flavor of many bearers can be completely caught within any disjunction of sharply distinguished kinds of contexts. The third kind of situation is one in which a word or some other bearer of dispositional meaning is quite new or, for some other reason, seems to have approximately the same meaning for every context. "Cyclotron," for example, seems to be such a word. To say that such a word is context-free, as some writers do, would however, be a mistake; the fact is rather just that the range of contexts in which such words can intelligibly occur is so narrow that the impact of all of the possible contexts is very nearly the same.

All of the ranges of contexts that have so far been discussed are applicable to and may be revealing regarding bearers of meaning in any of the modes of the dispositional way of meaning. Thus, while the wider ranges of contexts are most obviously applicable to bearers of meaning in the natural mode, in that what any human being who uses a bearer is disposed to use it to mean is certain to be influenced by conditions common to sentient and human experience; these contexts are also clearly applicable to bearers of meaning in the cultural and personal modes, in that neither what members of a cultural group are disposed to use bearers to mean nor what individuals use them to mean can be unaffected by conditions common to sentient and human experience. Similarly, while narrower ranges of contexts most obviously affect meanings in the cultural and personal modes, in that what members of cultural groups and even independent minded persons are disposed to use bearers to mean cannot but be affected by the conditions that determine or constitute cultures and by specific kinds of contexts; narrower ranges of contextual material apply also to meanings in the natural mode, in that what all men are disposed to use a given bearer to mean cannot but be affected in specific applications by the specific conditions in which it occurs. Concerning this latter point, it is interesting to note that Sigmund Freud, who has been one of the strongest advocates of meanings in the natural mode, specifically acknowledges the relativity of such meaning to the cultural contexts in which they occur.

However, while all ranges of contextual materials are relevant to the meaning of a given bearer in such fashion that particular notice of any one of them may be revealing with respect to a meaning of that bearer, the narrower ranges are the ones that are most often crucial. The broader ranges are for the most part presupposed and the narrower ones are more likely to be specifically noticed and mentioned. But while complete accounts of meaning require mention of all ranges of contexts, mention even of the narrower ranges can sometimes be omitted when the likelihood of ambiguity is excluded.

3. Contexts of Bearers of Meaning in the Causal Way

The major differences between the intentional and dispositional ways of meaning, on the one hand, and the causal way, on the other, have been seen to be considerable. Other differences between these two sets of ways are differences between the relations of contexts to other factors in instances of the intentional and dispositional ways of meaning and in instances of the causal way of meaning.

One such difference consists in the fact that whereas in instances of meaning in the intentional and dispositional ways bearers of meaning can be fairly sharply distinguished from their contexts, in instances of meanings in the causal way context and bearer are more or less continuous with one another. Thus, for example, for purposes of a given inquiry, a certain uttered or inscribed sentence may be quite clearly a bearer of meaning in the intentional way while the remainder of the paragraph or discourse in which it occurs, together with accompanying conditions, may equally clearly belong to the context of that bearer. Again, the English word "red" is clearly a bearer of meaning in the dispositional way while sets of words with more or less similar meanings and sets with opposing meanings, together with the sorts of settings in which the word may be used, are clearly contextually relevant to it. However, if certain clouds mean rain, it is not usually just those clouds that cause, and hence in the causal way mean, rain; it is rather those clouds under certain conditions. While the more focal aspects of a total situation can be thought of as bearing the meaning and wider aspects as constituting a context, no sharp boundary can be drawn between the two.

A second difference between the relation between contexts and other major factors in instances of the intentional and dispositional ways of meaning, on the one hand, and instances of the causal way, on the other, is as follows: in instances of meaning in the intentional and dispositional ways, the relation of the context to the eventual determination of the meaning is that of a set of associated factors to an act or a disposition to act that involves factors which, though they can be construed— in the broad sense of "causal" in which "causal meaning" is defined —as causal, are nevertheless sufficiently distinctive to lead us to speak ordinarily of the relation in question in language other than that of causality. Thus, while it is not incorrect to say that my past experiences cause me to intend, in saying that "I am ill," to say that I am suffering from a physical disorder; one would be more likely to say that my past experiences led me to intend to say that. Similarly, while one may say that geographical conditions help to cause Eskimos to use their word for "seal" to convey certain meanings, one is more likely to say that geographical conditions lead or influence them so to do.

When a bearer of meaning in the causal way is a particular fact or event, the context is, as in instances of particular bearers of meaning in the intentional way, already fully determinate when the event occurs. Thus, if Jones's being ill means that he will not be at the meeting, all the circumstances that affect his illness's having that meaning already exist as soon as the illness comes to have that meaning. If the rolling of this billiard ball in a certain way means that another ball will drop into a certain pocket, all the circumstances that are required to secure the result are already determined as soon as the ball's rolling in this way comes to have that meaning. The situation is similar whether the bearer is a physical, social, or psychological event. If this is so, while the bearer's having the meaning it does may depend on many circumstances, it is not relative to circumstances in the sense that the meaning would be one thing in one set of circumstances and another in another. Rather the meaning simply is what it is in the circumstances that have in fact been given. What the meaning would be in other circumstances is another question applicable not so much to the bearer itself as to events of its kind which might occur in other circumstances. Thus, in ascribing a meaning to a particular in the causal way, as in ascribing one to a particular in the intentional way, there is no need to say that the bearer has a certain meaning relative to a certain kind of context. All one needs to say is that the bearer has the meaning it does in the context it has, for only one context is directly relevant, and that context is equally relevant whether it is mentioned or not.

When the bearer of meaning in the causal way is not a particular fact or event but either an enduring object or a type of thing or event, just as when a bearer of meaning in the dispositional way is of one of these kinds, the relevant context is not given with the bearer as already determinate when the bearer originates. Rather the context may be of any of a number of alternative kinds and the meaning also involves alternative possibilities according to the kind of content that is chosen. The meaning is thus relative to the kind of context in that, for one context, it will be of one sort and, for another, of quite a different sort. Accordingly, as in the case of meanings of type bearers in the dispositional way, any adequate account of a meaning of a type bearer in the causal way must mention the kind of context for which that meaning is relevant; and any full account of the meanings of such a bearer must indicate the various meanings for the various relevant kinds of contexts. Thus clouds mean rain when they occur at the juncture of substantive variations of temperature and pressure. When they occur at locations of even temperatures and pressures, they may mean prolonged overcasts; and when they occur in a variety of other circumstances, they may have other meaning in the causal way. Wet streets mean rain if the sidewalks and grass are also wet. If not, they may mean the recent presence of the street sprinkler. In other circumstances, wet pavements mean that there has been a fire down the street. The adding of sodium nitrate to the contents of a test tube means one thing when the initial content of the tube consists of hydrocholoric acid and quite another when the initial content is potassium sulphide. The trajectory of a rocket with a velocity of 15,000 miles per hour east to west at an average distance of 100 miles above the surface of the earth will be quite different from that of the same rocket similarly related to the moon.

The contexts that are relevant to meanings in the causal way can, as in the case of meaning in the intentional and dispositional ways, be appropriately regarded as physical, social, psychological, and semiotic. Since the causal relations that are most firmly established are physical ones, to which the relevant contexts are largely physical, both the common man and the scientist are likely to focus attention on the physical contexts of bearers of meaning in the causal way. Indeed, a large part of the work of experimental scientists consists in sorting out the physical contextual variables that are relevant to meaningful causal relations. However, since a substantial part of the life of every man is preoccupied with social relations and with reactions of his own to which social and psychological contexts as well as physical ones are relevant, social and psychological contexts play in the end as prominent a role in determining the causal meanings to which we attend as do physical ones. The causal meaning of a domestic quarrel is contingent upon previous social relations of the parties involved, and the meaning of threats of war can in no sense be measured apart from insights into the previous struggles of the contending nations. Any kind of odd or unusual behavior, or for that matter most normal behavior, can be intelligibly interpreted only in the light of networks of psychological principles together with knowledge of the psychological histories of the persons involved. Meaningful sentences uttered or inscribed, rituals, and other symbols having intentional and dispositional meanings also have causal meanings. When they do, the semiotic contexts of their intentional and dispositional meanings become indirectly also contexts of their causal meanings. Thus, if your report of the death of my friend has a certain meaning in terms of its effects upon my emotions and activities, the context that helped to determine your intentional meaning also helps to determine the causal meaning of your report. Again, if in telling a friend of some absentminded act of his own, a college professor remarks that he's a stupid fellow, the causal meaning of his remark will be of one sort; but if, in an attempt seriously to evaluate himself, he makes the same remark, the causal meaning may be of quite another sort. Similarly, if, in a conversation about character someone remarks that a certain man is good, the intentional and causal meanings will be of one sort; but if the same remark is made in a conversation about safe cracking, the intentional and the causal meanings will be very different.

One matter pertaining to the psychological contexts of bearers of meaning in the causal way requires special notice, namely the human interest that tends to attach to a bearer's having the meaning in the causal way that it has. For one thing, the existence of such an interest in a bearer's having a certain meaning in the causal way sometimes plays a part in the bearer's actually having that meaning. If one is interested in getting a new Pontiac and an increase in salary is needed to make that possible, then his interest in the Pontiac has an obvious bearing upon the increase's meaning that he gets the Pontiac. However, such actual participation of interests in the determination of causal relations on which causal meanings depend is confined to causal relations in the realm of human action and does not constitute the most pervasive role of interests with respects to causal meanings. This most pervasive role of interests consists in the fact that almost all of the causal meanings that people choose to mention are causal meanings that depend on causal relations in which people are interested whether or not these interests have anything to do with bringing these relations into being. Indeed, to such an extent does human interest attach to causal meanings that people mention, that to say that something has a certain meaning but no one has the slightest interest in it, is a very odd thing to say. Even when other interests are lacking that of curiosity is likely to be present.

For such reasons as these one may be inclined to suppose that a meaning's being a subject of human interest is a necessary part of the context of a bearer that has a meaning in the causal way. Such a supposition would, however, be a mistake. In many instances of meaning in the causal way, the interest that people take in the meaning has no effect whatever on the causal relation on which the meaning depends. The clouds do (or do not) mean rain regardless of my interest, and the billiard ball's rolling means just what it means regardless of my wishes. Actually, the effect of human interest with reference to meanings in the causal way is for the most part that of leading to and influencing *ascriptions* of meaning rather than meanings. It is largely the role of human interest with reference to such ascriptions that makes saying that something has a certain meaning in the causal way but that nobody is interested odd; for if nobody is interested, why report the fact? But, however odd it may be to say that something has a certain causal meaning about which no one cares, to say such a thing is not self-contradictory. If someone says that the fact that a certain pebble's having been repeatedly exposed to frost means that it will crack but nobody has the slightest interest in that, the reply is that if nobody has the slightest interest in this meaning, it's odd that one should mention this meaning but that the pebble's repeated exposure has this meaning all the same. Indeed, it seems very likely that countless events in which no one is interested or knows about nevertheless have meanings in the causal way and that the difficulty of mentioning what no one cares about is an egocentric predicament of ascriptions of meanings in the causal way that places no limitations upon meanings in that way themselves.

4. Contexts of Bearers of Meaning in the Implicative Way

That here are two couples of things means that here are four things, and that one thing's being to the right of another and still another thing's being to the right of the first thing means that third thing's being to the right of the second would seem to be instances of meaning in the implicative way requiring no contexts. On the basis of such cases as these one may be inclined to say that bearers of meaning in the implicative way at any rate need no contexts and are not affected by any. Moreover, it does seem that since the relations on which meaning in the implicative way depends are basically formal, the bearers of meaning in the implicative way are not likely to require such complex and indefinitely wide ranging contextual backgrounds as bearers of meaning in the causal way often require. It is also clear that the term "context," having been designed to refer to the patterns of words or texts within which a given word or set of words occurs, has to be stretched somewhat to apply to the settings of things having meanings by virtue of their implications. Nevertheless, bearers of meaning in the implicative way do have settings apart from which their implicative meanings would not come off, and these settings may in an appropriately expanded sense be properly referred to as contexts. In situations in which my-being-a-parent means that I am a father and Smith's-sponsoring-Schmidt means that Smith is sponsoring an alien, that contextual assumptions to the effect that I am male and that Smith is an alien are both needed and plausible is likely to be evident. However, even in such instances as those of the two couples and of one thing's being to the right of another, implicative meaning depends in some degree on contextual backgrounds as well as focal factors; for apart from rather complex mathematical systems of numbers and space relations to which the focal factors belong, the presence of two couples would not mean four things nor would one thing's being to the right of another and still another's being to the right of the first mean that the third was to the right of the second.

What are the contexts of bearers of meaning in the implicative way? In the preceding chapter, while the bearers of meaning in the implicative way were said broadly to include many kinds of statements, facts, events, situations, and principles, what carried the weight of the meaning in this way was seen to be basically propositions formulating these statements, facts, events, situations, principles, etc. This consideration suggests that while the contexts of meanings in the implicative way may also be broadly said to include statements, events, situations, facts, and principles; they are best thought of as consisting basically of propositions correlatable with those statements, facts, events, situations and principles and representable as uniting with propositional bearers of implicative meanings to imply such meanings.

The modes of impact of contexts upon the eventual determinations of implicative meanings vary with the particularity or generality of the bearers of meaning in the implicative way very much as corresponding modes do with the corresponding properties of bearers in other ways. Thus when, on the one hand, the bearer of meaning in an instance of the implicative way is particular, the context is already determined when the bearer occurs, and accordingly the meaning is not relative to a choice of contexts. It is also unnecessary either to know or to mention the context in order for the meaning to obtain, or for a corresponding ascription of meaning to be true, though of course knowing and mentioning the context may help in ascertaining the meaning or in explaining the ascription. Apart from the contextual fact of my being male, my being a parent would not mean that I am a father. But my being male was in fact already determined when my being a parent was determined. My being male makes its contribution to the implicative meaning of my being a parent, whether known or mentioned or not, though knowing and mentioning it will of course help one to discern or to test the implicative meaning. Similarly, Schmidt's being an alien is a necessary contextual foundation of Smith's-sponsoring-him's implicatively meaning that Smith is sponsoring an alien, but Schmidt's being an alien is already a part of the situation in which Smith sponsors him and does not need to be selected out of available alternatives. It sufficiently supports the implication that Smith's action implies sponsorship of an alien whether or not it is mentioned or even noticed.

When, on the other hand, the bearer of meaning in the implicative way is general, the meaning is relative to the context in the sense of depending on which of alternative possible contexts is chosen. Hence, the context must be known if the meaning is to be known and the context must be mentioned if the corresponding ascription of meaning is to be adequate. Thus someone's being a parent means implicatively that that person is a father only if a context is chosen in which the person in question is a male, and Smith's sponsoring someone means implicatively that Smith is sponsoring an alien only if the one whom Smith sponsors is an alien. One's being eliminated in the first round of a particular tournament may mean implicatively that one does not play in the second round, for the contextual reason that that tournament is conducted by rules which prohibit such a thing; but one's being defeated in a tournament means that one is excluded from the second round only if the tournament under consideration is conducted by rules that prohibit play in the second round under such conditions.

The contexts that are relevant to meanings in the implicative way include much the same kinds of physical, social, psychological, and semiological factors as enter into the contexts of meanings in other ways. Thus, my being a parent's meaning that I am a father hinges upon the physical fact of my being male; and a body revolving-about-the-sun's being a planet is contingent upon the physical fact of its being above a certain size. That that man was Jewish means that in Germany of 1935 he would be exposed to certain disabilities depends on certain sociological facts about the Germany of that period; and that Smith was a Republican meant that he could not be elected in Harlem in 1964 depends on certain socio-political contextual facts concerning Harlem in that year. That the screen pattern was exposed for only a thousandth of a second meant that no one could recognize it depends on contextual psychological facts about perception. That that animal is a vixen means that that animal is a fox depend on the con-textual semiotic fact that "vixen" means female fox; and that an animal's being a mule means that it is not purebred hinges on the semiotic fact that a mule is by definition a hybrid. In addition, however, to the four foregoing kinds of contextual material that are prominent in other ways of meaning, another kind of material that plays a smaller role in the other ways of meaning is always present and often prominent in the contexts of meaning in the implicative way, namely, logical principles. Whether or not these principles are grounded in semiotic principles as their eventual basis, I shall not at present try to say. In any event, such is their role in instances of the implicative way of meaning, that they require separate consideration here. The principles in question include not only principles of formal logic but also principles of logics of languages and of specific disciplines. These principles may enter into the contexts of implicative meaning either as premises or as modes of inference. Thus, that I shall be defeated if I defend the amendment means that I shall be defeated, depends on the contextually assumed logical premise that either I shall defend the amendment or I shall not. My being-a-parent's mean-ing my being a father depends on the contingent contextual fact of my being a male but that the two facts together mean my being a father depends on the logical relations of being male, being a parent, and being a father. Smith's-defending-Schmidt's mean-ing that Smith is defending an alien depends upon Schmidt's being alien; but it also depends upon some such logical principles as that whatever stands in certain relation to something else, stands in that relation to something having the properties that what it stands in that relation to has. In every other instance that has been cited or can be cited, a fact that has a certain meaning in the implicative way has that meaning, not only by virture of its own character and that of facts that can be thought of as contextual, but also by virtue of basic logical principles through which propositions based on the initial and contextual facts imply that meaning.

With regard to the contexts of bearers of meaning in the implicative way, somewhat the same sorts of remarks concerning the role of interest may be made as were made with regard to contexts of bearers of meaning in the causal way. To such an extent are the implicative meanings which one notices or comments upon, meanings selected along lines of human interest that one is likely to think that a meaning's being humanly interesting is a condition of its being a meaning in the implicative way at all. It is odd to say that something has a certain meaning in the implicative way but that that is no concern to anyone. However, upon reflection, one must recognize that any proposition has vast numbers of implications; and that while only a few of these are likely to be humanly very interesting, they all represent meanings of the proposition in the implicative way. Odd as it may be to remark that an implication about which no one cares is implicatively meant, it can scarcely be denied that whatever something implies it also means in the implicative way.

5. *Contexts of Ascriptions of Meaning*

In concluding this account of contexts of bearers of meaning, I wish to say something about the relation between the contexts of the sorts of bearers of meaning that have thus far been considered and the contexts of statements that ascribe meaning to bearers of meaning. A bearer that has a meaning but is not an ascription of meaning, may be referred to as the first order bearer of meaning; a statement ascribing a meaning to something may be referred to as a second order bearer of meaning; and an ascription of a meaning to a second order bearer of meaning may be referred to as a third order bearer of meaning. Thus one may speak of and compare the contexts of first, second, and even third order bearers of meaning.

Contexts of the first order bearers of meaning often have effects upon meanings as background factors that usually do not come into sharp focus and are not referred to by statements that constitute first order bearers of meaning. Thus, the utterance, "I am hungry," is likely to be produced and understood only in a complex of physiological and social conditions which it neither mentions nor necessarily leads anyone to attend to. Lightning means thunder only in view of a variety of meteorological factors which, however, do not need to be noticed by persons who know this meaning of lightening or be mentioned by those who mention this meaning.

While second order bearers of meaning sometimes, as will be seen, include references to the contexts of first order bearers of meaning; they do not ordinarily refer to their own contexts. Second order contexts, however, deeply influence the interpretations that second order bearers of meaning ascribe to first order ones, for the situation in which a statemen is made invariably affects the meaning of the statement. For this and other reasons, one is often tempted to read the contexts of second order bearers of meaning back into meanings of first order bearer of meaning. Thus, upon noticing the surprise caused by my saying "....."; I may add that what I really meant was "-----", which seems sensible now but hardly expresses just the content of the earlier intention. Similarly, taking account of popular reactions to the President's statement, his staff may say what he meant was ".....", which in the light of the conditions under which the interpretation is given seem plausible, but which strictly speaking does not express what was intended, or even suggested by the context, at the time of the original statement. The context of an ascription of meaning remains, despite all temptations to see it otherwise, quite distinct from the context of a first order bearer of meaning; and however much it may be used in discovering or discussing the meaning of the first order bearer, it has nothing whatever directly to do with the meaning of such a bearer. This fact is readily apparent when the first order bearer of meaning and the ascriptions of meaning based on it are widely separated in time. Thus, neither our historical knowledge nor our feelings about Caesar's words have any part in the context of his famous "*Veni, Vide, Vinci,*" nor do our reactions or any subsequent events play any role in the context of the words of the Declaration of Independence. The distinctness of the contexts of ascriptions of meanings from those of first order bearers must, however, also be duly recognized when the two bearers are closely connected in time; for the former are contexts of statements about initial statements, and they may be either true or false without in any way affecting the original statements or their contexts. The two contexts may indeed contain common elements; but, in orientation and in principle, they are entirely different.

The contexts of first order bearers of meaning can no more be assimilated to those of corresponding second order ones than can the contexts of second order ones be assimilated to those of first order ones. The circumstances that prompted Caesar's words are no part of the context of my ascriptions of meaning to his words, however essential a part they are of the contexts of his words; and the circumstances that led me to speak as I did just now are no part of the context of my present explanation of what I meant, however essential a part they may be of the context of my initial utterance.

Nevertheless the contexts of first order bearers of meaning are highly significant for ascriptions of meaning. Ascriptions of meanings to particulars often refer to, or depend upon, noticing the contexts of the bearers to which they ascribe meanings, and ascriptions of meanings to types must, if they are to be complete, take account of the contexts of the bearers to which they ascribe meanings. Thus, I may remark that my previous statement, in the context in which it was made, meant so and so; and in explaining the meaning of the word "governor," I shall have to say that in the context of politics, it means highest official of a region, while in the context of technology it means regulator of a machine. Since most ascriptions of meaning purport primarily to explain meanings of first order bearers and since the contexts of such bearers are always important and sometimes indispensable guides to the meanings of these bearers, ascriptions of meanings to first order bearers always entail responsibility for taking full account of the contexts of these bearers; and often such ascriptions become increasingly illuminating as they become increasingly specific in actually referring to the contexts of the bearers of meaning that they purport to interpret.

The bearers of meaning whose meanings are affected by the contexts of second order bearers of meaning are, of course, second order bearers themselves, i.e., statement ascribing meanings to first order bearers of meaning. Hence contexts of second order bearers of meanings play the same sort of vital role in the determination of second order meanings as first order bearers do in the determination of first order meanings. Thus, if I say that justice means giving everyone his due, it matters a good deal to what I mean by saying it whether I say it in a context of an exercise in defining English words, in a context of quoting a famous saying, in one of giving a judicial decision, in one of working out the effects or implications of a word or action, or in some other context. Similarly, if someone asserts that war would mean ruin, the meaning of his assertion will vary a good deal according to whether the setting is that of showing what is implicit in words, planning a national policy, seeking to further one's own industrial designs, or some other sort of setting.

Among the most significant functions of the contexts of ascriptions of meanings to first order bearers of meaning is that of disclosing the way of meaning in which meaning is being ascribed to the bearer. Usually, as has been previously seen, the form of an ascription of meaning to a first order bearer throws some light upon the way of meaning involved, and often the context of such a bearer throws further light upon the subject; but these factors often fail to clear up possible confusions on what way of meaning is involved. Hence, in order to ascertain the way in which a meaning is being ascribed to a bearer in any given instance, it is often necessary to take note of the context of the ascription, which in helping to disclose the intent of the ascriber also helps to disclose the way in which he intends to ascribe the meaning. Thus, whereas one cannot say concerning an isolated quotation of the sentence " 'Justice' means giving everyone his due," whether the sentence ascribes meaning in the intentional way or meaning in the cultural dispositional way to justice; if the sentence is quoted in a context of discussion of someone's meaning in a given speech, then the sentence ascribes a meaning in the intentional way, and if the sentence is quoted in a context of discussion of the meaning of words in English, the sentence surely ascribes a meaning in the dispositional way. A statement to the effect that a body's fall to the surface of the earth from a height of thirty-two feet means the elapsing of an interval of one second may equally well be an ascription either of causal or of implicative meaning; but if the statement is made in reply to a question in which the constant of acceleration near the surface of the earth is given, the way of meaning indicated is implicative. One need scarcely add that this function of contexts of second order bearers of meaning in disclosing ways of meaning greatly facilitates the endeavor to apprehend meanings themselves of first order bearers of meaning; for, as was seen in the preceding chapter, one can never ascertain the meaning of any bearer of meaning with any degree of assurance without some apprehension of the way of meaning involved.

The statements in which one actually refers to or describes the contexts of second order bearers of meaning, i.e., ascriptions of meaning to ascriptions of meaning, are bearers of meaning of a third order. Thus when one says that " 'triangle' means three sided," his statement is a second order bearer of meaning and its context is a second order context; but when one goes on to say that that statement means that the word "triangle" in English is commonly used of figures bounded by three sides, his statement is a third order bearer of meaning and its context is a third order context. However, third and higher order bearers of meaning and their contexts need be of no special concern here, for the bearers and contexts which for the most part are encountered are of the lower orders of bearers of meaning and no new principles of any special interest emerge at the higher levels.

CHAPTER IV

STIMULI AND MEANINGS

Among the features of meaning situations most closely associated with meanings are the environmental stimuli that prompt the production of bearers of meaning. The problem of the present chapter is that of the role of such stimuli in meaning situations, and especially that of the relation of such stimuli to meanings.

1. Some Accounts of Meaning Emphasizing Stimuli

Since the production of bearers of meaning in the intentional and dispositional ways is often prompted by environmental stimuli, and since bearers of meaning in this way express their own meanings, the identification of stimuli to the productions of bearers of meaning with meanings themselves is by no means initially implausible. That at least some meanings are to be identified with stimuli to their production has been suggested by a number of psychologists and philosophers. Whether or not these writers are able adequately to support this suggestion, they may at any rate be expected to have given careful scrutiny to the role of stimuli in meaning situations. Accordingly, I shall introduce the present inquiry concerning the role of stimuli in meaning situations by considering the views of a few of these writers. Of the three writers to be considered, one is a psychologist and two are philosophers.

a. B. F. Skinner's book *Verbal Behavior* is not specifically a book about meaning. From the outset it is confined to verbal bearers of meaning; and even with reference to these, its concern is not so much to describe their meanings as to explain why we produce them—an enterprise in which Skinner considers such concepts as those of reference and of meaning to be more a hindrance than a help. Nevertheless, the areas of experience with

91

92   THE CONCEPT OF MEANING

which Skinner is concerned are identical with certain kinds of
meaning situations, and Skinner considers the concepts that he
presents—especially that of stimulus—to be more than adequate
substitutes for those of meaning and reference. Occasionally he
indicates fairly specifically how he considers the concepts he
develops to be related to meanings and references. Hence, his
account seems, despite its disclaimers, to involve a partial assimilation of meaning to stimulus and may be expected, in any case,
to include interesting suggestions concerning the role of stimuli in
meaning situations.

Verbal behavior, according to Skinner, is a mode of "operant
behavior," i.e., behavior which is distinct from "activities.....primari-
ly concerned with the internal economy of the organism;" it has
"an effect upon the environment which has a return effect upon
the organism."[1] More specifically, "verbal behavior is behavior
reinforced through the mediation of other persons."[2] The kinds of
independent variables required to explain the dependent operants
of verbal behavior can be reduced to a very few including initial
response patterns, deprivations, and reinforcements. In general, the
procedure of language learning resembles that by which pigeons
can be fairly quickly taught to perform rather complex movements.
When an operant somewhat resembling the desired response occurs,
it is quickly reinforced by approval or the removal of a threat.
Subsequent closer approximations are similarly reinforced, deprivations being used when necessary to facilitate the reinforcements, until the desired verbal operant is well established.[3] The
success of the learning is measured by its strength or the probability
of its occurring at the proper times.[4] Once the operant has been
established, it continues to be reinforced by the responses of
listeners.[5] Verbal operants are, however, of different kinds, each
of which functions somewhat differently.

A *mand* is a type of verbal operant referred to in traditional
analyses as "commands," "entreaties," and the like. The word is
invented and has numerous affinities with "command," "demand,"

---

[1]B. F. Skinner, *Verbal Behavior* (New York: Appleton-Century-Crofts,
Inc., 1957), p. 20.
[2]*Ibid.*, p. 14.
[3]*Ibid.*, pp. 28 ff.
[4]*Ibid.*, pp. 22 and 28.
[5]*Ibid.*, pp. 33 f.

and "countermand." A mand then "is a verbal operant in which the response is reinforced by a characteristic consequence." It requires no specific stimulus, is "under the control of revelant conditions of deprivations or aversive stimulations," and "specifies its reinforcement."[6] Thus the mand "Bread" is a verbal operant reinforced by the characteristic of being given bread, which it specifies, and under the control of stimulation of deprivations of food.

In certain kinds of verbal behavior, the operant is under the control of verbal stimuli. Thus, "echoic behavior" is "verbal behavior....under the control of verbal stimuli [in which] the response generates a sound-pattern similar to that of the stimulus. For example, upon hearing the sound *Beaver*, the speaker says '*Beaver*'."[7] In "textual behavior" a reader is guided point by point by a text which may take "the form of pictures . . . ., formalized pictographs, hieroglyphs, characters, or the letters or symbols of a phonetic alphabet."[8] "Intraverbal behavior," though not guided point by point by verbal stimuli, is nevertheless specifically prompted by such stimuli through learned responses. Instances are the making of "the response *four* .... to the verbal stimulus *two plus two*, or *to the flag* to *I pledge allegiance*, or *Paris* to *the capital of France*."[9]

The most important of the varieties of verbal operants, and the crucial one from the point of view of what have traditionally been called reference and meaning, is what Skinner calls the "tact." The term is suggested by the word "contact." In the tact, the role of the condition of the agent, whether that of deprivation or satiation, is reduced to a minimum. The stimulus is largely in control though the audience also, as always, plays its part in shaping the operant.[10] "A tact may be defined as a verbal operant in which a response of a given form is evoked.....by a particular object or event or property of an object or event."[11] The scientific community focuses its expressions in tacts and endeavors to make these tacts possible; its interest is in stimuli rather than in the

---

[6]*Ibid.*, p. 36.
[7]*Ibid.*, p. 55.
[8]*Ibid.*, p. 65.
[9]*Ibid.*, p. 71.
[10]*Ibid.*, pp. 83 ff.
[11]*Ibid.*, p. 82.

conditions of agents. The stimuli that control tacts need not, however, be regarded simply as individual objects and events. A tact may be generalized so as to involve a whole class of things;[12] or it may be treated metaphorically so as to involve things like it in certain respects only.[13] In abstractions we endeavor to refine the stimulus to which the tact is a response.[14] "The referent of an abstract tact, if this term has any meaning at all, is the property or set of properties upon which the reinforcement has been contingent and which therefore controls the response."[15]

Although Skinner is reluctant to speak directly about reference and meaning, which he thinks should be replaced by his functional account,[16] he thinks that it is in the tact that what is valid in these notions is best represented. Thus in the tact "a given form is brought under stimulus control through differential reinforcement," so that "the probability that the speaker will emit a response of a given form in the presence of a stimulus bearing specified properties under certain conditions of deprivation or aversive stimulation....*so far as the speaker is concerned*..... is the relation of reference or meaning."[17] In so far as other varieties of verbal operants bear meanings or references, they depend eventually upon the same sort of reference. Thus, whereas many historical statements are directly controlled by other words and are therefore intra-verbal, the other words eventually should lead back to non-verbal stimuli as, for example, statements about Caesar lead "back to an instant in which a response was made to Caesar as a man."[18]

Verbal behavior beyond the minimal level of complexity requires, in addition to direct verbal responses, verbal responses to direct responses, functioning in such fashion as to order the initial responses and to indicate what the speaker is doing. Such second level verbal operants are referred to as "autoclitics." They include such descriptive autoclitics as "I said," "I recall," "I observe," "I agree," "I deny," such suffixes as "s," such assertive

---

[12]*Ibid.*, pp. 91 f.
[13]*Ibid.*, pp. 92 ff.
[14]*Ibid.*, pp. 107 ff.
[15]*Ibid.*, p. 113.
[16]*Ibid.*, pp. 7 ff.
[17]*Ibid.*, p. 115.
[18]*Ibid.*, p. 129.

STIMULI AND MEANINGS

95

autoclitics as "is," such qualifying ones as "not," and sound and word ordering autoclitic functions.[19] It is in terms of these autoclitics that complex verbal expressions are put together so as to be intelligible. Every speaker, moreover, constantly scans and edits his own speech behavior in the light, not only of his grasp of autoclitic relations, but also of the reinforcement of the response patterns of his speech community.

b. Bertrand Russell's theory of language is highly complex and involves many aspects which are rather remote from the sort of stimuli now in question. Even with regard to basic sentences expressing perceptions, Russell takes meaning to be definable as much by reference to responses to bearers of meaning as by reference to stimuli to the production of such bearers. However, with reference to one side, at any rate, of the meanings of these basic expressions, Russell at one point presents such a clear-cut stimulus interpretation that some of his remarks are well worth citing in the present context, even if they must be for this purpose, pulled out of their setting in more comprehensive theories of meaning that he from time to time suggests.

In an interesting passage in his *Inquiry into Meaning and Truth*, Russell treats a word as "a class of similar movements, of the tongue, throat, and larynx."[20]

The utterance and use of such words, he here suggests, is as much a part of learned bodily activity as is walking. To be sure, the building of complex sentences and the development of inferences by the use of words depends upon rules of syntax and logic that are far from elementary. However, the meanings of those basic sentences that express our perceptions and upon which all other propositions about the world depend, are grounded in simple psychological facts. On the passive side, these meanings are identifiable with responses to utterances; but on the active side, they are identifiable with stimuli to the production of such utterances. "The simplest kind of 'meaning,' out of which other kinds are developed" depends on an association between a word and a feature of the environment by virtue of which "the word 'means' this feature of the environ-

---

[19]*Ibid.*, Chapters 12 and 13.
[20]Bertrand Russell, *An Inquiry into Meaning and Truth* (London: George Allen and Unwin, 1940), p. 24.

ment."[21] At this level, "words have 'meaning' when there is an association or conditioned reflex connecting them with something other than themselves."[22] On the active side the relevant association of a word with a feature of its environment consists in the fact that the word's "utterance can be caused by the feature in question."[23] Thus, "I say 'fox' when I see a fox, because a fox suggests the word 'fox'."[24] Similarly, "if the toast is uneatable because it is old, you say 'hard'; if a ginger biscuit has lost its crispness, you may say 'soft'; if the bath scalds you, you say 'hot'; if it freezes you, you say 'cold'."[25]

The indicative mode of expression is the basic one and "in the indicative, a word A means a feature B of the environment if.....when B is emphatically present to attention, A is uttered or there is an impulse to utter A.... "[26] Even with reference to basic logical words an important part of the meaning lies in the stimulus. Thus, where "not" is used, the stimulus is usually a positive expression accompanied by a sensory experience incompatible with that expression; and where "or" is used, the stimulus tends to be hesitation between two propositions.[27]

c. The most sophisticated and carefully critical of contemporary presentations of the sort of view under consideration is that of Professor W. V. Quine in his book *Word and Object* and in several recent articles. Quine has long been reluctant to talk about meanings at all lest encouragement be given to illusory accounts of meanings as mysterious entities.[28] However, he thinks that no harm is done in talking about something's having a meaning or significance, especially provided such language is interpreted in respectable scientific language by reference to stimuli. Any interpretation of a meaning as a stimulus, Quine acknowledges, would have been, at the beginning of the century branded as psychologism, an attempt to reduce a logical category

---

[21]Bertrand Russell, *Human Knowledge* (New York: Simon and Schuster, 1948), p. 72.
[22]*Ibid.*, p. 72.
[23]*Ibid.*
[24]*Ibid.*, p. 113.
[25]*Ibid.*, p. 70.
[26]*Ibid.*, p. 71.
[27]*Ibid.*, Chapter IX.
[28]W. V. Quine, *From a Logical Point of View* (Cambridge: Harvard University Press, 1953), p. 11.

to a psychological one. However, since efforts to gain infallible
foundations for science, either by reducing meanings of physical
object terms to those of psychological terms or by translating
physical object terms into psychological terms, have now been
abandoned, there can no longer be any real objection to interpreting meanings in psychological terms. What is now being sought is
not infallibility but understanding of our language; and since
stimuli are the points at which the world impinges upon our
bodies, it is these that in the end hold the keys to the meaning of
our language.[29]

Since the meaning of any sentence is presumably what it
"shows with its translation,"[30] a genuinely empirical account of
at least some aspects of meaning may well be grounded in an
understanding of the sort of radical translation that a linguist
attempts for a language that is fundamentally different from his
own. Such a translation, Quine contends, must be built initially
upon attempts to notice and scientifically systematize and
record the verbal responses of natives to stimuli that the linguist
as well as the native can sense, supplemented, as soon as this is
feasible, by queries in the presense of a given stimulus concerning
whether or not a given verbal response applies. For example:
Let us suppose that when a rabbit appears a native says "Gavagai";
that every time the linguist asks in the presence of a rabbit if
the term "Gavagai" applies, the native replies in the affirmative;
and that when the linguist asks in the absence of a rabbit if the
term applies the native replies in the negative. By such occurrences,
queries and replies as these, the linguist may expect to approximate *stimulus meanings* for brief sentences. "The stimulus meaning of a sentence for a subject sums up his disposition to assent
to or dissent from the sentence in response to present stimulation."
This stimulus meaning is not "a dated particular event....but....a
repeatable event form" such that "the affirmative stimulus meaning of a sentence S [consists of].....all those stimulations that
would prompt assent to S."[31]

The sentences to which stimulus meaning is most nearly

[29]W. V. Quine, *Ontological Relativity*, Chap. 3.
[30]W. V. Quine, *Word and Object* (Cambridge, Mass.: The Technology
Press, and New York: John Wiley and Sons, Inc., 1960), p. 32.
[31]*Ibid.*, p. 34.

adequate are occasion sentences; i.e., sentences that would be prompted only by the presence of the appropriate stimuli. Over against these occasion sentences are *"standing sentences"* such as "The crocuses are out" and "The Times has come," which can be prompted by questions without the presence of the stimulations appropriate to them. Standing sentences are indeed often prompted by the stimuli to which they are appropriate, and some of them can be elicited only when they are in close proximity to such stimuli. But standing sentences are often influenced by other factors, and some of such sentences are but rarely and remotely connected with revealing stimuli. Obviously, "the less susceptible they are to prompted assent and dissent, the fewer clues are present in stimulus meaning."[32]

Even occasion sentences are sometimes partly separated from the stimulations that would normally prompt them by collateral factors such as accompanying signs and activities of local kibitzers. Moreover, some occasion sentences have only intrasubjective meanings. For example: whereas "Bed" is scarcely susceptible at all to intrusive information and is likely to be used largely in the same situation by all members of a language group, the use of "Bachelor" depends on the information at the disposal of the speaker and varies from speaker to speaker. Accordingly, it seems advisable to define a special class of observation occasion sentences the stimulus meanings of whose members are both intersubjective within a language group and determinable with minimal interferences from collateral factors. "Observationality" may be thought of "as degree of constancy of stimulus meaning from speaker to speaker,"[33] and "occasion sentences whose stimulus meanings vary none under the influence of collateral information may naturally be called *observation sentences*."[34] With regard to such sentences, "stimulus meanings.....do full justice to the meanings."[35] These sentences "wear their meanings on their sleeves,"[36] and it is for them "that the notion of stimulus meaning constitutes a reasonable notion of their meaning."[37]

---

[32]*Ibid.*, p. 36.
[33]*Ibid.*, p. 43.
[34]*Ibid.*, p. 42.
[35]*Ibid.*
[36]*Ibid.*
[37]*Ibid.*, p. 36.

This "version of observation sentences" allows "the sentences to be about ordinary things instead of requiring them to report sense data," for the occasion sentences on the stimulus meanings of which there is concensus in a group are very likely to be sentences about ordinary things. Such sentences, being "just the occasion sentences on which there is pretty sure to be firm agreement on the part of well-placed observers," formulate the principal data of the sciences;[38] and it is to them that we are most likely to appeal for evidence in disputes both in science and in our common concerns.

The fact that such standing sentences as "Bachelor" and "Unmarried man" vary as to stimulus meaning from speaker to speaker does not imply that stimulus synonymy cannot be achieved for them. Such synonymy can readily be achieved for at least any given individual, for "an individual would at any one time be prompted by the same stimulations to assent to Bachelor and Unmarried man, and similarly for dissent."[39] An extension of this synonymy to a whole language community can be achieved by the discovery that the relevant terms are stimulus synonymous for each member of the community. Further extension even to other linguistic communities can be achieved by finding a bilingual speaker for whom the terms are synonymous or by the linguist's becoming bilingual himself.[40]

The notion of stimulus synonymy may be made to lead into a notion of stimulus analyticity of sorts by saying that sentences are stimulus analytic when they hold "come what stimulation may," and this notion may be socialized by "calling socially stimulus-analytic just the sentences that are stimulus analytic for almost everybody." However, the tests involved do not rule out such sentences as "There have been black dogs," and no formal criterion even of stimulus analyticity is possible. Our intuitive feel of analyticity inevitably depends in fact on our reluctance to abandon "a pattern on which the communicative use of a logical particle heavily depends."[41]

The techniques that discern stimulus meanings of sentences can be extended in some measure to the discernment of

---

[38]*Ibid.*, p. 44.
[39]*Ibid.*, p. 46.
[40]*Ibid.*, p. 47.
[41]*Ibid.*, pp. 66 f.

truth-functional connections between sentences. Thus "the
semantic criterion of negation is that it turns any short sentence
to which one will assent into a sentence from which one will
dissent, and vice versa. That of conjunction is that it produces
compounds to which.....one is prepared to assent always and
only when one is prepared to assent to each component. That of
alternation is similar with assent changed twice to dissent."[42]

The range of applicability of stimulus meaning and the
techniques associated with its discernment are nevertheless very
limited. Only with reference to observation sentences, is stimulus
meaning to be equated with meaning, and even then, subject to
some restrictions concerning intrusive information. Stimulus
meaning is not applicable to any sentences but short ones, for
where longer units are concerned, confusion all too easily disrupts
connections of stimulus and expression. Moreover, stimulus meaning
is not applicable to terms as distinct from sentences. Even so
simple a term as "gavagai" which a native might use to refer to
rabbits can scarcely be equated in meaning with the English word
"rabbit." When the native uses his word as a part of a sentence,
he may equally well mean either "rabbits, stages of rabbits, integral
parts of rabbits, the rabbit fusion [or] rabbithood";[43] and no test
in terms of assent and dissent, with reference to presented stimuli,
can distinguish among these interpretations with any degree of
assurance. The main body of any language, including the meanings
of its terms and the manner in which they are put together to form
sentences and to facilitate inferences, is dependent on the language
system, which differs from language to language and especially
from culture to culture. While one can project and to some extent
test "analytic hypotheses" concerning the meanings of terms from
one language to another, there is never any one correct translation
of an isolated term or passage in a given language. To be sure,
whole translational systems may come out with similar results,
but no one vocabulary or grammar can claim to be the correct one
for the reason that there is no one correct one.[44] Even within a

---

[42]*Ibid.*, pp. 57 f.
[43]*Ibid.*, p. 52.
[44]*Ibid.*, pp. 68 ff. See also W. V. Quine, "Meaning and Translation" in
Jerry A. Fodor and Jerrold Katz, *The Structure of Language* (Englewood
Cliffs: Prentice Hall, Inc. 1964), pp. 21-32; and "Speaking of Objects" in
Proceedings of American Philosophical Association (Yellow Springs, Ohio,
1958).

given language, the rendering of another person's statement in indirect discourse must remain indeterminate in that no one rendition is the correct one.[45]

In our culture in general and, more specifically, in English, the development of language beyond the elementary level of stimulus meaning has included: a rough standardization of phonetic norms, divided reference and general terms as distinct from mass terms, demonstratives and the techniques of predication, devices for the formulation of relative clauses and indefinite singular terms, expressions for identity, and abstract terms.[46] Such devices, however, lead in certain circumstances to various well known confusions and anomalies such as vaguenesses; ambiguities of terms, syntax, and scope; and especially referential opacity in instances of modal expressions, indirect expressions and intentional verbs. Most of these difficulties can be handled for practical purposes by various devices within ordinary language.

For strict scientific and philosophical work, Quine recommends the use of a modified form of the canonical system of *Principia Mathematica* in which all singular terms are eliminated by suitable devices, all indirect discourse is paraphrased, and the sole remaining constructions are predication, universal quantification, and the truth functions. Such a system cannot, to be sure, represent reality point by point; and, even if it did, we should have no way of recognizing the fact. At best, it represents the simplest among many possible constructions connected with empirical data at various points and on the whole becoming more satisfactory as its various devices are gradually improved.

The data by which the whole is tested, the points at which it touches reality, are, however, in the end, observation sentences, whose meanings are, as has been seen, stimulus meanings. Such sentences fit into the systems of science as "eternal sentences," whose singular terms have been replaced by general ones, and whose relativity is removed by specifying time and place coordinates.[47] But all such sentences are, after all, derivative from observation sentences; and apart from the stimulus meanings of

---

[45]W. V. Quine, *Word and Object* (Cambridge, Mass.: The Technology Press, and New York: John Wiley and Sons, Inc., 1960) p. 219.
[46]*Ibid.*, Chapter III.
[47]*Ibid.*, pp. 193 f.

observation sentences on which they rest, the sentences of science
would remain uninformative.

2. *Roles of Stimuli in Meaning Situations*

As in instances of all of the factors considered in this and
the next four chapters, stimuli to the production of bearers of
meaning are relevant primarily to intentional and dispositional
meanings rather than to causal and implicative ones; and the
writers who have emphasized the roles of any of these factors in
meaning situations have been primarily concerned with situations
in which intentional and dispositional meanings are prominent.
Accordingly, in discussing the roles of stimuli and the other factors
in question in meaning situations, I shall focus upon situations
involving intentional and dispositional meanings. Subsequently, in
systematic discussion of meanings, I shall reintroduce discussion
of causal and implicative meanings alongside that of intentional and
dispositional meanings.

That Skinner, Russell, Quine and others who have emphasized
the roles of stimuli in meaning situations have made significant
suggestions concerning the manner in which words are learned and
combined will be evident to any thoughtful reader of the works of
these writers or even of such brief sketches of samples of these
works as the foregoing. The purpose of introducing these sketches
is, however, to use them, not to illuminate the modes of word
learning and language structure, but to throw such light as they,
together with fresh consideration of meaning situations, can upon
conceptual issues concerning the relations of meanings to other
factors in meaning situations, the manner in which meanings may be
discerned, and the relations of stimuli and meanings themselves.

Stimuli to the production of bearers of meaning seem clearly
to be so related to the larger contexts of bearers of meaning as to
play the role of observable foci, in which vast ranges of contextual
factors that underlie and maintain meanings converge toward the
production of bearers of intentional and dispositional meanings.
This is an important role; for, in themselves, the contextual factors
in question manifest no notable order and appear as little more
than random fragments of all that occurs. However, in a specific
stimulus to the production of a given bearer of a certain meaning,

background and contextual factors converge in a single observable event from the perspective of which they can be seen as ordered patterns directed toward the production of the relevant intention and bearer of meaning. Thus when Quine's native is prompted by the presence of a rabbit to say, "Gavagai"; the sun, the sky, the trees, the wind, the brush, his fellow tribesmen, the visiting linguist, previous experience of rabbits and training concerning what to say when he sees a rabbit, and much else impinges upon the native's experience. However, in the moving, brown object in the brush, all of these factors come to focus in a stimulus that prompts his intentional utterance. When an astronomer, upon receiving certain radio signals says, "Sirius," the situation is even more complex but essentially similar. Many astronomical facts and laws enter into the background of his utterance, and very complex elements of scientific training are involved; but all of the background factors converge in the present stimulus signal and lead through it toward his intentional utterance.

Not only do stimuli to the production of bearers of meaning play the role of observable foci for the entire backgrounds and contexts of bearers of intentional and dispositional meanings, they also function as immediately observable prompters of the intentions that produce these bearers and eventually determine these meanings. Although it is by no means inconceivable that intentions determining meanings sometimes occur apart from stimuli, it seems clear that most such intentions, and most dispositions to have such intentions are prompted by stimuli. Indeed, recent experiments seem increasingly to suggest that, apart from environmental stimulation, human activity tends to come to a standstill altogether. Even when stimuli prompting a given meaningful utterance are not immediately apparent, a little patience in the search for them is likely to disclose them; and when the relevance of stimuli to such utterances is not at once clear, further investigation usually indicates significant connections. That the intentions that determine meanings, and the bearers that have them, are in fact for the most part prompted by observable stimuli greatly facilitates the quest for observable clues to meanings; for whereas the intentions that eventually determine intentional and dispositional meanings—though manifested in various behavioral ways—are not directly observable, the stimuli that prompt them are. Such stimuli are in fact the last observable occurrences preceding the "internal" phases of the intentional determination of meanings, and accordingly they are especially likely to be revealing with respect to such meanings. To search for objective tests for intentional and dispositional meanings is always, among other things, to try to locate stimuli prompting the production of meaningful utterances, gestures and the like.

Because stimuli to the production of bearers of meaning play the role of observable prompters of meaning determining intentions and bearers of intentional meaning, they also very often—though by no means always—play the role of referents of bearers of intentional and dispositional meanings. The need to communicate, out of which meaning situations arise, is in considerable measure rooted in the needs of different organisms to attend to the same features of the world; and since, in a meaning situation it is the stimulus that attracts the attention of the agent, it is in often the same stimulus to which he intends, in producing the bearer, to direct the attention of the respondent. Thus when Quine's primitives on seeing a rabbit say "Gavagai," they very likely refer to rabbits; and when Russell's hunters on seeing foxes say "Fox," they are likely to refer to foxes. If a speaker of English repeatedly says "Dark cloud" whenever he sees a dark cloud, an occurrence of "dark cloud" in his discourse is likely to refer to a dark cloud; and if a speaker of a primitive language repeatedly says "Tonza" when he sees a wolf, an occurrence of "Tonza" in his discourse is likely to refer to a wolf. To be sure, when I see a rabbit, I may think of meat and, remembering that the gas has been left on in the oven under the roast, say, "My roast!" Or, the astronomer, seeing the moon and recalling current predictions, may say "Eclipse." But such instances of using bearers to refer to things remote from the stimulus are likely to occur in quite complex situations; and, as Quine's account suggests, many short utterances plainly refer to that which stimulates them.

Although meanings can, for reasons subsequently to be noted, scarcely be construed as particular stimuli, there is no reason why they may not sometimes be construed as repeatable patterns manifested in stimuli. Indeed, since stimuli are what prompt both the bearers that have meanings and the intentions that eventually determine them, there are good reasons to think that meanings may sometimes well be so construed. Moreover, since their own stimuli are often what meaningful expressions refer to, and since a primary function of such expressions is often to refer to these stimuli, the reasons for construing meanings of at least some expressions as patterns that are in fact manifested in stimuli to the production of these expressions are very strong. That the stimulus meaning of a brief sentence of a certain sort may be of this order seems to be what Quine is claiming when he remarks that such a stimulus meaning "is not a dated particular event...but a repeatable event form." And Skinner seems to suggest something of the same sort, at any rate concerning the meaning of an abstract term, when he writes that such a term refers to "the property or set of properties upon which the reinforcement has been contingent and which therefore controls the response."

By virtue of their playing all of the roles thus far indicated in meaning situations, stimuli to the production of bearers of meaning may very well be thought of as the most satisfactory of directly observable clues to particular intentional and dispositional meanings. By virtue of being observable foci of the backgrounds and contexts of bearers of meaning, they tend to concentrate in themselves whatever light can be thrown on meanings by these contextual factors. And by being observable prompters of meaning-producing intentions and often of expressions that refer to them, they sometimes lead the inquirer to attend to objects and events in the repeatable patterns in which meanings may be found. Yet in so doing they remain, unlike intentions, fully observable. To be sure, they are not the only observable clues to meanings. Such clues can also be found in responses to bearers of meaning and in referents of those bearers other than stimuli. But then responses are only indirectly related to meanings by way of their effects; they inform us directly of how bearers are taken and, only indirectly of what bearers mean. And while referents other than stimuli can indeed be very informative regarding meanings, they are themselves likely to be difficult to discern and often they are discernable only by way of prior discernment of meanings. Accordingly, any quest for observable clues to intentional and dispositional meanings will do well to begin with stimuli to the production of bearers of meanings, and any account of such meanings that is to be operational may well take such stimuli as focal factors.

3. *The Non-Equivalence of Stimuli and Meanings*

Although the roles of stimuli to the production of bearers of meaning in meaning situations are such as to link stimuli closely with meanings and to render them very useful for the disclosure of meanings, stimuli are by no means to be equated with meanings. This fact is recognized in some degree by Quine, who is aware of the severe limitations of stimulus meanings as such; it is also acknowledged in a different way by Russell, who finds other factors in addition to stimuli also directly relevant to meanings. However, just because the links between stimuli and meanings are as close as they are, it is all too easy to press the notion of the coincidence of stimuli and meanings beyond the point justified by the character of the concepts involved. Accordingly, it would seem to be worthwhile, quite apart from any attempt to reply to specific claims of the writers mentioned, to indicate some of the main considerations that preclude the equating of stimuli to the production of bearers of meaning and meanings.

a. The consideration should be kept clear that meanings seem never to be stimuli regarded as particulars. Quine explicitly recognizes this when he equates stimulus meanings, not with particular events, but with "repeatable event form[s]." I am not sure that any reputable writer has ever explicitly insisted that meanings were equatable with particular stimuli, but some writers have failed to keep the fact clear that they were not; and when that fact is kept clear, one of the main reasons for wanting to equate meanings with stimuli—i.e., belief that a nominalistic theory of meaning may be possible—is removed. That some meanings are not particular stimuli is readily apparent in instances in which particular stimuli are simply not available to constitute meanings of evidently meaningful expressions, such as negative and abstract statements. That no meanings are particular stimuli is strongly suggested by the fact that meanings are not particular stimuli even in those cases in which stimuli very closely connected to meanings and actually referred to by bearers of meaning are present. When, on being confronted with a pentagon, a red box, or a bear, one says "That's a pentagon," "That's a red box," or "There's a bear"; one is stimulated by, and refers to, the pentagon, the box or the bear, and there is even a certain coincidence of the content of the stimulus and the meaning. But in such instances one has no inclination to point to the pentagon, the box, or the bear, and to say that that is his meaning or some part of his meaning. If there is anything about the stimulus that is coincident with the meaning or any part of the meaning, it is not the particular object or event before the speaker but rather the object or event form.

b. A consideration that tends to show that stimuli, construed not as particulars but as object or event patterns, are often not equatable with intentional meanings is that such stimuli and intentional meanings are, in many instances basically remote from one another and connected with one another in only accidental and tenuous ways. When, on seeing the smoke from a neighbor's chimney, a housewife says "Goodness, my meat must by now be burning," the stimulus that prompts her has little to do with her meaning. When the bright sunshine prompts the professor to speak of his brilliant students, or the red rose on the rostrum leads the Fourth of July orator to make amusing remarks about the Russians; the stimulus has even less to do with the meaning. And, in general, one would seem to be safe in saying that the cases in which stimulus patterns coincide with meaning patterns are much rarer than those in which they do not.

c. Whether or not the repeatable forms constituting contents of stimuli and those constituting contents of intentional meanings coincide, the two are determined in quite different ways and the whole of which the one is a part is by no means the same as that of which the other is a part. What makes certain repeatable forms stimuli to the production to bearers of meaning is that their instances prompt such production whereas what makes repeatable forms intentional meanings is that they are intended, in the production of bearers of meaning, to be apprehended by respondents as intended. This consideration helps to explain how the event forms prompting certain verbal expressions can be as different from those meant by such expressions as the two are in the instances of the housewife's statement about her meat, the professor's about his students, or the orator's about the Russians. It also shows why, even when event forms constituting contents of stimuli coincide with those constituting contents of meanings, the stimuli and meanings involved are by no means the same. A fox event form as stimulating the word "fox" is one thing; the same event form as intended to be apprehended by a respondent as intended is another. The two may indeed have a common element, but as wholes they are quite different.

d. Even if it were possible to equate meanings of one-word utterances with stimuli to their production, no parallel equation seems possible with reference to words of a language or to sentences of more than a single word. One reason for this has been suggested by Quine, who points out that the word "gavagai" that his primitives use for rabbits could, as a word in a sentence, equally well mean "rabbits, stages of rabbits, integral parts of rabbits, the rabbit fusion [or] rabbithood." Every language in actual use involves such complexities of expression and such niceties of meaning that any attempt to equate its meanings with stimuli to the production of its expressions appears to be doomed from the outset; and Quine himself stresses the impossibility of adequate translation. If meanings of complex verbal expressions are to be equated with stimuli, then stimuli must be linked with such expressions either by nature or by some sort of conditioning; but the fact is that even moderately competent users of any language can be shown to be capable of using and understanding thousands of novel combinations of words that are surely not linked with their meanings by nature and concerning which there has been no opportunity for the requisite conditioning. Whether or not, by way of such meaning hypotheses as Quine suggests or the sorts of indirect conditioning that Skinner suggests, the vast gaps that seem to separate the meanings of complex verbal expressions from their stimuli can be narrowed remains to be seen. Clearly no attempts thus far made to equate meanings of complex verbal expressions with their stimuli has gotten very far; and, with regard to any attempt in the foreseeable future to establish such an equivalence, it is difficult to see how it could avoid the sort of devastating objections raised in Noam Chomsky's review of Skinner's *Verbal Behavior*.[48]

---

[48]Noam Chomsky, A review of B. F. Skinner's *Verbal Behavior,* in *Language,* 35, No. 1 (1959), pp. 26-58. Reprinted in Jerry A. Fodor and Jerrold Katz, *The Structure of Language* (Englewood Cliffs; Prentice Hall, 1964), pp. 547-578.

CHAPTER V

RESPONSES AND MEANINGS

Bearers of meaning are, as has been seen with reference to all instances of intentional and dispositional meanings and as will be seen with reference to many instances of causal meanings, oriented either directly or indirectly toward responses of one kind or another. Hence, responses must be thought of as significant factors in meaning situations. Since writers who have given substantial roles to responses in their discussions of meaning are especially likely to be sensitive to whatever functions such responses to bearers of meaning may have in meaning situations, I shall, before directly inquiring into the character and function of such responses in meaning situations, seek such leads as can be found from some writers of this sort.

1. Some Accounts of Meaning Emphasizing Responses

Most of the writers, prior to the present century, who have recognized the importance of responses in meaning situations have construed the relevant responses in largely cognitive terms and subordinated these responses to cognitively construed intentions of agents. Thus, for example, John Locke represents words as "signs of internal conceptions.....whereby......the thoughts of men's minds might be conveyed from one to another," "the instruments whereby men communicate their conceptions and express to one another those thoughts and imaginations they have within their own breasts."[1] Similarly, Thomas Hobbes declares that "names are signs not of things, but

---

[1]John Locke, *Concerning Human Understanding* in *The Great Books of the Western World* (Chicago: Encyclopedia Britannica, 1952), Vol. 35, pp. 251 and 254.

of our cogitations," and "that the sound of this word *stone*
should be the sign of a stone, cannot be understood in any sense
but this, that he that hears it collects that he that pronounces it
thinks of a stone."[2] However, since views similar to those held
by these writers are to be considered in a later chapter I shall
not say much about them here.

Many philosophers and psychologists of the present century
have become distrustful of all introspectable data and inclined to
link meanings with behavioral responses, and it is with views of
these writers that I am at present concerned. Some of the
writers in question take the responses relevant to meanings to be
direct though implicit. Others take these responses to be largely
dispositional. Some writers of both groups take emotional factors
to be important parts of the responses relevant to meanings.

a. The immediate forerunner of a very substantial part of
contemporary thought of the kind in question is John B. Watson.
Watson's is the boldest and most uncompromising statement of
the view that meanings are to be equated with behavioral
responses to whatever has meaning. The nub of Watson's position
is formulated in the following statement from his *Psychology from
the Standpoint of a Behaviorist*: "Exhaust the conception of
action—i.e., experimentally determine all of the organized responses
a given object can call forth in a given individual, and you have
exhausted all possible 'meanings' of that object for that individual."[3]

b. While Bertrand Russell tends in one aspect of his thought,
to identify the meanings of elemental indicative sentences with
stimuli to the production of these sentences, he tends, in another,
to identify them with responses to these sentences. Thus, as a
second requirement of a sentence A's meaning B, in addition to
"there being an impulse to utter A," is that "when A is heard it
arouses what may be called an 'idea' of B, which shows itself
either in looking for B or in behavior such as would be caused
by the presence of B." The demand is that the apprehension of
the expression have "effects analogous, in certain respects, to the

---

[2]Thomas Hobbes, *De Corpore*, chap. 2, par. 5 as reprinted in *Body,
Man, and Citizen*, ed. by R. S. Peters (New York: Collier Books, 1962), p.
34.

[3]John Watson, *Psychology from the Standpoint of a Behaviorist* (Phila-
delphia: Lippincott, 1919), p. 366.

sensible presence of the object."[4] Thus "when I utter the word
'fox', and when you, having not yet seen the animal, hear the
word......, you look for the fox...." or in some other way assume
a "belief" attitude. The only requirement for "external reference"
in an expression is "that the occurrence has some of the effects
that would result from the sensible presence of that which is its
external reference."[5]

   c. Like the psychologist Watson and the philosopher Russell,
the linguist Leonard Bloomfield, who identifies meaning on another
side with stimuli to bearers of meaning, identifies meaning on one
side with direct responses to bearers of meaning. Thus, Bloomfield
defines "the *meaning* of a linguistic form as the situation in which
the speaker utters it and the response which it calls forth in the
hearer."[6]

   The identification of meanings with direct responses is,
however, as has often been pointed out, subject to serious
difficulties. In response to a given bearer of meaning, any one of
many things, or possibly nothing at all, may be done. If I am
informed that the grass in the yard is high, I may get out the
lawn mower, call the yard man, express regrets, delay action, or
take no action at all. In order to meet this sort of difficulty,
Watson undertakes to show that many of the relevant responses
are minute muscular contractions below the level of ordinary
observability. A more recent effort to deal with the variability
of overt behavioral responses in much the same manner, by
appeal to implicit responses, is that of Charles Osgood.

   d. An adequate view of meaning must, Osgood thinks, avoid
the subjectivism of mentalistic views and at the same time be
definite enough to distinguish sign behavior from other related
types of behavior. This result can, he thinks, be achieved by
regarding meaning as a *portion* of a response pattern which
becomes diverted from its normal role in such a pattern to be
connected with a sign and to become a self-stimulus to another
response. Osgood's formula is as follows: "A pattern of stimulation
which is not the object is a sign of the object if it evokes in an

---

4Bertrand Russell, *Human Knowledge,* p. 71.
5*Ibid.,* pp. 113 f.
6Leonard Bloomfield, *Language* (New York: Henry Holt and Company,
1933), p. 139.

organism a mediating reaction, this (a) being some fractional part of the total behavior elicited by the object and (b) producing distinctive self-stimulation that mediates responses which would not occur without the previous association of the non-object and the object patterns of stimulation."[7] Thus, for example, although the natural response to a spider may be a certain pattern of anxiety behavior, some part of this pattern may come to be connected with the term "spider" and may become a self-stimulus to certain overt behavior. Similarly, while a hammer is in practice connected with actual clutching and pounding motions, some fragmentary parts of such motions may come to be connected with the word "hammer" and may become self stimuli to various other motions.[8] The partial response is the meaning. Meanings have, for Osgood, various dimensions including not only representational ones but also feeling and volitional ones. Much sign behavior consists, Osgood thinks, not just of signs, but of "assigns," that is to say, instead of consisting of partial responses directly to stimuli, it consists of partial responses to other signs. Meanings can be measured, but they are not measured very well by such factors as overt motions and skin reactions. Better results are obtained by word-association tests in which the subject is asked whether the word is more nearly weak or strong, rough or smooth, etc. Osgood has worked out tests of the requisite kind in considerable detail in collaboration with George Suci and Percy H. Tonnenbaum in *The Measurement of Meaning*.[9]

Even when direct responses to bearers of meaning are reduced to minute physiological responses or to the partial responses discussed by Osgood, the identification of meanings with direct responses continues to be open to serious objections even from the point of view of the sort of scientific empiricism with which they are designed to accord. As Roger Brown has pointed out, there is very little empirical evidence for the kinds of partial responses that Osgood relies upon, abstract terms such as "*man*, animal, and triangle" are very difficult to represent in

---

[7]Charles E. Osgood, *Method and Theory in Experimental Psychology* (New York: Oxford University Press, 1953), p. 696.

[8]*Ibid.*, p. 697.

[9]Charles Osgood, George Suci, and Percy H. Tonnenbaum, *The Measurement of Meaning* (Urbana: The University of Illinois Press, 1957).

Osgood's terms; and, at very best, Osgood has "pushed the mediating response back into the nervous system where no one will undertake to look for it."[10]

e. Because of such difficulties as these, many recent writers who emphasize the role of responses in meaning situations take the relevant factors to be not direct responses but dispositions to respond in any of complex varieties of ways. Of the advocates of such dispositional accounts, I shall present two. The first, Charles Morris, has, over a period of thirty years, worked more systematically with problems concerning meaning situations than any other writer. A sketch, first, of some leading ideas of his general "semoitic" and then, more specifically, of his idea of meaning as dispositional response should be helpful in the orientation of features of meaning situations subsequently to be considered as well as in that of the feature now under consideration. The second of the two writers to be considered, Charles L. Stevenson, is important in the present context because of the detailed and sensitive character of his analysis of dispositional responses, especially on their "emotive" side.

Semiosis, or "the process in which something functions as a sign," Morris tells us, is "a mediated-taking-account-of."[11] Its basic ingredients are these: the "mediator" or "that which acts as a sign," the-taking-account-of" or "that effect on some interpreter in virtue of which the thing in question is a sign to that interpreter," and "what is taken account of" or "that which the sign refers to." These ingredients may be referred to respectively as the *"sign-vehicle," "the interpretant"* and "the designatum"[12] or "signification."[13] To these may be added the interpreter himself. Thus, "a traveller [the interpreter] prepares himself to deal appropriately [the interpretant] with the geographical region [the designatum] in virtue of a letter [the sign-vehicle] received from a friend."[14]

---

[10]Roger Brown, *Words and Things* (Glencoe: The Free Press, 1958), pp. 101 f.

[11]Charles Morris, *Foundations of the Theory of Signs* (Chicago: University of Chicago Press, 1938), pp. 3 f.

[12]*Ibid.*, pp. 3 and 4.

[13]See Charles Morris, *Signification and Significance* (Cambridge, Mass.: The M.I.T. Press, 1964), p. 2.

[14]Charles Morris, *Foundations of the Theory of Signs*, p. 3.

Semiotic, or theory of signs, which is the science dealing with semiosis, has three main branches. *Syntactics* inquires into "the formal relation of signs to one another;"[15] it deals with combinations of signs without regard for their specific significations or their relations to the behavior in which they occur."[16] *Semantics* is a study of "the relations of signs to the objects to which the signs are applicable;"[17] it "deals with the significance of signs in all the modes of signifying."[18] *Pragmatics* is the study of "the relation of signs to interpreters;"[19] it "deals with the origin, uses, and effects of signs within the behavior in which they occur."[20]

Sign vehicles may be used in three different ways: designatively, with regard to "the nature of the environment in which the organism operates;" appraisively, with regard to "the impact or relevance of this environment for the needs of the organism;" or prescriptively, with regard to "the ways in which the organism must act upon the environment in order to satisfy its needs.[21] A sign in the designative mode describes a part of the environment, a sign in the appraisive mode evaluates it, and a sign in the prescriptive mode proposes a line of action with regard to it. Thus, when a bystander warns a traveller of an obstacle in the road to a certain point, his words may "designate a condition of the road, appraise this condition as an obstacle to further progress, and prescribe the discontinuance of the response of driving to the point in question."[22] Similarly, in instances in which a dog is conditioned to expect food upon the sounding of a buzzer, "the buzzer perhaps designates food in a certain place, appraises this positively in relation to hunger, and prescribes the response of acting in a certain way."[23]

Sign vehicles may either indicate or characterize their designata. When they characterize these designata, they do so either

---

[15]*Ibid.,* p. 6.
[16]Charles Morris, *Signs, Language and Behavior* (New York: Prentice-Hall, Inc., 1946), p. 219.
[17]Charles Morris, *Foundations of the Theory of Signs,* p. 6.
[18]Charles Morris, *Signs, Language and Behavior,* p. 219.
[19]Charles Morris, *Foundations of the Theory of Signs,* p. 6.
[20]Charles Morris, *Signs, Language and Behavior,* p. 219.
[21]*Ibid.,* p. 62.
[22]*Ibid*
[23]*Ibid.*

iconically, by resembling them, or symbolically, by being connected with them by arbitrary conventions. Sentences are combinations of indexical and characterizing signs according to rule.[24] Natural objects or events become signs of other natural objects or events; for example, thunder becomes in this way a sign of lightning.[25]

The broad varieties of interpretants answering to the designative, appraisive and prescriptive modes of the use of sign-vehicles are as follows. Answering to the designative mode, is "a disposition to react to the designated object as if it had certain observable properties;" for example, when told "that there is a black object in an adjoining room, one is set for certain visual experiences on entering the room."[26] Answering to the appraisive mode, is "a disposition to act toward a designated object as if it would be satisfying or unsatisfying," i.e., "a disposition to respond by object preferences," as when a child, told by its mother that a medicine is "nummy num," "is set for something that he will favor."[27] Answering to the prescriptive mode, is "a disposition to act in a certain kind of way to the designated object or situation," i.e., "a disposition to respond by behavior preferences," as when a person trying to open a door is told to press down on the knob, and "is disposed to perform that kind of action" expecting in so doing to achieve the desired result.[28]

The designata or significations of signs are not, as is sometimes supposed, "actually existing objects which are denoted...[but]...such things which the sign *can* denote; i.e., such objects or situations which according to the semantical rule or usage could be correlated to the sign vehicle by the semantical relation of denotation.[29] For a sign to denote is for it to refer to an actually existing object. Thus while signs denote by way of their designata and all signs have designata, not all signs have denotata. The main varieties of designata or significations, answering to the designative, appraisive, and prescriptive factors in sign use are respectively "simulative properties of the object;"

---

[24]Charles Morris, *Foundations of the Theory of Signs*, pp. 21 ff.
[25]*Ibid.*, p. 12.
[26]*Signification and Significance*, p. 6.
[27]*Ibid.*
[28]*Ibid.*
[29]*Foundations of the Theory of Signs*, pp. 25 f.

"reinforcing properties of the object," i.e., "the capacity of an
object to increase the probability of the performance of a response
made to it;" and instrumental properties of the act prescribed,
i.e., its capacity to facilitate the achievement of associated ends.[30]
In line with this account, values can be construed in terms of an
"objective relativism" grounded in the significata of appraisive
signs as "properties of objects......relative to preferential behavior."[31]

    With specific reference to meaning, Morris points out that
the term "meaning" has been variously used to refer to designata,
denotata, interpretants, sign implicates, and the processes of
semiosis,[32] and indeed, "any and all phases of the sign processes."[33] Because of the resulting confusion, he thinks that the
term might well be abandoned.[34] Certainly meaning is, he thinks,
neither a "Platonic idea" nor an "idea inhabiting a special domain
of mental entities;" for in neither case would it be accessible to
intelligible inquiry.[35] Nevertheless, meaning, as "a semiotical term
and not a term in the thing language,"[36] can be given a satisfactory
interpretation according to which meanings are accessible to
scientific inquiry.[37] Basically the meaning of any sign is to be
equated with "*both* its signification and its interpretant."[38]

    Hence, a further understanding of the response aspect of
Morris's view of meaning will require further consideration of
those dispositions to respond that constitute for him the
interpretant of signs. Earlier accounts of interpretants in terms
of responses have been defective, Morris thinks, mainly in their
misguided attempts to equate such interpretants with direct
responses to signs as substitute stimuli and in their failures to
recognize the goal-seeking character of the responses constituting
interpretants. If the responses in question were direct and not
goal-directed, the Pavlovian dog, for example, would be required
to respond to the bell, as it does to food, by eating it; and a

---

[30]*Signification and Significance*, pp. 8 f.
[31]*Ibid.*, p. 18.
[32]*Foundations of the Theory of Signs*, p. 43.
[33]*Signs, Language and Behavior*, p. 19.
[34]*Ibid.*, p. 19 and *Foundations of the Theory of Signs*, p. 44.
[35]*Ibid.*, p. 43.
[36]*Ibid.*, p. 45.
[37]*Ibid.*, pp. 45 ff.
[38]*Signification and Significance*, p. 9.

drug would be as much a sign as a word.³⁹ These difficulties are
avoided by thinking of the interpretant as a "disposition to
respond" in terms of a goal-directed activity in suitable circumstances, "a habit of the organism to respond, because of the sign
vehicle, to absent objects which are relevant to a present prob-
lematic situation as if they were present.⁴⁰ The disposition in
question may involve long chains of responses or "response-
sequences," such as those involved in a dog's chasing, killing,
and eating a rabbit. It may, moreover, include a wide range of
behavior sequences, the completion any one of which will be a
fulfillment of it. That is to say, it must be defined in terms of a
"behavior-family." Thus, the interpretant in which the response
aspect of any meaning consists becomes "*a disposition.....to respond
under certain conditions by response sequences of [a] behavior
family.*"⁴¹ In addition to avoiding the errors of taking the crucial
responses to be direct and mechanical, this sort of dispositional
interpretation, Morris holds, avoids the errors of thinking "that
a sign must itself be a response,"⁴² of neglecting the role of the
context,⁴³ and of supposing that the response sequence must be
complete before it comes to have any interpretative value.⁴⁴
Initially, and whenever we seek to check our results, we must
ascertain dispositions by observing patterns of overt behavior,
and even fragments of such patterns may be helpful; but once we
have established general correlations between patterns of observable behavior and verbal behavior, verbal reports can themselves
become means of discerning the dispositions in which meanings
consist.⁴⁵

f. While Charles Stevenson's principal concern with meanings has been with the meanings of evaluative terms, he has also
developed with considerable care a more general theory of meaning.
I shall first sketch the main features of his general theory and
then refer briefly to his account of the meanings of evaluative
terms.

³⁹*Signs, Language and Behavior,* pp. 6 f.
⁴⁰*Foundations of the Theory of Signs,* p. 30.
⁴¹*Signification and Significance,* p. 30.
⁴²*Ibid.,* p. 15.
⁴³*Ibid.*
⁴⁴*Ibid.,* p. 16.
⁴⁵*Ibid.,* p. 14.

Stevenson recognizes a variety of senses of "meaning" including, for example, the one in which the meaning of a sign is that to which people refer when they use the sign.[46] He is, however, primarily concerned with a psychological, causal sense of "meaning" in which the meaning of a sign, though having introspectable aspects, can be interpreted largely in causal, behavioral terms. Such a causal interpretation, he finds, includes both stimulus and response aspects;[47] but his interest is centered in the latter, and attention will be directed to the latter in the account that follows.

The attempt to characterize the meaning of a sign simply as "the psychological reactions of those who use the sign" is, Stevenson thinks, promising but lacking in clarity and incapable of explaining the comparative constancy of meanings of a sign amid the bewildering fluctuations of people's responses to the sign. Thus "a sense is needed in which a sign may 'mean' less than it 'suggests'."[48] Such a sense can be described, not by reference to people's responses to a sign, but by reference to people's dispositions regarding a sign or the sign's dispositions with reference to people's responses.

For something to have a dispositional property is for it to have a property such that certain correlated responses occur when it is present under suitable attendant circumstances, and for these responses to vary in predictable ways with variations in certain of these circumstances. The dispositional property itself has a base on which it depends, but that base need not be known in order for the dispositional property to be known. Thus, coffee has a dispositional property of stimulating increased activity that may be recognized quite apart from knowledge of the exact cause of the stimulation; and this property remains constant, despite varying degrees of stimulation, in that for each increase in the amount of coffee, there is an increase of stimulation.[49] If a disposition to respond in a certain way is thought of as a "first order" disposition, a disposition to acquire that disposition will be thought of as a second order disposition. Thus,

---

[46]C. L. Stevenson, *Ethics and Language* (New Haven: Yale University Press, 1940 and 1960) p. 42.

[47]*Ibid.,* p. 57.

[48]*Ibid.,* p. 43.

[49]*Ibid.,* pp. 45 ff.

if magnetism is taken as a disposition of the first order, then the disposition of a metal to *acquire* magnetism....will be a disposition of the second order.[50]

This account of dispositional properties suggests the following definition of meaning from the point of view of the hearer: "The meaning of a sign, in the psychological sense required, is.....a dispositional property of the sign, where the response, varying with attendant circumstances, consists of psychological processes in a hearer, and where the stimulus is his hearing the sign."[51] In terms of this definition "a sign can remain constant even though its psychological effects vary."[52] Moreover, for the purposes in hand, it doesn't matter whether the dispositional property is said to be such a property of the sign or "of the persons who *use* the sign."[53]

The meaning now defined in terms of psychological response includes at least two quite distinct aspects; an emotive one and a descriptive one. "Emotive meaning is meaning in which the response is a range of emotions." The emotion involved consists of feelings and attitudes, the latter being considered to include " 'desire,' 'wish,' 'disapproval,' etc."[54] The emotive meaning of a term is, from the response point of view now in question, its disposition to evoke feelings and attitudes in certain hearers under suitable circumstances. The strength of the functioning of emotive meaning in any given situation is not merely that of the adding on of feelings associated with a sign; it is rather that of the setting off of a long prepared reaction. The use of the emotive terms is "like a spark that ignites prepared tinder."[55]

The descriptive aspects of response meaning are defined in terms of the cognitive effects of the use of words. These cognitive effects are in turn to be explained as conditional dispositional properties relating to action. Such dispositional properties become sufficiently definite to yield, in many instances, fairly precise meanings. This they do by way of their interconnections through the repetition of verbal rules such as the rule that "100 comes

[50]*Ibid.*, p. 53.
[51]*Ibid.*, p. 54.
[52]*Ibid.*, p. 54.
[53]*Ibid.*, p. 55.
[54]*Ibid.*, p. 60.
[55]*Ibid.*, p. 61.

after 99," that "10 times 10 is 100," and that a great aunt is "a sister of a parent of one of the parents."[56] Accordingly, "the 'descriptive meaning' of a sign is its disposition to affect cognition, provided that the disposition is caused by an elaborate process of conditioning that has attended the sign's use in communication, and provided that the disposition is rendered fixed, at least to a considerable degree, by linguistic rules."[57]

Emotive and descriptive meanings may, of course, attach to the same signs. Sometimes the emotive meaning of a term is relatively independent of the descriptive meaning in that it does not change with changes in the descriptive meaning and may continue to hold even when the descriptive meaning has changed. This consideration makes possible persuasive definitions by which a speaker leads his audience to accept an altered definition of a term in order to attach the original motive power of the term to the content of the new definition.[58] The opposite procedure, that of altering the emotive meaning of a term while keeping its descriptive meaning constant, is also possible.[59] Thus, for example, "a group of people.....might leave the descriptive meaning of 'democracy' unchanged, and gradually let it acquire, for their usage, a much less laudatory emotive meaning [or] they might keep the strong laudatory meaning unchanged, and let 'democracy' acquire a descriptive sense which made reference only to those aspects of democracy (in the older sense) which they favored."[60] Sometimes, instead of being largely independent of descriptive meaning, emotive meaning is dependent upon descriptive meaning in the sense that it changes with descriptive meaning "after only a brief 'lag'."[61] Always, the two varieties of meaning are aspects of meaning of a sign rather than two different meanings. In metaphor, "the attendant circumstances preventing the metaphor's literal meaning from being realized in any ordinary way, serve thereby to intensify the form in which each term's emotive meaning is realized."[62]

---

[56]*Ibid.*, p. 69.
[57]*Ibid.*, p. 70.
[58]*Ibid.*, Chapter IX.
[59]*Ibid.*, p. 72.
[60]*Ibid.*
[61]*Ibid.*, p. 73.
[62]*Ibid.*, p. 75.

The principal application of the response theory that Stevenson develops, and indeed the one with a view to which he develops the theory, concerns ethical terms and especially the term "good" in the generic sense, which Stevenson takes to be basic. "Good," in the sense which Stevenson undertakes to characterize, must be so defined as to recognize that goodness is "a topic for intelligent disagreement," is "magnetic," and is "not discoverable solely through scientific method."[63] The term has both descriptive and emotive aspects. To a considerable extent the emotive aspects depend upon the descriptive one; and for this reason, it is nearly always possible to bring reasons to bear upon ethical disagreements. The distinctively ethical aspect of the term "good" is, however, the emotive one; and the disagreements in attitude which arise in this aspect of the use of the term are fundamental in the sense that when they are settled, ethical disputes tend to terminate.[64] According to one mode of analysis that approximates the significance of common usage, " 'This is good' is synonymous with 'I approve this; do so as well.' "[65] The first, or indicative, part of the statement answers to the descriptive aspect of the meaning, and the second, or imperative, part answers to the emotive part. The imperative is, however, only a rough approximation of the emotive, for the term "good" involves much more subtle suggestions that cannot be conveyed in an imperative. Indeed, there is no exact synonym for this aspect of "good," for emotive terms tend to have their own quite distinctive flavor. Another analysis of the term "good" that is equally applicable to actual usage but brings out a different aspect of meaning may be put in the following way: " 'This is good,' has the meaning of 'This has the qualities, or relations' X, Y, Z...., except that 'good' has as well a laudatory emotive meaning which permits it to express the speaker's approval and tends to evoke the approval of the hearer."[66] Such an account of the meaning of "good" provides for the recognition of considerable, and even detailed, descriptive content by virtue of which something is said

---

[63]C. L. Stevenson, "The Emotive Meaning of Ethical Terms" in C. L. Stevenson, *Facts and Values* (New Haven: Yale University Press, 1963), p. 15.
[64]*Ethics and Language*, Chapter 1.
[65]*Ibid.*, p. 81.
[66]*Ibid.*, p. 207.

to be good but, at the same time, continues to give due recognition to the crucial emotive aspect of the meaning of "good."

2. The Non-Equivalence of Responses and Meanings

Such accounts of meanings and responses as the foregoing
bring to focus three major questions that are deeply embedded
in the character of meaning situations and require special
consideration here. Can responses be equated with intentional or
dispositional meanings? If not, what are the major roles of
responses in meaning situations? And what are the roles of
emotions, attitudes, and emotive meanings in meaning situations? These three questions, in the order indicated, determine
the themes of this and the two succeeding sections.

Although the role of responses in meaning situations is so
vital that most of the meanings that mainly concern us would
never occur if there were no responses, attempts to equate
responses with meanings inevitably run into difficulties that in
the end preclude any such equivalence. One of these difficulties
consists in the quite different modes of the eventual determination
of responses, on the one hand, and of intentional and dispositional
meanings, on the other.

The eventual determination of intentional and dispositional
meanings, not only differs from that of responses, but lies on
the opposite side of the stimulus-response relation. To be sure,
the intention of an agent in making a particular utterance is
directly affected by his expectation concerning probable
responses and hence is indirectly affected by previous responses;
but his intention on a present occasion is already formed before
any response to his particular utterance takes place and, indeed,
regardless of whether or not any response occurs at all. Thus,
when someone says "Shut the door," the intention determining
his meaning is formed before any one makes any responding
move and whether or not anyone ever does. Similarly, while the
dispositions of members of culture groups are affected by
anticipations of responses to various terms and other symbols
and hence, indirectly by past responses, and while, in a given
culture, dispositions to use expressions and dispositions to respond
to them may become so well adjusted to one another that each

may be used as a guide to the other; what determines the dispositional meaning of any bearer is, as has been previously shown, people's dispositions to use it rather than their responses to its use or even their dispositions to respond to its use.

A second obstacle to the equating of intentional and dispositional meanings with responses consists in the differences between the cognitive contents of such meanings and those of responses to the bearers of these meanings. The cognitive content of a response to a bearer of intentional meaning is often widely at variance with the meaning of that bearer. Speaking quite literally, I may say that the day is dark; but what my respondent takes me to mean may be that business is bad or that the world is going to pieces. A father, impressed with the artistry of a villain in a television drama, may say, "The man is good"; but his son may be astonished at how anyone could say that such a man was good. A government official wishing to warn the enemy that his nation is about to unleash its full might, may declare that his people have taken about all they can endure; but what the enemy gets may be that the speaker's people are on the point of giving up the fight. So frequent, indeed, are the occasions and so many and varied the sources of misunderstanding that it is more surprising that the cognitive contents of intentional meanings of bearers and those of responses to them should coincide as often as they do than that they do not always do so.

When the cognitive contents of dispositional meanings and of responses to the bearers of these meanings are being compared, differences are as a rule not likely to be very great for the reason that dispositions to use and to respond to bearers of meaning within culture groups tend to become adjusted to one another. However, since the dispositional meanings of terms are eventually determined by agents who use these terms whereas responses are eventually determined by respondents, differences between cognitive contents of dispositional meanings and responses cannot be completely eliminated. They are evident in persistent misunderstandings between generations and between subculture groups within a given culture and, in the manner in which members of any group are disposed, owing to their biases in their own behalf, to use some terms in one way and to respond to them in another.

A third obstacle precluding the equating of intentional and dispositional meanings with responses is that, even in instances in which the cognitive contents of such meanings and of responses to their bearers are much alike, such responses almost invariably include a great deal that is not included in the corresponding meanings. While someone's response to a given utterance may include apprehension of precisely the meaning the agent intended, it is also very likely to include a great many associated ideas as well as feelings, impulses, and even overt actions that were no part of the intended meaning. Thus, when someone remarks that the door is shut, a respondent may think, not only of the door in question and its closed condition, but also of the doors of the cathedral in Florence or of those of his childhood playhouse or even the fancied doors of the dawn. He may also either rise to open the door, settle down comfortably in his chair, or feel guilty. When the flagman signals that the tracks are clear, his respondent may, not only get the message, but also think of his boyhood semaphor experiences, of bullfights, and of school flag raisings. He may, in addition, open the switch or be angry with the flagman for thinking that he did not know that the tracks were clear. The responses that members of a group are disposed to make to type words and other bearers of dispositional meanings are also, even in the cases in which their cognitive contents are closely correlated with dispositional meanings, likely to contain a great deal that does not belong to these meanings.

Thus, responses in our culture to such words as "hero" and "saint" tend to carry with them penumbras of favorable feelings and impulses that cannot be construed as parts of their meanings, and such words as "fool" and "liar" are likely to yield unfavorable feelings and actions which are real and important but hardly parts of the meanings of these terms. The sight of the Statue of Liberty regularly stirs in returning travellers strong emotions, and the waving of Old Glory may regularly cause American troops to rally; but these feelings and actions can scarcely as such be parts of the dispositional meanings of the relevant symbols even though they depend on such meanings. These responding feelings and attitudes depend upon dispositions of respondents to respond rather than, as dispositional meanings do, upon dispositions of agents to intend.

They belong to the force of the bearers in question rather than to the meanings of these bearers.

While the view that intentional and dispositional meanings are to be equated with dispositions of respondents to respond to bearers of meaning is by no means the same as the view that these meanings are to be equated with the actual responses of respondents, some of the same sorts of obstacles that stand in the way of the latter view also stand in the way of the former. First, whereas intentional and dispositional meanings are eventually determined by the intentions and dispositions of agents to intend, in using bearers, to lead respondents to apprehend meanings; dispositions to respond are eventuallly determined by the environmental, physiological, and psychological factors that shape the dispositions of respondents with respect to bearers of meaning presented to them. If I say "The day is dark," what I mean depends in the end upon what I intend to lead my respondents to apprehend as my meaning, and what speakers of English mean by "dark" depends on their dispositions in using this term in various kinds of contexts; but what my respondent's dispositions are in responding to my remark is a matter of his psychology not mine, and what the dispositions of those who understand English are to respond to words, types, and symbols depends upon their situations as respondents not as agents. Second, the cognitive contents of intentional and dispositional meanings may be different from those of dispositions to respond to the bearers of such meanings. To my remark that "I am hot" you may, at different times, be disposed to respond in a half dozen different ways, without the meaning's having changed; and because dispositions of members of groups to use bearers of meaning depend on factors different from those determining their dispositions to respond to these bearers, even the common cognitive contents of dispositions with respect to the use of such ordinary words as "I" and "hot" can, and do, sometimes differ from those of dispositions with respect to responses to them. Third, even when the cognitive contents of dispositions to respond to bearers of intentional and dispositional meanings coincide in the main with such meanings, these dispositions to respond still nearly always include a great deal that is not included in these meanings as such. They include everything in the dispositions of respondents to respond to bearers that is not either intended by agents to be apprehended as their meanings or such that agents are so disposed to intend it; and if either the psychological backgrounds or the actual responses of respondents are any indication of these dispositions to respond, these dispositions include a great many possible ideas, feelings, and impulses that agents neither intend nor are disposed to intend to have apprehended as their meanings, even when these agents have at other times been respondents with respect to the same words and symbols. When I say that you are late, you may be disposed to think me critical of you and to become angry in a way which I do not intend at all; and speakers of English may be disposed in general upon hearing the word "you" to be psychologically placed on guard in a way that speakers as such are not disposed to intend.

Thus far, I have been concerned with the view that intentional and dispositional meanings can be equated with responses or with dispositions to respond to stimuli. I want now to make a few remarks concerning the view that some causal meanings of stimuli other than bearers of intentional or dispositional meanings can be equated with responses to such stimuli. This view is, I take it, somewhat more plausible than the views that identify intentional and dispositional meanings with responses. No such extraneous factors intervene between the responses in question and the eventual determinations of the corresponding meanings as intervene between responses and the eventual determiners of intentional and dispositional meanings; and no such deviations are found between these responses and the corresponding meanings as are found between intentional and dispositional meanings and responses. If a causal meaning of Jones's shoving Smith is that Smith strikes Jones, the eventual determination of this causal meaning lies in Smith's reaction; and this meaning cannot be at variance with that reaction since it is essentially a characterization of that reaction. Nevertheless, it will not quite do simply to equate even responses to stimuli that are not bearers of intentional or dispositional meanings with causal meanings of these stimuli. The reason is not that other factors intervene or that discrepancies occur but just that even causal meanings operate upon a different logical level from that of responses. The causal meaning is not just the response as such but that the response occurs. The causal meaning of Jones's shoving Smith is not Smith's response but that Smith responds in this way. The causal meaning of that blow is not this knee jerk but that this man's knee jerks. The causal meaning of your outburst is not my irritation but that I am irritated.

3. Role of Responses in the Discernment of Meaning

If responses to bearers of meaning are not equatable with meanings, what is their role in meaning situations, especially as regards the light that they can throw upon the disclosure of meanings? This question is best approached, not by attempting to consider meaning situations in general, but by considering separately each of the types of meaning situations in which responses have been seen to be relevant, namely, those involving intentional and dispositional meanings and those whose meanings depend upon responses to stimuli other than bearers of intentional or dispositional meanings.

a. Bearers of intentional meaning are produced with the intent to yield responses which include at least apprehensions of meanings intended. Whenever they are responded to as bearers of intentional meanings, responses to them are built upon the respondent's apprehension of something as meant by the agent. But responses to bearers of intentional meaning may, and usually do, include a great deal besides what is either intended by agents or apprehended as so intended. They include many ideas not so intended or apprehended and also emotions, impulses, and verbal and overt activities. Quite frequently they include activations of dispositions that only gradually unfold contingently upon various attendant circumstances. They are total reactions of respondents often including, but by no means confined to, apprehensions of what agents intend to have apprehended as their meanings.

If this is the character of responses to bearers of intentional meanings, it is readily understandable why such responses should deviate as widely as they have been seen to do from the meanings intended. Between what the agent intends to make apprehensible and the respondent's response, there intervene not only the bearer of meaning, which may itself be ill chosen, but also psychological and cultural idiosyncrasies of the respondent. Even when the respondent correctly apprehends what the agent

128 THE CONCEPT OF MEANING

intends, his response often adds to that correct apprehension extraneous cognitive, emotional, and volitional factors; and these can be quite different from what might be expected on the basis of what he takes to be the meaning.

However, if responses to intentional meanings are neither equatable with such meanings nor contain sure apprehensions of them, they, nevertheless, contain within themselves the sorts of apprehensions or takings-of-something-to-be-meanings-intended upon which the whole receptive side of the process of communication depends, and upon the cessation of which agents would soon cease to intend to make anything apprehensible at all. Moreover, there are good reasons for thinking that the apprehensions included in responses to bearers of intentional meanings are often successful apprehensions of the meanings intended. Such, on the one hand, are the natural links between many objects and events commonly used to convey meanings and the meanings intended that successful communication can often be carried on even between people of different cultures. And such, on the other hand, are the symbolic and linguistic capacities of any given culture group that the members of such a group regularly succeed in apprehending at least the major drift of what their fellows intend to convey. Breakdowns in communication, however frequent, remain the exception rather than the rule. Husbands and wives, parents and children, friends and neighbors, and even bitter enemies usually manage to understand one another rather well and scientists gain remarkable degrees of precision in their communications with one another.

Not only do responses contain takings that are in considerable part correct apprehensions of intended meanings, they also often include behavioral elements that can serve as useful guides to meanings for persons who do not have, or for special purposes do not wish to use, more direct means of access to intentional meanings. Despite all personal and social idiosyncracies of individuals, some regularities obtain between what people apprehend and resulting behavior; and such irregularities as occur can in fact be explained and adjusted by way of broader regularities within which they fall. Hence, insofar as people apprehend intentional meanings correctly, the manner of their behavior will often afford significant clues to the intentional meanings to which they are responding. If in response to a certain utterance someone closes a door or raises a window, the meaning of the utterance may be surmised from the character of the response. If in response to an utterance a respondent attacks the speaker, one sort of meaning is suggested; if he begins to beat his wife, another sort of meaning is suggested; and if he searches his pockets, still another is suggested. Moreover, if a subtle observer can trace out a respondent's behavior patterns in detail, he may surmise fairly precisely what meaning that respondent takes to have been meant and hence, provided the circumstances of communication are favorable, what meaning the agent means.

b. When the meaning situations under consideration are those involving dispositional meanings of types and enduring particulars, the roles of relevant responses are similar to the roles of responses in meaning situations involving intentional meanings. Such responses are total reactions including cognitive as well as emotional and volitional aspects that may be revealing with reference to the meanings of the bearers which prompt them. However, responses to bearers of dispositional meanings are to be thought of, not as particular responses that individuals make, but as kinds of responses that individuals or members of groups are ready to make in suitable circumstances. Moreover, while cognitive contents of these responses are in principle capable of deviating from the meanings which the relevant bearers are usually intended to mean, powerful forces are at work bringing and keeping these cognitive response contents and the meanings commonly intended in the use of these bearers in line with one another. First, the processes of teaching and learning, concentrated in the youth of the members of the group but also continued through life, tend to keep dispositions to take bearers of meaning to have certain meanings and dispositions to use them, in accord with one another. Second, distortions brought about in special circumstances that cause the manner in which an individual takes a bearer of meaning to deviate from the usual norms tend to be ironed out by the more frequent occurrence of more nearly normal circumstances. Third, idiosyncratic uses of, and responses to, bearers of meaning are likely to yield inconvenient results that tend to bring dispositions to use bearers of meaning and dispositions to respond to them into line with one another. Fourth, the same individuals are both users of bearers of meaning and respondents to them, and their dispositions to use a given bearer of meaning and to respond to the same bearer of meaning tend constantly to adjust to one another. For such reasons as these, the responses that people are disposed to make to words and other bearers of dispositional meanings tend to be highly reliable clues to dispositional meanings; and accordingly, insofar as behavior is a reliable clue to apprehensions of meanings, the behavioral aspects of these responses come to be publicly verifiable clues to these meanings.

c. When the meaning situation under consideration is one in which a stimulus other than a bearer of intentional or dispositional meaning has a meaning by way of a response, the connection between the response and the meaning is so direct that to be aware of the response as such is already to apprehend the meaning. The response is then not properly said, as in the other cases, so much to contain the meaning as rather, in a manner subsequently to be discussed, to exemplify the meaning or to be characterized by the meaning. Thus, if I observe that Jones responds to his pinching shoe by removing it, I already know that a meaning of the pinching shoe is that Jones removes it; and if one understands that the United States increases its defense budget in response to an increase in the Soviet budget, one already knows that a meaning in the increase of the Soviet budget is that the United States increases its budget. One may not always know just what occurrence is a response to a given event; but once he does, he has already apprehended at least one causal meaning of that event in that he has apprehended an effect which immediately governs a meaning.

In the light of the foregoing account of responses in meaning situations, it is now possible to say something about why, despite evident differences between meanings and responses, intelligent inquirers have often been inclined to equate intentional and dispositional meanings with responses. One reason for this inclination consists in the fact that a response that is revelant to a bearer of intentional or dispositional meaning includes a respondent's apprehension of, or disposition to, apprehend something as a meaning of such a bearer, and that accordingly in many instances it includes a successful apprehension of such a meaning itself. A further reason consists in the fact that even in cases of bearers of intentional and dispositional meanings, observable behavioral aspects of responses are sometimes excellent clues to meanings. The insufficiency of these two reasons is, however, as plain as their initial plausibility. A third reason for the identification of intentional and dispositional meanings with responses to their bearers consists in the fact that, not only other stimuli, but even bearers of intentional and dispositional meanings often yield responses that directly disclose causal meanings. Not only may Jones's shoving Smith mean that Smith strikes Jones, but Jones's saying that Smith is a fool may mean that Smith strikes Jones; and in the latter case, as in the former, that Smith strikes Jones is a meaning of the preceding occurrence. However, it should be plain that this third reason no more justifies the equating of intentional and dispositional meanings with responses than do the other two. One can indeed correctly say that bearers of intentional and dispositional meanings yield causal meanings by way of responses to them; but this affords no ground for saying that the causal meanings so yielded may be identified with the intentional or dispositional meanings of these bearers. Smith's striking Jones does indeed directly disclose a causal meaning of Jones's utterance, "You are a fool," namely, that Smith strikes Jones, but that causal meaning is by no means equatable either with the meaning intended in Jones's utterance or with the dispositional meaning of the English expression, "You are a fool."

It should also be clear now why behavioral responses to bearers of meaning may well be drawn into operational accounts of meanings. To be sure, when particular bearers of intentional meanings are concerned, behavioral responses may be too varied to be very helpful in revealing meanings. But when the more general bearers of dispositional meanings, such as word types, are involved and discrepancies between uses and responses tend to be ironed out, behavioral responses as correlated with laws of behavior may go a long way toward supplying publicly observable data for inquiry concerning meanings. These data may be further refined and made more relevant by focusing attention not upon responses directly but upon the dispositions to respond that responses manifest. Moreover, findings regarding meanings arrived at in this way have at least some advantages over those arrived at by examining stimuli alone in that it is often easier to determine what is a response to a bearer of meaning than it is to determine what is the stimulus to such a bearer. In any case, when these two kinds of data, those grounded in stimuli and those grounded in responses, are correlated, the objective bases available for inquiring into dispositional meanings are substantial though the fact must not be lost sight of that the stimuli and responses thus searched out and correlated cannot themselves constitute meanings but are at best accompanying factors that may serve as useful clues to meanings.

4. *Emotive Meaning and the Place of Emotions and Attitudes in Meaning Situations*

Although much that has been said in both the preceding chapter and the present one bears to some extent upon problems concerning the place of emotions and attitudes in meaning situations, so much discussion has in recent years been devoted to what has been called "emotive meaning" that some special attention to these problems seems to be required. I shall accordingly consider directly the roles of emotional and attitudinal factors in meaning situations and the applicability of the notion of "emotive meaning" to these factors.

Most bearers of meaning emerge from a background of feelings and attitudes as well as thoughts and issue in responses that prominently include feelings. Even scientific meanings are not without promptings and responses of an emotional order. Throughout most of the history of inquiry concerning meaning, these facts have been inadequately recognized. Inquiries in anthropology, sociology, psychology, linguistics, and other disciplines have, however, in the present century, brought these facts to the fore. A major purpose of some earlier proponents of the notion of emotive meaning, including many logical positivists, was to provide a repository in which non-cognitive meanings could be placed so as to render scientific meanings free of emotional and attitudinal encumbrances. Subsequent proponents of the notion, such as Stevenson, have been more constructively concerned to present emotive meanings, including meanings of moral terms, in balanced perspective rather than simply to preserve the purity of science.

In the years since the publication of Stevenson's *Ethics and Language,* a good many philosophers of language in England and America, prompted in part by the work of emotivists and in part by broader interests of their own, have been less concerned to develop a concept of emotive meaning than to examine in detail the whole matter of the specific functions of linguistic expressions including those involving emotive and attitudinal factors as well as others. In the pages that follow, I shall, making ample use of the suggestions of these later writers as well as of emotivists themselves, try to sketch some of the major roles of emotional factors in meaning situations. Such an endeavor should bring to light considerations that may be helpful not only in the orientation of emotional and attitudinal factors in meaning situations but also in the evaluation of the notion of emotive meaning.

The major functions of emotional and attitudinal factors in meaning situations seem to be the following: First, the psychological situations in which our intentions to produce bearers to express our meanings emerge are often highly charged with emotional and attitudinal factors and are rarely, if ever, entirely devoid of them. Accordingly, our expressions of meaning in the intentional way are nearly always at very least prompted by, and intimately associated with, such factors. Moreover, since meanings in the dispositional way depend upon, and manifest themselves in, expressions of meaning in the intentional way, they too may properly be said to rest upon, and to be intimately associated with, such factors. Thus if I say that "Senator X acts like a fool" or that "Captain Y is a great guy," I am very likely to be prompted by feelings which are intricately interwoven with what I mean; and words such as "fool" and "great" have long since come, through such usage as my present usage, to be disposed to be used under the impact of emotive promptings and with emotional connections.

Second, the responses that we make, and the kinds of responses we are disposed to make, to linguistic expressions often include substantial emotional and attitudinal factors and are rarely altogether without such factors. The response of Senator X and his friends to my remark about his making a fool of himself will no doubt include, not only apprehension of what I said, but also some rather strong feelings and perhaps words and deeds as well. The same will be true, though somewhat less emphatically, in the case of my remark about Captain Y. Even a remark about the contents of a test tube is not likely to be met with entire apathy, especially if further results hinge upon it. Since bearers of meaning are produced in the light of anticipations of responses, the emotional responses that follow utterances and inscriptions invariably have an impact upon dispositions to use these bearers. Moreover, since substantial proportions of the terms of a language are taught and used in circumstances in which they are likely to yield emotional and attitudinal responses, verbal expressions come to have emotive dispositional properties with reference both to use and to response that are quite as much a part of the capacities of these expressions as are any cognitive content they may have.

Third, since from a given verbal expression causal inferences can often be made to the fact that the speaker had a certain emotional or attitudinal reaction or that a respondent will have such a reaction, that someone has a certain emotional or attitudinal experience can often be said literally to be a meaning of an expression in the causal way. Thus my statement about Senator X meant that he became angry and my statement about Captain Smith meant that he was much pleased. "What's the meaning of the word 'fool'?" "Well, one meaning is that if you use it of a person he's likely to become angry." "What's the meaning of the expression 'great guy'?" "One meaning is that if you use it of anyone he's likely to be at least a little pleased."

Fourth, verbal expressions are often used to refer to emotions and attitudes or to attribute them to ourselves or others. Such references and attributions may themselves be emotionally neutral or they may be full of feeling. They are very often directly or indirectly prompted by situations involving emotions, and they would scarcely come to be used or understood at all save for the fact that the people who use and understand them have at one time or another the emotions referred to or attributed. Thus, one may say that he, or someone else, is, or has been, afraid or sad, or that fear of sadness can have a depressing effect. In so saying, he may, or may not, in fact be afraid or sad; but apart from some experiences of fear and sadness in him and his hearers at some time or other, such things would scarcely come to be said or understood at all. Most languages have considerable vocabularies of words suited to talking about and ascribing emotions. Some of these terms such as "afraid" and "sad," are themselves basically neutral in terms of their dispositions to arise from or to generate emotional responses; but others, such as "malevolent" and "sadistic," are likely to arise from or lead to emotional responses in the process of referring to or attributing emotions and attitudes.

Fifth, utterances that emerge from emotional contexts are often—though not always—intentional expressions of emotion. On the one hand, the instinctive cry of a wounded animal is scarcely an intentional expression of emotion and neither is the grimace of an unconscious man or the crying of a new-born baby; but, on the other hand, neither is one's dispassionate statement that he is in pain or that he dislikes an enemy. An intentional expression of one's emotion requires as a minimum, on the one hand, that the agent have at least some inkling that the bearer of meaning he produces is likely to lead to an apprehension on the part of a respondent of his having the emotion and, on the other hand, that the emotion be at least in some degree actually present. One says or does what at least to some minimal extent he anticipates will convey an impression that he feels what he does. To talk about the expression of an emotion, is, however, all too general a way of talking. Expressions of emotion are of many kinds. In expressing an emotion one may be pleading or commanding, condemning or condoning, courting or castigating, or doing any one of many other expressive acts each of which involves its own special modes of cognitive import and emotional overtone. For every such kind of action most languages contain considerable arsenals of terms with dispositional emotive charges varying degrees at the disposal of the user of the language.

Sixth, many utterances and inscriptions that yield emotional responses, as well as some others, are intended so to do, and many words in most languages have dispositional capacities to yield such responses. The mere fact that an utterance or inscription does, in fact, yield an emotional response does not imply, of course, that it was so intended; but when it was so intended, the emotional response is as much a part of what the agent intended as is the respondent's understanding of what the agent intended to say. Moreover, the capacities of words to produce emotional responses is as much a part of the power of words as is the power to bring about understanding. If, trying to get you to stand up and fight, I say, "It looks as though you were afraid of him," the result I intend in terms of your emotional response is indeed an even more important part of my intention than my intention that, as a means to this, you understand what I say. Similarly the potential emotional impact of the word "liar" upon anyone to whom it is addressed is likely to be a good deal more dynamic than is the effect of the term upon the understanding of that person.

However, while such considerations as the foregoing are sufficient to show how ill-balanced traditional accounts of meaning had become, through neglect of the emotional and attitudinal factors in meaning situations, and how significant was the achievement of those who stressed the notion of emotive meaning in giving due recognition to such factors; nothing in these considerations justifies the claim that the meanings of some terms includes a "a range of emotions" or that the expression "emotive meaning" can be used without misrepresenting the character of meaning situations. Indeed, there seem to be good reasons for holding that meanings include no such ranges of emotions and that the term emotive meaning represents a misconstruction of the role of emotions and attitudes in meaning situations. In the pages that follow, I wish to offer some considerations in support of this contention.

In the first place, elements in meaning that have been regarded as purely emotive are usually found to be in some measure grounded in cognitive elements in meaning situations. This consideration, now duly recognized by some proponents of the notion of emotive meaning is amply illustrated in the history of the development of the notion of emotive meaning. The earliest proponents of the notion were inclined to think of certain terms, including evaluative and metaphysical ones, as being altogether emotive in meaning. Subsequent proponents of the notion saw underlying the emotive meanings of these terms considerable cognitive content and thought that, in many instances, reasons grounded in such contents could be given for the emotions and attitudes in which the emotive meanings consisted. Thus to say that a piece of meat was good was not to express mere arbitrary liking for the meat but to express such liking because the meat was found to be tender, tasteful, etc.; and to say that one ought to contribute to a certain cause was not arbitrarily to express a prompting to give to that cause but to express a prompting to give because the cause was suited to meet certain needs, etc. Already the recognition of cognitive grounds for emotive ingredients in meanings has been carried a long way, and it can be carried farther. When one recognizes that the criteria for the applicability of a term can vary widely according to times, places, persons and contexts and that disagreement on the applicability of terms appear quite irrational in the absence of disagreements concerning criteria and situations, one should be ready to search a long time for cognitive roots of differences concerning the applicability of a term before putting the difference down to pure emotion. When one does so search, sufficient cognitive explanations are usually found to be much more readily at hand than one initially supposes. Two people differ radically on the goodness of an act, and both seem to describe the act in the same way; but it turns out that one was weighing motives heavily and the other was not. Two others differ on the beauty of a poem, but one was concerned with rhythm and the other with suggested mental pictures. Two people differ on the creativity of a book but one has noticed sources that the other overlooked. Such considerations as these are not incompatible with the claims of Stevenson, who recognizes with reference to his second pattern account of good that a full list of criteria may be given in each case.

Now I do not wish to say that there are in meaning situations no prompting emotions not traceable to cognitive suggestions and no emotional responses not explainable by cognitive apprehensions, and I surely do not wish to say that intentional and dispositional meanings may not have emotional accompaniments. I do not even wish to say that we do not intend to express emotions by our words both through and apart from the cognitive import of these words. What I do wish, in the second place, to say is that the roles of emotions that come into meaning situations are better described in other ways than by including emotions in meanings and calling them emotive meanings. The roles that should be assigned to emotions in meaning situations are such roles as those suggested in the foregoing account of the roles of emotions in meaning situations. Emotions may be causes or effects of bearers of meaning. They may, as causes or effects, directly yield meanings in the causal way. They may be referred to and attributed to persons. They may accompany the intentions that prompt the production of bearers of meaning or be parts of the responses intended, or produced, by such bearers either through, or independently of, cognitive meanings. But to include them in meanings themselves is to conflate aspects of meaning situations that are more clearly seen through an analysis that distinguishes those aspects; it is also, for reasons subsequently to appear, to distort the notion of meaning itself.

In the third place, despite the intricate interweaving of meaning and emotional factors in the origins and results of utterances and inscriptions, meaning and emotion are sufficiently separable to facilitate a clear distinction between those functions of language in virtue of which it yields meanings and those in virtue of which it expresses or produces emotions. This holds true even in those cases, such as evaluative statements, in which the intimacy of meaning and emotive factors is greatest and *a fortiori* in all other cases as well. If I say that a picture is hideous, I both mean that the picture has certain characteristics and at the same time express dislike for it and suggest that you should dislike it too. But while it would be odd for me to say that the picture was hideous but I didn't dislike it or think you should, there would be no self-contradiction in my saying that; and certainly there would be no self-contradiction in my suggesting that I disliked it and expected you to do so but that it wasn't hideous. The situation is similar with respect to moral evaluation. If I say that a certain action is good, I mean that the action has certain characteristics and I strongly suggest that I approve it and that you should too; but while it would be odd to say that the action was good but I didn't approve it or think you should, there would be no self-contradiction in saying that. If I say that a certain kind of act is always right, while I suggest, in so doing, that I have a certain impulse to do that kind of thing, and should be deemed perverse if I did not, still I do not contradict myself in admitting that I have no such impulse. In all such cases, however intimate the psychological ties of meanings and emotions, a logical distinction remains possible that permits us not indeed to get rid of the emotional factors but to recognize emotive functions of language as important in their own right and distinguishable from meaning functions however closely the two may be related to one another. The meaning of an expression is one thing; its force, as John Austin shows, is another. My intending to produce in my respondent certain emotions and attitudes by no means justifies the inclusion of those emotions and attitudes in what I intend him to apprehend as my meaning. Indeed, it is only by way of his understanding certain meanings as my meanings that I ordinarily expect to produce such attitudes and emotions in him at all.

A fourth objection to the notion of emotive meanings is the consideration that intentional and dispositional meanings, on the one hand, and emotions (at any rate where actual emotions as distinct from types of emotion are concerned), on the other hand, are not only distinguishable from one another but on different logical levels from one another; so that the notion of emotive meaning becomes, in those versions at any rate that emphasize actual emotional responses, a basic logical mistake, even a sort of contradiction in terms. For a bearer to have a meaning in the intentional way is for an agent to intend to make that meaning apprehensible to someone as his meaning, and for a bearer to have a meaning in the dispositional way is for someone to be disposed to intend in using it in certain contexts to make such a meaning apprehensible to respondents. But while one can make a meaning apprehensible to another or be disposed to do so, and while one can make the fact or character of his emotion apprehensible to another, one can scarcely make his emotion itself apprehensible to another. Meanings can be apprehended, shared, conveyed, and repeated, and so also can types or characters of emotions; but actual emotions are particular occurrences in particular individuals which, while they can be stimulated, increased, discouraged, diminished or even known, cannot be made apprehensible, shared, or conveyed as meanings can. They may, accordingly, prompt, or be prompted by, expressions of meanings but they can never be included in meanings.

If the notion of emotive meaning is as misleading as has been suggested, how did so many competent philosophers come to employ such a notion? The story is no doubt complex, but at least these factors appear to be prominent in it. One is a legitimate and long overdue recognition of the great importance of emotional and attitudinal factors in meaning situations. Another is a sound recognition that a given bearer of meaning can be causally connected with "ranges of emotion," both at its origin and in its consequences, that directly yield causal meanings. Still another is an assumption, born of the period of psychological inquiry in which the notion of emotive meaning was promulgated, that all meanings are to be placed in causal frameworks. If all meanings are basically causal and some meanings appear to consist of emotional factors causally connected with bearers of meaning, it is quite natural to think of the whole gamut of emotive factors in meaning situations as ranges of emotions meant. Unfortunately for this line of thought, however, intentional and dispositional meanings cannot be assimilated to the causal pattern without losing their distinctive intentional and dispositional character; and in any case the emotions that are causally connected with bearers of meaning are not themselves the meanings of these bearers though they often directly yield causal meanings of these bearers.

If what has now been said about emotive meaning is essentially sound, the concept of emotive meaning as such and the claim that some meanings include ranges of emotion will need to be replaced by detailed analysis of the function of emotive factors in meaning situations. However, no abandonment of the major emphasis of emotivists on the role of emotion in meaning situations or of their quest for the discovery of the character of that role is called for. What is called for is rather a redirection of inquiry to work out the various functions of language including very significant non-cognitive ones. Actually, it appears that a number of former advocates of emotive meaning are now content to recognize that their major point has been adequately made and to have the thrust of their arguments absorbed in the current detailed effort to work out the specific functions of language without any longer contending for the apparently dubious notion of emotive meaning.

CHAPTER VI

REFERENTS AND MEANINGS

One can scarcely make an intelligible statement without intending to refer to something, and a large proportion of the expressions that people commonly use can be used to refer. Hence referents, or things referred to, are important features of meaning situations intricately interwoven with meanings. They have been more often identified with meanings than any of the other features of meaning situations thus far considered; and whether or not such an identification is correct, some understanding of what their roles in meaning situations are, is essential to any adequate understanding of meanings.

In the first section of the present chapter, I shall call attention to some important things that can be, or have been said about referents and meanings by inquirers disposed in some manner to assimilate meanings to referents. In the second section, I shall discuss directly the character of reference and referents. In the third section, I shall consider the problem of the assimilation of meanings to referents and in the fourth, the relations of referents and meanings to one another.

1. Some Views Concerning Referents and Meanings

a. Among the most prominent and primitive of all expressions are names and descriptive expressions referring to particular observable objects and events. The words a child is first taught are those referring to his mother, his father, his bottle, his rattle, his crib, his hands, feet, eyes, ears, nose, and some of the simple things he and others do, such as crying, smiling, shaking hands, etc. Primitive peoples make extensive use of names for specific objects and events and seem reluctant to use general expressions signifying wide varieties of things. Indeed, they often use different expres-

sions to refer to different stages of the same object or event.
Accordingly, it is not surprising to find an ancient writer speculating thus concerning the origin of at least a part of language: "So
out of the ground the Lord God formed every beast of the field
and every bird of the air, and brought them to man to see what
he would call them; and whatever the man called every living
creature, that was its name."[1]

On the basis of such considerations as the foregoing, a naïve
reference theory of meaning, to the effect that the meaning of a
term was just those observable objects and events to which it
referred, might be formulated. I do not know that any serious
inquirer has ever confined his thought within any such naive
naming theory for very long, but almost everyone is at times disposed to equate the meaning of a term with what it refers to. Such
a view has at any rate the merit of pointing out tangible features
of meaning situations related to bearers of meaning in a way closely
analogous to the way in which meanings are related to them and
capable in many instances of disclosing meanings. However, such
a view is altogether incapable of dealing with the meanings of
even the simplest general terms such as "red" and "square" not to
speak of abstract terms or fictitious entities. Hence, if the assimilation of meanings to referents is to be at all plausible, this naïve
naming theory must, in one way or another, be considerably
modified.

b. One rather drastic way of coping with the problem of
general and other troublesome terms within a referential theory
of meaning is to adopt the extreme "platonistic" view that every
expression has as its meaning a character or universal to which it
refers. According to such a view, not only abstract terms, but all
general terms and even names and descriptions would refer to
universals constituting their meanings. Thus, not only would
"virtue" and "justice" mean the universals to which they refer,
but "John," "America," "red," "man," and "good" would also
mean characters referred to by these terms. However, apart from
the question of whether or not meanings are ever identifiable
with referents, such a view is, among other things, quite incapable
of giving any satisfactory account of the apparently unmistakable

---

[1]Genesis 2:19, *The Oxford Annotated Bible* (New York and Oxford:
The Oxford University Press, 1962).

reference of most proper names and definite descriptions to individuals, or of such facts as that when I say that John is tall and that the man on my left is still taller, the names and descriptions used are used to refer to actual individuals rather than to characters exemplifiable by individuals.

c. A subtle way of meeting the difficulties of assimilating meanings to referents by way either of a naïve meaning theory or an extreme platonism is that of analyzing ordinary sentences into more refined ones that refer, neither to ordinary individuals nor to universals, but only to elemental objects which are readily apprehensible. An important step in the direction of such an analysis was taken in Bertrand Russell's celebrated theory of descriptions in which he undertook to reduce sentences containing definite descriptions, and hence sometimes seeming to refer to things that did not exist, to compounds of simple sentences containing nothing with which one could not be acquainted. Thus Russell undertook to reduce the sentence "The present King of France is wise," which seems to refer to a nonexistent king, to be a compound sentence to the effect that there is at least one person who is a king of France, at most one person who is a king of France, and not any person who is king of France and is not wise[2] Subsequently in *The Philosophy of Logical Atomism*[3] Russell undertook to carry his analysis further by making the eventual elements of expressions even more elemental. In this effort he was influenced by the now celebrated logical atomism of Ludwig Wittgenstein's *Tractatus Logico-Philosophicus*.

According to the doctrine of Wittgenstein's *Tractatus*, the world consists of facts; and all facts either are, or are analyzable

[2]G. E. Moore, "Russell's Theory of Descriptions" in P. A. Schilpp, *The Philosophy of Bertrand Russell* (New York: Harper and Row, 1963), pp. 195 ff. See also Bertrand Russell, "Reply to Criticisms" in *op. cit.*, p. 690; Bertrand Russell and A. N. Whitehead, *Principia Mathematica* (Cambridge: Cambridge University Press, Second edition, 1925), Vol. I, pp. 30 ff. 66 ff., and 173 ff.; Bertrand Russell, *Introduction to Mathematical Philosophy* (London: Allen and Unwin, 1919), chap. 16; and "On Denoting" *Mind*, XIV (1905), reprinted in Herbert Feigl and Wilfrid Sellars, *Readings in Philosophical Analysis* (New York: Appleton-Century-Crofts, Inc., 1949), pp. 103-115.
[3]Bertrand Russell, *The Philosophy of Logical Atomism* (1918) in W. P. Alston and George Nakhnikian, *Readings in Twentieth Century Philosophy* (Glencoe: The Free Press, 1962), pp. 298-380.

into elemental facts. The facts consist of "simple," "unalterable," and "subsistent" objects that "make up the substance of the world" and "fit into one another like links in a chain."[4] Elemental names are the names of such objects. Indeed "a name means an object" and "the object is its meaning."[5] Elemental propositions manifest elemental facts. More complex propositions, properly analyzed into their constituent elemental ones, depict the structural features of the world. However, while such a view helps to resolve some ancient riddles about apparent references to nonexistent objects and affords us some fresh insights into the structure of languages, the analyses it offers us are by no means translations of what our referring statements mean; at best they substitute for sentences that we understand quite well, indefinitely long sequences of sentences of which we can deal with but small portions at a time.

d. Theories than abandon the naïve naming theory but preserve the identification of referents and meanings may take a form different from those of treating referents as either universals or elemental objects, by treating the references through which things become referents, not as direct intentional relations, but as indirect causal ones. Such an indirect reference theory was developed by C. K. Ogden and I. A. Richards in their book, *The Meaning of Meaning*, has subsequently been elaborated in the movement referred to as General Semantics, and has been, in one way or another, reflected in the writings of a great many inquirers.

Although Odgen and Richards list sixteen different interpretations of meaning and recognize that meaning can in one sense be construed as a referential relation,[6] they take meaning in the sense in which a bearer is said to have a meaning to be something that a sign or symbol *refers* to by an indirect causal relation. They specifically repudiate the notion that a referent is directly referred to by a symbol, and present the referential relation as a triangular one in which a symbol is connected by a set of causal relations

---

[4] Ludwig Wittgenstein, *Tractatus Logico-Philosophicus,* Tr. B. F. McGuinness (London: Routledge and Kegan Paul, 1961), 2.021, 2.02, and 2.03.

[5] *Ibid.,* 3.203.

[6] C. K. Ogden and I. A. Richards, *The Meaning of Meaning* (New York: Harcourt Brace & Co., First Published 1923), pp. 185 ff.

with a thought or reference, which in turn is causally connected with a referent.[7]

A sign factor and its referent alike belong to a recurring referential context, so that when a part of the context occurs alone it tends to cause a felt gap and to stimulate a reaction as to the whole. Thus, a reference may be described as a "engram" or residual trace of an adaptation made by the organism to the stimulus. For example: If having often struck matches before and seen the striking followed by a flame, my present striking of a match becomes a sign referring by way of residual traces of a flame;[8] the psychological context constitutes a reference; the present external context is a sign; and the referent, which constitutes the meaning, is the flame to which the psychological context is adapted. "The meaning of A is that to which the mental process of interpreting A is adapted."[9]

Such an account of meaning is said by its authors to be suited to the standpoint of the speaker, in that "when we speak, the symbolism we employ is caused partly by the reference we are making,"[10] and also to that of the hearer, in that "when we hear what is said, the symbols cause us to perform an act of reference and to assume an attitude which will......be more or less similar to the act of the speaker."[11] It is also said to be capable of covering generalizations in that it shows how they arise from invariable sequences as, for example, the belief that match scrapes are followed by "flames" is grounded in exceptionless series of instances of the following of scrapes by flame.[12] The account is, moreover, said to explain how false statements can be meaningful. In such statements, the reference or meaning "will be the set of the scattered referents of the true simple beliefs which it contains."[13] "Thus, if we say, 'This is a book' and are in error our reference will be composed of a simple indefinite reference to any book, another to anything now, another to anything which may be here, and so on. These con-

---

[7]*Ibid.*, p. 10.
[8]*Ibid.*, pp. 52 f.
[9]*Ibid.*, p. 200.
[10]*Ibid.*, p. 10.
[11]*Ibid.*, p. 11.
[12]*Ibid.*, pp. 64 ff.
[13]*Ibid.*, p. 73.

stituents will all be true, but the whole reference to this book
which they make up together.....will be false, if.....what is there is
actually a box or something which fails to complete the three
contexts, book, here, and now."[14]

Drawing considerably upon ideas developed by Ogden and
Richards, Russell, and Wittgenstein, Alfred Korzybski, founder
of the Institute of General Semantics, held that the meaning of
an expression is to be found in one or more physical objects or
events to which it is linked through a more or less complex
reference rooted in the human nervous system. Upon this basis
Korzybski built, in his *Science and Society*, a system of "General
Semantics," which he believed to be not only theoretically sound but
also of great practical and therapeutic value. All previous philoso-
phies of language, as well as much common misuse of language,
he thought, were rooted in a misguided "Aristotelianism" which
wrongly identified subjects and predicates, introduced the false
doctrine of the excluded middle, erroneously separated thoughts
and feelings, broke the natural links between the human organism
and the world, hypostatized abstractions, and relied upon intensional or property definitions instead of developing extensional definitions by listing individuals as examples.[15] A first step in the cure
for such semantic ills is, Korzybski believed, to recognize that the
basic meaning of any sensible expression lies in the atomic and
subatomic particles and events to which it refers. A further step
is to recognize the multidimensional character of every meaning
and to define terms extensionally by reference to individuals and
quantities rather than intensionally by qualities. Abstractions,[16]
achieved by progressively leaving out of consideration for various
purposes some ingredients of a basic reference, has of course its
legitimate and useful place in thought and language. It leads back
from scientific object, to ordinary thing, from thing to word,
and from word to word about word. However—and this is a prime
requirement for the cure of semantic ills—people must constantly
remember that they are abstracting and keep reminding themselves

[14]*Ibid.*, p. 72.
[15]Alfred Korzybski, *Science and Sanity,* Second edition (Lancaster, Penn-
sylvania: The International, Non-Aristotilian Library Publishing Company,
1941), pp. xviii ff.
[16]*Ibid.*, Chap. 24.

of the "semantic differential," that is, of what they have left out.[17] The greatest benefit that could come to mankind would be that children should be trained from the beginning to be aware of the semantic differential and keep pressing back to basic referents. If such a habit could be established many forms of individual insanity and much of mass insanity that leads to wars and needless strife could be overcome.[18]

Two of the most widely read of the works written largely under the influence of Korzybski are Stuart Chase's *The Tyranny of Words*, and S. I. Hayakawa's *Language in Thought and Action*. In *The Tyranny of Words*, Chase insists that the roots of many of our current problems lie in our treating signs and symbols as though they had the properties of their referents. His insistance is that only as we are diligent in tracing down the referents of our terms, can we expose the emptiness of terms lacking referents and grasp the impact of meaningful terms.[19] Chase applies his quest for referents to wide ranges of expressions including those of science, politics, economics, law and international relations. In the second edition of *Language in Thought and Action*, Hayakawa reformulates the main lines of Korzybski's semantics in contemporary popular terms and undertakes to apply it to current problems. He suggests that Korzybski was opposed, not to Aristotle,[20] but to some interpretations of him and, not to two-valued logic, but to a practical habit of oversimplifying issues in terms of dichotomies.[21] He builds a "ladder of abstraction" upon Korzybski's model, and fits some aspects of recent accounts of operational definitions and emotive meanings into the scheme of general semantics.[22] Gathering the linguistic habits he considers objectionable under the label "intensional"[23] and those he considers desirable under the label "extensional,"[24] he assembles a sub-

---

[17]*Ibid.*, Chap. 25.
[18]*Ibid.*, Chap. 31.
[19]Stuart Chase, *The Tyranny of Words* (New York: Harcourt Brace and Co., 1938), especially Chapters 7 and 8.
[20]S. I. Hayakawa, *Language in Thought and Action* (New York: Harcourt Brace and World, Inc., 1964), p. 248.
[21]*Ibid.*, pp. 239 ff.
[22]*Ibid.*, pp. 183 ff. and 85 ff.
[23]*Ibid.*, pp. 278 ff.
[24]*Ibid.*, pp. 303 ff.

stantial wealth of illustrative material and comments upon such topics as the functions of the language of poetry and that of advertising in modern civilization. The General-Semantics movement has its own publication called ETC2 and continues to reflect the ideas and practical admonitions of its founder.

Such attempts indirectly to assimilate meanings to referents as those of Ogden and Richards and writers influenced by them have supplied initially plausible accounts of some simple statements involving references to objects and events and of substantive terms in such statements. They have also thrown significant light upon the manner in which the quest for referents can illuminate meanings of complex and false sentences and even of fictional, general, and abstract terms. However, their accounts of these latter meanings remained strained and unconvincing, and their accounts of meanings even of simple sentences and clearly referential terms are, for reasons that will subsequently appear, quite inadequate.

e. Partly because of an increasingly evident inadequacy of all theories that attempt fully to explain meanings even indirectly in terms of referents, a number of recent writers have renewed and developed a type of thought concerning meaning which, on the one hand, identifies one aspect of meanings with referents, but on the other hand, also recognizes and even insists upon, another very different aspect of meanings. In the remainder of the present section, I shall indicate something of the character of relevant ideas of two earlier writers who helped to impress the point of view under consideration upon contemporary thought concerning meaning, namely, John Stuart Mill and Gottlob Frege. I shall then go on to sketch some relevant ideas of two current representatives of this point of view, C. I. Lewis and Rudolf Carnap. It is, however, worthy of mention that a number of other writers, including some, such as Morris, Quine, and Russell, whose views have been discussed in other connections, have contributed significantly to the development of the point of view in question.

(1) John Stuart Mill divides all expressions or names, as he calls them, into connotative and non-connotative or denotative. "A non-connotative term is one which signifies a subject only or an attribute only." Thus *John, London, England, whiteness, length* and *virtue* are all non-connotative. "A connotative term is one which denotes a subject, and implies an attribute." Thus

"white, long and *virtuous* are connotative."[25] The denotation of a term is for Mill whatever it is used to "signify directly" or refer to. It's connotation is what it "implies, or involves or indicates."[26] "All concrete general names are connotative and hence ordinarily have both denotations and connotations."[27] Thus, *man*, for example, "denotes Peter, Jane, John and an indefinite number of other individuals of whom, taken as a class, it is the name." It connotes "corporeity, animal life, rationality and a certain animal form" and does not apply where any one of these attributes is missing.[27] Proper names are non-connotative or denotative only; and for this reason they have no meanings. Indeed, Mill quite explicitly insists concerning all terms that "the meaning resides not in what they denote but in what they connote."[28]

(2) In the thought of Gottlob Frege, a grouping of aspects of meaning situations somewhat similar to that of Mill, though quite different in some aspects, is developed. Having earlier equated the meaning of an expression with what he called its content, Frege came, in his essay "On Sense and Reference" and in his subsequent writings, to view the meaning that he had previously thought of as content under the dual aspects of *Sinn* and *Bedeutung* or sense and reference. In general, the reference of an expression is what it refers to, stands for, signifies, or designates (i.e., its referent);[29] and the sense of an expression is its "mode of presentation,"[30] what the expression expresses. An expression *"expresses* its sense, *stands for* or *designates* its reference."[31] An expression that has a sense may, of course, lack a reference (e.g., when its object does not exist); but anyone who takes the expression seriously supposes that it has a reference.[32] Both the reference and the sense of an expression must be distinguished from "the associated idea" or "internal image";[33] for

---

[25]John Stuart Mill, *A System of Logic* (London: Longmans, Green and Co., Ltd., New Impression, 1961), p. 19.
[26]*Ibid.,* p. 20.
[27]*Ibid.,* p. 19.
[28]*Ibid.,* p. 2.
[29]Gottlob Frege, "On Sense and Reference," translated by Max Black and Peter Greach in *Translation from the Philosophical Writings of Gottlob Frege* (Oxford: Basil Blackwell, 1952), pp. 56 ff.
[30]*Ibid.,* p. 57.
[31]*Ibid.,* p. 61.
[32]*Ibid.,* pp. 58 and 62.
[33]*Ibid.,* p. 59.

"the same sense is not always connected, even in the same man, with the same idea."[34] "A painter, a horseman, and a zoologist will probably connect different ideas with the name Bucephalus," but the sense may be the same for all.[35]

The specific character of the references and senses of expressions depends upon the kinds of expressions under consideration. The reference of a name or noun phrase is ordinarily an object referred to as, for example, "The Moon" has for its reference the moon itself and the "Evening Star" has for its reference the planet Venus. The sense of a name or noun phrase is its mode of presentation. For example, a sense of "The Moon" is indicated by the phrase "satellite of the earth"; and a sense of "Evening Star," by the expression "star that appears in the early evening." The reference of a predicate or concept expression is itself a concept.[36] Thus for example, the concept expressed by "x is green" is presumably the reference of the predicate "is green." The sense of a predicate expression is, according to J. B. D. Walker's plausible interpretation of Frege's view, "the contribution it makes to the sense of a sentence in which it occurs." Thus, " 'the sense of the expression is dead' is the contribution made by this expression in ....., e.g., the sentence 'Caesar is dead' to the thought of the sentence."[37] Since sentences are ordinarily made up of expressions that have references they, too, may be expected to have references;[38] and since the intent of sentences is to arrive at truth, the references of sentences can be taken to be their truth values, i.e., the True and the False. Thus, the reference of "5 is a prime number" is the True, and the reference "4 is a prime number" is the False. "All true sentences have the same references and so . . . do all false ones";[39] for example, the sense of the sentence "5 is a prime number" is the thought that 5 is a prime number.[40] Since equivalent references cannot be substituted in sentences in indirect discourse without altering the

---

[34]*Ibid.*
[35]*Ibid.*
[36]*Ibid.*, p. 43. See also J. D. B. Walker, *A Study of Frege* (Oxford: Basil Blackwell, 1965), pp. 78 ff. and 84 ff.
[37]*Ibid.*
[38]Gottlob Frege, "On Sense and Reference", p. 63.
[39]*Ibid.*, p. 65.
[40]*Ibid.*, p. 62.

REFERENTS AND MEANINGS 151

truth values of the whole sentences, the reference of a sentence in indirect discourse becomes what is ordinarily the sense of that sentence, i.e., the thought expressed by it. Thus in "Copernicus believed that the planetary orbits are circles," the reference of the subordinate sentence is not the True but the thought that the planetary orbits are circles.

(3) In the main, C. I. Lewis's account of meaning follows the lines suggested by Frege's thought with some modifications and further developments. In Lewis's thought, what Frege called reference becomes roughly denotation or extension, and what Frege called sense is broken down, within a broadly intentional meaning, to include signification and intension or connotation; but the parallels are not exact, and intension itself is further subdivided. Each of four major modes of meaning, Lewis finds, is applicable to terms, propositions, and predicates or propositional functions.

With reference to a term: "the *denotation*.....is the class of all actual things to which the term applies;" "the *comprehension*.....is the classification of all.....consistently thinkable things to which the term would be correctly applicable;" "the *signification*.....is that property in things the presence of which indicates that the term correctly applies, and the absence of which indicates that it does not apply;" and "the *intension* is . . . . the conjunction of all other terms each of which must be applicable to anything to which the term would be correctly applicable."[41] Thus, for example, the term "man" denotes the class of actual men, comprehends all possible men, signifies, among other things, animality, and includes in its intension "the *term* 'animal'."[42] Terms, such as "being," that apply to anything consistently thinkable have universal comprehension and zero intension; and terms, such as "round square," that are not applicable to anything consistently thinkable have zero comprehension and universal intension.[43]

With reference to a proposition: "the extension or denotation..... is the actual world, in case it is true," and "null or zero," in case it is false; the *signification* is "the state of affairs referred

---

[41]C. I. Lewis, *An Analysis of Knowledge and Valuation* (La Salle, Illinois: The Open Court Publishing Company, 1946), p. 39.
[42]*Ibid.*, p. 43.
[43]*Ibid.*, pp. 47 ff.

to;" the comprehension is "any consistently thinkable world which would incorporate the state of affairs it signifies;" and the intension is "whatever must be true of any possible world in order that this proposition should be true of it."[44] For the proposition "Mary is making pies," the denotation is the actual world as characterized by Mary making pies, the signification is the state of affairs consisting in Mary making pies; the comprehension is any possible world characterized by Mary making pies; and the intension is whatever is implied by Mary making pies. The basic reason for saying that the extension or denotation or a proposition is the actual world rather than the specific state of affairs signified is that since many predicates are neither true nor false of that state of affairs, the law of the excluded middle would fail if the denotation were confined to the state of affairs.[45] For all analytically true propositions, the comprehension is universal and the intention, zero; and for all self-contradictory statements, the comprehension is zero and the intension, universal.[46]

With regard to predicates or propositional functions: "The *extension*.....is the class of existents..... of which this predication is truly predicable;" "the *comprehension*.....is the classification of things consistently thinkable as being characterized by this predicate;" "the intension[is].....all that attribution of this predicate to anything entails as also predicable to the thing;" and "the *signification*.....is the essential property which anything must have if the predicate.....should apply to it."[47] The predicate "being red" denotes all existing red things, comprehends all possible red things, signifies the character of being red, and has as its intension whatever is implied by being red, e.g., being colored. The predicate being a cube with seventeen edges has zero comprehension, and the predicate "being not human or being an animal" has universal comprehension.[48]

Since all analytic propositions would, insofar as the definitions thus far given are concerned, have exactly the same intensional meaning, namely, zero, a further refinement within intensional meanings must be marked out, and may be appropriately referred

---

[44]*Ibid.*, pp. 51 ff.
[45]*Ibid.*, p. 52.
[46]*Ibid.*, p. 57.
[47]*Ibid.*, pp. 63 ff.
[48]*Ibid.*, p. 64.

to as "analytic meaning." Roughly, two statements have the same analytic meanings when and only when each of their terms have the same meanings and their syntax is basically the same.[49] Since language is designed to apply to the world, a further distinction is required with reference to intensional meaning, between linguistic meaning and verbal meaning. The verbal intension of an expression consists of the linguistic expressions that must apply if that expression is to apply. One might know the whole linguistic intension of an expression and still have no real understanding of the expression. The *sense meaning* of an expression consists of the criteria in mind for the application of that expression. It should be construed not as an image but rather as a rule or a schema.[50]

(4) In his important book, *The Logical Syntax of Language* (1934), Rudolph Carnap contended that meaningful language was either object language designating objects and events or syntactical language characterizing object language. Meaningful language that seemed to be of some third kind, he took to consist of disguised syntactical sentences. However, in his subsequent book *Meaning and Necessity* (1947 and 1956), Carnap substantially broadened his perspective concerning language and presented what he thought of as a new method of meaning analysis which "takes an expression, not as meaning anything, but as possessing an intension and an extension."[51]

The significant expressions of a language are, Carnap holds, basically either individual expressions, predicates, or declarative sentences. The extensions of these expressions are to be defined by reference to designated individuals, classes and truth values. "The extension of an individual expression is the individual to which it applies."[52] The extension of a predicate expression is "the class of those individuals to which it applies."[53] And "The *extention of a sentence* is its truth-value."[54] The intensions of expressions are to be defined by reference to individual concepts,

---

[49]*Ibid.*, pp. 83 ff.
[50]*Ibid.*, pp. 134 ff.
[51]Rudolf Carnap, *Meaning and Necessity,* Second edition (Chicago: University of Chicago Press, 1956), p. iii.
[52]*Ibid.*, p. 401.
[53]*Ibid.*, p. 11.
[54]*Ibid.*, p. 26.

properties, and propositions. Thus, "the intension of an individual expression is the individual concept expressed by it."[55] The intension of a predicate expression is "the corresponding property," the term "property" being regarded as equivalent to "quality," "character," "characteristic," and the like and included under the term "concept."[56] "The intension of a sentence is the proposition expressed by it."[57] In referring to the extension of predicates as "classes," to the intensions of expressions as "concepts," "properties," and "propositions," and to all of these as "entities"; Carnap intends, not to add to the metaphysical furniture of the world, but simply to use ordinary English words to talk about the expressions that we use in talking about the world.[58]

Having defined the extensional and intensional meanings of various kinds of expressions, Carnap goes on to the related but different matter of the character of extensional and intensional contexts. A sentence is extensional with respect to an expression included in it, Carnap holds, if the expression is such that the replacement of the expression by an equivalent one transforms the sentence into an equivalent sentence; and a sentence is intensional with respect to an expression included in it if it is not extensional and if the replacement of the expression by a logically equivalent one (i.e., one equivalent by virtue of semantical rules only) transforms the whole sentence into a logically equivalent one.[59]

f. In recent years a great deal of illuminating discussion of reference and referents has been carried on by writers who are not in the least disposed to identify referents with meanings. However, since the main contribution of such discussion can readily be embodied in the systematic discussion of reference and referents that follows, I shall not undertake to develop the trend of this discussion here.

[55] *Ibid.*, p. 41.
[56] *Ibid.*, pp. 19 ff.
[57] *Ibid.*, p. 27.
[58] *Ibid.*, pp. 22 f. See also Rudolf Carnap, "Empiricism, Semantics and Ontology," *Revue International de Philosophie*, II (1950), reprinted in Leonard Linsky, *Semantics and the Philosophy of Language* (Urbana: University of Illinois Press, 1952), pp. 207-228.
[59] *Ibid.*, pp. 46 ff.

2. Reference, Bearers of Reference, and Referents

By considering examples of referential and meaning situations together with leads suggested by such accounts of reference and referents as the foregoing, I wish now to consider systematically three important problems, each bearing in its own way upon the character of reference, bearers of reference, and referents. The first is that of the character of reference, bearers of reference and referents. The second is that of the extent to which meanings can be assimilated to referents. The third is that of the specific character of the relation between meanings and referents insofar as that relation can be discussed prior to specific discussion of the character of meanings. I begin in the present section with the first problem asking what reference is, and what sorts of things can be said to be referred to.

a. The term "reference" can be used either of the relation between what refers and what is referred to, and hence as essentially equivalent to "referring" or of what is referred to, and hence as equivalent to "referent." Upon this ambiguity hinges a good deal of confusion between what may be called a relational sense and an object sense of the term "reference." In the endeavor to avoid such confusion, I shall, from now on, confine the use of "reference" to the relational sense and use the term "referent" where the object sense is intended.

Even the relational term "reference" and the various associated forms of the verb "to refer" have many different uses.[60] In one such use of the term "refer" that is emphasized by many philosophers, only those expressions refer whose principal function is to direct attention to some individual event that is to be further characterized. This use of the term is helpful from the point of view of distinguishing between substantive and predicative functions of expressions within sentences and probably for some logical and ontological purposes as well. However, since it fails to recognize referential functions in many meaningful expressions that in a very common and straightforward sense refer, it is not

---

[60]Cf. James V. Cornman, *Metaphysics, Reference and Language* (New Haven and London: Yale University Press, 1966), pp. 142 f.

very helpful for the purpose of drawing a basic distinction between meaning and referring. I shall, accordingly, be mainly concerned with a broader use of the term "reference" and associated verbs in which an expression is said to refer if it functions to direct attention to something whether or not that is its principal function, and whether or not what it refers to is individual or is to be further characterized. The function of the verb "to mean" in the non-referential sense in which an expression means a meaning rather than a referent, contrasts with that of the term reference and associated verb forms in the indicated sense in that whereas for an expression to mean something is for it to function so as to alert someone to a meaning without, as a rule, directing attention to that meaning or indeed necessarily to anything else either; for an expression to refer in the indicated sense is for it to function, presumably by way of a meaning, to direct attention to something.

One important feature of reference is that, like meaning, it always involves a bearer. Where there is reference there must be something that carries the reference, something through which the reference is accomplished. This bearer of reference is appropriately said to refer to that referent. Thus, if someone says that "John is my brother" or "The woman in that blue dress is tall," "John" will properly be said to refer or have reference to a certain man; and "the woman in the blue dress," to a certain woman. Similarly, if a military commander places a magnetic pointer at a certain location on a map, the pointer as thus used will ordinarily be said to refer directly to the location on the map to which it points, and to refer indirectly to a corresponding geographical location. Virtually all inquirers concerning reference recognize this feature of reference.

A second important feature of reference is that it always involves an agent and is in a basic sense accomplished by an agent. Events in nature are causes and effects of one another, and often they resemble one another; but they never refer to one another or, as such, have references. The falling of a tree into a lake causes but does not refer to the resulting splash, and a natural stone profile on the side of a mountain resembles but does not refer to the face of a man. Even artifacts produced by agents as a result of careful plannings usually refer neither to their causes nor to the functions nor to anything else unless someone uses them so to to. Words and symbols have reference, strictly speaking, only as someone uses them to refer.[61] To have achieved at least partial recognition of the interventions of agents between bearers and referents is one of the significant accomplishments of the indirect reference theory of Ogden and Richards.

A third noteworthy feature of reference in the sense under consideration is that it is always intentional. It may indeed involve causal, pictorial, and even ontological factors, but it is never any of these to the exclusion of dependence upon the intention of an agent. Heartbeats and knee jerks may be revealing but they do not refer. Drawings and diagrams resemble things and events but they do not by themselves yield references to anything. Bearers of reference may exemplify universals, but they do not ordinarily refer to universals and they cannot do so apart from agents' intentions that they should. Words and symbol types as such may be well suited to refer to things or events and they are commonly used to refer. They may even be appropriately called referring expressions; but they do not actually refer to anything except as someone uses them so to do. This intentional character of reference is obscured by the causal theory of Ogden and Richards which regards a match's being scratched to be a paradigm of reference. Apart from an agent's intention to use a match-scratching to refer to something, the scratching would not refer to anything; and neither, apart from an intention, would an uttered or inscribed linguistic expression. The intentional character of reference is also obscured by a logical atomism that takes similarity of structure to suffice for reference and by a platonism that takes exemplification to suffice for this purpose.

A fourth, and more distinctive feature of reference is that the intention upon which it depends is always an intention openly to direct the attention of a respondent to that which is referred to. An agent's referring to something is not a characterizing of that thing, an orientation of that thing to other things, a statement about that thing, a drawing out of causal consequences or implications of that thing, or a behavioral or emotional response to that thing. It is rather the agent's undertaking to direct

---

[61]Leonard Linsky, "Reference and Referents," in Charles E. Caton, *Philosophy and Ordinary Language* (Urbana: University of Illinois Press, 1963), pp. 74 ff.

someone's attention to that thing. The agent may indeed build upon his reference to the thing to which he refers a characterization, description, statement or course of action; and his reference may be achieved in part through using a characterization or a description; but his reference to the thing, far from being identical with any of these, is just an attempted direction of attention to the thing. Insofar as, in saying that the man on my right is tall, I am referring to a certain man, my intention is to direct attention to a certain man, not to say anything about him; and what I do say about him, in referring to him and thereafter characterizing him, is incidental from the standpoint of the reference. Moreover, if in saying that he is tall I am in any way referring to his tallness, to that extent I am undertaking to direct attention to that feature of him, even though for other purposes I may be doing other things regarding him.

The intention of the agent who refers to something, is not, moreover, to direct the attention of the respondent to the referent stealthily or without the respondent's knowing what he is doing. It is rather to direct the respondent's attention to the referent in such a way that the respondent will be able to recognize that the agent is in fact directing his attention to the referent and that the agent intends so to do. A person who engages in "hidden persuasion," may subtly draw attention to something without intending the respondent to know what he is up to but he is hardly referring to the thing in question. One does not need to say "I refer to" so and so in order to refer to it, but he does need openly to direct attention to it, and a part of what he does is to disclose what he is doing.

One further feature of reference that requires mention is that reference depends upon factors beyond itself in that nothing can count as reference unless there exists something else (a referent) to which it refers. References have indeed their own intentionally determined structures but they are not self-contained. If they are to be references at all, they must have referents whose existence as such—though not as referents—is independent of them. No referent is indeed contained in a reference; but apart from a referent, no reference can refer. Referents need not be precisely as corresponding references represent them but referents must always exist if there is any reference. Otherwise there may be attempted reference but no referring. Just what the character of a referent is will become clearer in subsequent discussion of referents themselves.

In the light of the foregoing considerations a working definition of reference in the sense under consideration can be formulated as follows. A thing or event x has reference to a certain thing or event y if and only if an agent in producing the thing or event x intends to direct the attention of a respondent to the thing or event y in such fashion as to lead the respondent to recognize both what the agent seeks to direct his attention to and that the agent so seeks to direct his attention.

If the foregoing account is essentially correct, reference can be infelicitous in a number of different ways without actually falling short of what is required to constitute reference. The agent, though fully intending in producing the bearer of reference to refer to some particular thing or event, may have expressed himself badly. The expression may be hopelessly ungrammatical or inarticulate or inaudible or odd or ideosyncratic or a slip of speech. Moreover, the respondent may be preoccupied or drowsy or otherwise inattentive. Even if both the agent and the respondent do their best, the referent may, through no fault of either, be quite different from what it was represented in the reference to be. The referent may, indeed, belong to an altogether different existential level from that indicated by the form of reference employed. For example: it may, unbeknown to the agent, be a mirror image of an ordinary object rather than such an object; or it may be a product of collective imagination rather than a part of the physical world. While in any case of attempted reference one or more of such infelicities as the foregoing may prevent one's saying that an object-as-described-by-the-agent has been referred to, the occurrence of such an infelicity need not imply that no reference has been made or even prevent one from subsequently indicating what has been referred to.[62] If I say "That Oldsmobile is shiny," when in fact it is a Ford, and if I say, "That rig is big," when I meant to say, "That pig is big," my references are infelicitous; but I have nevertheless made a reference in each case, in the one case, to the Ford and in the other, to the pig.

b. What kinds of things refer, have references, or are bearers

---

[62]Cf. Leonard Linsky, *Ibid.*

of references? Three suggestions appear in this connection to be
worthy of special notice. One is that bearers of reference for the
most part either are, or are closely related to, linguistic expressions. Primarily, words signifying objects and events about which
something is said are what refer. In the main, other things that are
used to refer function, when they refer, much as linguistic expressions do, and usually either represent, or are accompanied by,
linguistic expressions. A girl who bears herself in a certain way
to draw attention to her charms is not referring to herself, nor is a
musician who plays feelingly in expressing his joy in a sunset
referring to the sunset. A gesture may well refer to something, but
usually it is used as words would be used or else it is used in
conjunction with words. Arrows and other pointers are also often
used to refer but usually in integral relation with verbal utterances.
    A second suggestion concerning bearers of reference is that,
for the most part, they are also bearers of intentional meaning.
This suggestion derives at least some initial plausibility from the
close analogy between something's meaning intentionally and its
referring. Like meaning intentionally, referring depends upon
agents, is a function of particular bearers, is eventually determined
by intentions, is grounded upon anticipated responses, and is
expected to be recognized for what it is. The suggestion that bearers
of reference are generally also bearers of intentional meaning is,
however, best supported by considering examples. As has already
been seen, bearers of reference are nearly always linguistic
expressions or other particulars functioning as such expressions do.
Among linguistic expressions that refer, all of the descriptive expressions actually used to refer are obviously intentionally meaningful.
When, in speaking or writing, one uses any such expressions as, "the
man at the head of the table," "my oldest brother," "the brown
book," or "the flood of 1961" to refer to something, he is clearly
using expressions that have intentional meanings. The sorts of
expressions actually used to refer but which least obviously have
intentional meanings would seem to be proper names and
demonstratives, but reasons have already been seen for thinking
that even these have intentional meanings in certain contexts.
While a proper name merely as an expression within a linguistic
community has little or no meaning save that of being an
expression suitable for the designation of a male or female person,
an animal, a location, etc; a name as actually used in a context,

as an expression that refers must be, is in most instances rich with meaning both for user and respondent, and would be of no use for reference if it were altogether without a meaning that serves as a criterion for identification of the referent. Similarly, not only do "this" and "that" have common meanings indicating the thing before the speaker or just now referred to, but in the particular contexts that are relevant to reference, they also involve much more explicit meanings. If even names and demonstratives must have at least minimal intentional meaning in order to serve as bearers of reference, it seems to be reasonably safe to say that nothing can so serve without having some intentional meaning. To be sure, bearers of dispositional meaning such as the word types "man," "animal," "house," and even "squareness" are types available for use in referring; and in connection with certain contexts they can be called referring expressions. But to be available to refer, or even to be a referring expression in the sense indicated, is not actually to refer. The fact is that the expression "referring expression" is ambiguous, and that both what is available for use in referring and what actually refers are currently sometimes called referring expressions must not be allowed to mislead one into supposing that bearers of dispositional meaning as such refer or have references.

The third of the suggestions that I am presenting concerning what kinds of things refer or have reference is more controversial than the other two and runs counter to such current doctrines as that only expressions standing for individuals refer, that only expressions in substantive positions refer, that if predicates refer at all they refer to classes, and that if sentences refer at all they refer only to truth or to falsity. The suggestion is that linguistic expressions of many different kinds that are bearers of intentional meaning are also bearers of reference.

This suggestion receives some initial plausibility from the previously mentioned close analogy of meaning and referring, but it must in the end be tested by cases. If reference is narrowly construed, after the manner of some current theories, as applicable only to what has as its primary function to refer; then, by definition, only a very limited range of bearers of meaning can be included in bearers of reference. However, if reference is thought of in line with a more natural wider use that is also more illuminating with regard to the relation of reference and meaning, as I suggested at the outset of this section it should be, then none of the varieties of bearers of intentional meaning need be excluded at the outset. Regarding any given bearers of meaning, the question of its reference is simply whether or not one can intelligibly ask and correctly answer questions concerning what it refers to.

That intentionally meaningful proper names, pronouns, definite descriptions, and some indefinite descriptions in actual use generally refer to definite individuals is scarcely likely to be seriously questioned. "John," as actually used, in all probability refers either to John or to someone or something that the speaker takes to be John; so also does "he" when it introduces a statement following a statement about John. "The man in the blue shirt," as actually used, is almost certain to refer either to a particular man who is wearing a blue shirt or to someone or something that the speaker takes to be a man wearing a blue shirt. Even "a man," or "a member of the faculty," when used to convey the information that a particular individual has, or has had, a certain characteristic or has done something, may refer to a specific individual.

When such intentionally meaningful terms as "man," "Athenians," "cats," and "houses." are actually used in the making of general statements, as they often are, following such terms as "all," "some," and "a," they obviously do not always refer in the sense of directing attention specifically to known individuals; for in cases of statements beginning with "all," many of the individuals involved may not yet even exist, and in cases of statements beginning with "some," there is usually no designation of which members of the indicated class are relevant. Nevertheless, the terms in question do often function in general statements to direct attention to members of classes, even though not to specifically indicated ones. Hence, in the broad sense of reference now under consideration, they are, in the instances under consideration, used to refer.

While such abstract terms as "redness," "squareness," "justice," and "virtue" as used in uttered or inscribed sentences obviously do not refer to individuals, one can, and often does, ask concerning such terms used in this manner what they refer to. "When you say that justice is characteristic of this state, to what does the term 'justice' refer?" "When you say that square-ness is in the shape of many figures, what does 'squareness' refer to?" One replies to such questions by mentioning certain properties of states and figures; and whether the properties in question are thought of as particular aspects of particular states and figures or as some kinds of universals, they do seem to be what the ex-pressions in question direct attention to and hence to be properly said to be referred to by these expressions.

In the narrower sense of "reference" mentioned at the outset, predicate terms do not, of course, refer; but in the broader sense under discussion, they do seem often to refer. While predicate terms as expressions in a language no more refer than do any other expressions in that capacity, predicate terms in actual use often seem as clearly to refer as do subject terms in actual use. Certainly, concerning such expressions, one often quite sensibly asks to what they refer. When someone says, "That billboard is square," "That house is white," or "That man is courageous," one readily inquires what "that billboard," "that house," or "that man" here refers to; but one can, and often does, inquire in much the same fashion what "square," "white," or "courageous" here refers to. Moreover, an important function of predicate expressions seems clearly to be to focus attention, not indeed upon their own meanings and not upon the subjects of the sentences to which they belong, but upon particular pro-perties of things referred to by the subjects of these sentences. Thus "square" refers to the particular shape of the particular bill-board; "white" refers to the particular color of that house; and "courageous" refers to a specific characteristic of that man.

One further variety of bearers of meaning in the intentional way requires comment, namely, uttered and written sentences. Two widely favored views are, on the one hand, that such sentences have no referents and, on the other hand, that their referents are simply truth and falsity. Both answers seem, however, to run counter to linguistic experience. People can, and often do, inquire concerning the referents of spoken and written sentences; and fairly definite referents can often be pointed out in reply. The referents in question seem, moreover, to be, not just truth or falsity, but specific states of affairs answering to the sentences in case the sentences are true and answering at least in some respects to the sentences in case the sentences are false.

Consider, for example, the following: (a) "The book is on the table." "To what are you referring?" "I'm referring to my chemistry book's being on top of my large study table." (b) "The president is busy." "To what are you referring?" "I'm referring to the president's being just now engaged in a conference with the Secretary of State." (c) "My pen is full of ink." "To what are you referring?" "To my pen's having an ample supply of ink." "You can't be because your pen is empty." "Well then at least I was referring to my pen in whatever condition it was, though since it has no ink in it I could not, as you say, have been referring to it's being full." (d) "Is your suitcase packed yet?" "To what are you referring?" "I'm referring to the present condition of your suitcase and asking whether or not it is that of being packed." A good many problems arise concerning the kinds of cases cited, and others would arise concerning different kinds that could be cited. However, in all such cases, to indicate a state of affairs as referred to would appear to be considerably closer to the import of our actual use of language than to say that sentences had no referents at all or none more specific than truth or falsity.

The suggestion here being offered that not one but many kinds of bearers of meaning are also bearers of reference or have referents is one that is congenial to most of the writers considered earlier in the chapter who tend to identify meanings with referents. Indeed, since for them in large measure to mean is to refer and meanings are referents, they tend to claim that everything, or almost everything, that actually has intentional meaning is a bearer of reference. In these latter claims they may prove to be mistaken; but in insisting upon a range of references of expressions far wider than that of substantive expressions as such, they duly recognize a common use of the term "reference" in which reference is closest to meaning and by consideration of which a relation of reference and meaning can, accordingly appropriately be discussed.

c. What kinds of things can be referred to? If what has been said so far is correct, anything to which an expression may function to call attention may be referred to, and what can be thus referred to has already been said to include not only individual things and events but also properties, relations, and situations. A practical way of discerning the range of possible referents is to notice the range of that which can be designated by the part of a sentence that is most characteristically—though by no means exclusively—thought of as a referring part, namely, the subject of the sentence. Obviously persons and physical objects and events are often designated by subjects of sentences. But so also are properties, relations and situations. "The color of the hair is red." "The speed of the comet is great." "Superiority" is a matter of degrees." "Transitivity is not a logical relation." "The election outlook is dim for the Democrats." "My being a father is a great responsibility." Fictitious entities seem also sometimes to be designated by logical subjects of sentences and to be quite appropriately said to be referred to by various expressions. One may say that "Cerberus guarded the gates of Hades" and that "The dagger that hung in the air before Macbeth disturbed him." One may also say that "Cerberus" refers to the dog that guarded the gates of Hades and that "the dagger that hung in the air before Macbeth" refers to a dagger that Macbeth thought he saw. One may go on to say that injustice is difficult to achieve," that "beauty is rare," and that in the previous statement "justice" refers to one of the virtues and "beauty" to an aesthetic quality.

Granted that the range of what can be referred to is very great, to what extent is it essential that what is referred to exist? The most restrictive sense of the term reference would suggest that all referents must be individuals in space and time. An extremely broad sense of the term would suggest that what is referred to need never in any sense exist.[63] The sense of "reference" in which reference is most like meaning suggests that although what is actually referred to must in some sense exist, it need not exist in just the manner indicated by the character of the reference itself. When someone undertakes to refer to the present king of France or to John's children when John has no children, his purported reference has no referent, and we are inclined to say that while he thought he was referring to the present king of France or to John's children he could not have been doing so because there is no present king of France and John has no children. However, when Macbeth refers to the hallucinatory dagger before him even though no real dagger is before him, he is not failing to refer but is referring—however mistakenly—to what he sees. Similar-

---

[63]Cf. C. E. Caton, "Strawson on Referring," *Mind,* LXVIII (1959), pp. 539-544.

ly when a child who has not yet learned to distinguish fact from fancy refers to Cerberus, while he cannot be referring to a real dog guarding the gates of Hades, since there is no such dog, he is referring not just to nothing at all but rather to Cerberus as represented in ancient myth that has been related to him.

Some interesting issues concerning the relation of the existential status of purported referents to the truth of statements are involved in the criticisms of Russell's "theory of descriptions" included in P. F. Strawson's much discussed article "On Referring."[64]

Here Strawson suggests that because he mistakenly regarded meanings as referents and failed to distinguish statements from sentences, Russell had erroneously equated the statement "The present King of France is wise" with a false statement to the effect that one and only one person was now king of France and was wise whereas in fact the original statement was, by reason of the non-existence of the purported referent of its subject, neither true nor false. Strawson seems here to be quite correct in pointing out the errors of confusing meaning with referent and failing to distinguish sentence and statement. He seems also correctly to hold that there are contexts in which the non-existence of the purported reference of a subject expression renders a sentential expression neither true nor false but without destroying the meaning of the expression. Nevertheless Strawson's account of the relation between the existence of referents as subject terms and the truth of statements seems to be only a part of the story, and why this is so becomes readily apparent when one considers, not just the cultural meanings of utterances upon which Strawson focuses, but also the intentional meanings which are most closely connected with references. In some contexts, to be sure, the agent presupposes the existence of the referent of the subject term without specifically intending to lead his respondent to apprehend this presupposition; and hence in case the referent does not exist he may simply withdraw the statement. But in other contexts, instead of merely presupposing the existence of the referent of the subject term, the agent specifically intends to lead his respondent to understand that this referent exists, so

[64]P. F. Strawson, "On Referring", *Mind,* L (1959), pp. 320-344.

that in case the referent does not exist he must acknowledge that what he meant was false. This occurs if, for example, an eighteenth century French general calls out to his faltering troops, who are uncertain whether or not their king still lives, "The King of France is wise." It also occurs when a swindler says to his victim that the ten thousand dollars that community leaders have already invested in his project assure the soundness of his project and when Don Juan lures a girl to his apartment by saying to her that his (non-existent) wife wishes to meet her. In some contexts, one neither presupposes nor intends to imply the existence of the referent of the subject term of his statement but intends to lead his respondent to apprehend that such a referent does not exist, so that the truth of his statement depends on the non-existence of this referent. This occurs for example, when in order to quiet the superstitious one says that dragons are to be dreaded only by fools. It also occurs in multitudes of instances of logical exercises in which statements are regarded as true by reason of the non-existence or even inconceivability of the purported referents of their subjects. All the immortal men that there are must be good, for the reason that the are no such men; all round squares must be red for the reason that there are no such squares; and all of them must be blue for the same reason.

One more remark concerning referents seems to be called for in order to link them with factors previously mentioned, namely, that referents are often identical with stimuli to the production of bearers of meaning. When Quine's primitive on seeing a rabbit says, "Gavagai," what prompts him to speak is what he refers to. And when I say, "The rapid approach of that car is a threat to all of us," what prompts me to speak is what I refer to. The sort of coincidence in question is, of course, not always to be found between stimuli and referents, for what stimulates an expression may have little to do with what it refers to. Prompted by the excessive heat of the room at the party, a guest may say that his chauffeur is awaiting him; and stimulated by the urge for a higher salary, the professor of history may write a monograph on the causes of the Crimean War. However, when stimulus and referent do coincide, the coincidence may be helpful in the quest for intentional meanings for the reasons that stimuli are generally more readily locatable than referents and that referents are more intimately interwoven with intentional meanings than are stimuli.

3. The Assimilation of Meanings to Referents

The foregoing considerations concerning reference, bearers of reference, and referents, construed in the ways in which these concepts are most like meaning concepts, should significantly facilitate the inquiry, now to be undertaken, concerning why some philosophers should have been inclined to assimilate meanings to referents and why such an assimilation cannot be carried through.

a. One set of factors that has inclined some philosophers to assimilate meanings to referents is the existence of an impressive series of parallels between intentional meaning, bearers of such meaning, and such meanings, on the one hand, and reference, bearers of reference, and referents, on the other. Both intentional meanings and references depend upon agents. Both involve anticipation of responses that recognize what is meant or referred to as meant or referred to. Both depend upon bearers. Bearers of intentional meaning and bearers of reference are both for the most part linguistic expressions. All bearers of reference are also bearers of intentional meaning, and most bearers of intentional meanings are also bearers of reference. Moreover, intentional meanings and referents are alike dependent for their respective character as intentional meanings or referents upon intentions of agents.

A second set of factors inclining philosophers to assimilate meanings to referents consists in a series of ambiguities attaching to terms connected with meaning and reference. One such ambiguity concerns the verb "to mean." Whereas the verb is most often used in a sense in which what is meant is a meaning, it is, as has been previously noted, sometimes used in a sense in which what is meant is a referent; and while the latter sense of "to mean" is radically different from the former, and has been carefully excluded from the present inquiry, thought can all too easily shift back and forth between the two. Thus, for example, a physician may say to his assistant, "That man is diabetic," and then go on to explain, "I mean the man on the right" ..... "What I mean is that his pancreas is diseased." Since what is meant in his first use of "mean" is clearly the man referred to, one may all too easily assume incorrectly that what is meant in his second use of the term is an illness referred to. A second sort of ambiguity facilitating the assimilation of meanings to referents is rooted in parallel "process-product" ambiguities of the terms "meaning" and "reference." "Meaning" may be used either of something's meaning a certain meaning or of the resulting meaning itself. In like manner "reference" may be used either of one thing's referring to another or of the thing referred to. In view of these parallel ambiguities, thought slides readily from recognition of the intimate linkage of meaning and reference as processes to a mistaken assumption that meanings and references (referents) as products are equally intimately linked. A third ambiguity encouraging the assimilation of meaning to reference lies in the character of the semantic term "denotation." In modern technical discussion, on the one hand, the denotation of a term is commonly thought of as the class of things to which the term applies, and this class is often regarded as consisting of the referents of the term. In ordinary discourse, on the other hand, the denotation of a term is its primary meaning. But in using the term "denotation" in the technical sense one tends to hold on also to the ordinary usage thus absorbing the notion of meaning into that of possible referent and hence by this route also assimilating meanings to referents.

It may, however, be doubted if either the close parallels between meaning and reference or their reflection in verbal ambiguities would have sufficed to lead philosophers to assimilate meanings to referents were it not for a third set of factors, namely, the close connections of language with the world and the sound determination of "tough-minded" philosophers so to keep this connection in sight as to preserve the down-to-earth intelligibility of common sense and scientific language. The earliest expressions of primitive people and of little children are closely tied to the specific objects in conjunction with which they occur; and no matter how complex or abstract linguistic expressions become, their applications to the world must never be lost sight of if language is to continue to perform any useful function. Moreover, to discern the referent of an expression often fulfills the purposes which one seeks to fulfill in seeking to discern the meaning of an expression.

It must be remembered that most recent referential theories of meaning have been developed in an era immediately preceded by a period of absolute idealism in which meanings of terms tended to be blurred and the connections of language with the world to become tenuous. That in such a situation advocates of referential theories should have endeavored, even in face of the evident implausibility of naive referential theories, to restore some firmness to philosophical accounts of meaning by linking terms with observable things and events is accordingly understandable, as is also their tendency to carry their efforts in this direction to excess.

b. While such considerations as the foregoing help to disclose the vitally important roles of reference and referents in most meaning situations, they in no way justify the assimilation of meanings to referents, and that such an assimilation is not possible has now come to be widely—though not universally—recognized.

The main reason for rejecting an assimilation of meanings to referents is the radical difference between the functions of meaning and referring that remains even when the latter is interpreted in the way in which it is most like meaning. For an expression to mean in the sense in which an expression means its meaning is for it to function so as to alert, or be disposed to alert, someone to a meaning by way of which it may direct attention to something, characterize something, describe something, ask a question, make a request, suggest a line of action, or do any of many other things. However like meaning referring may be, it differs from meaning in that an expression may mean its meaning without directing attention to that meaning or to anything else and in that the directing of attention to something in which referring consists is only one of the many further functions that can be performed by way of meaning functions. This fundamental reason for declining to assimilate meanings to referents is amply supported by other related reasons.

(1) Even if the attempt to assimilate meanings to referents could be achieved with reference to intentional meanings it could at best be only indirectly relevant, if at all, to dispositional meanings. To be sure, words and sentences as such can properly be said to be referential in the sense of being capable of referring, but neither words nor sentences actually refer save as actually

used. One can, of course, quite as readily say of an uttered or spoken expression that its referent is this or that as that its meaning is this or that. But whereas one can speak without qualification of a meaning of word or sentence type, one speaks of what the type *could* or normally *would* be used to refer to.

(2) Whereas the referent of an expression is contingent upon facts external to the referential function that institutes it, the intentional meaning of an expression is not contingent upon facts external to the meaning function that institutes it. What a given bearer of intentional meaning means depends in the end wholly upon the intention of the agent. What the referent of a primary bearer of reference is depends to be sure partly on the intention of the agent but it also depends on the character of the external world and will vary according to what the facts turn out to be. If someone says, "There comes a tall man in a blue sweater," what he means remains unaffected if the man turns out to be short and is wearing a green shirt and no sweater. But the referent of the expression cannot remain unaffected; for it is now clear that while the speaker was indeed referring to a man, he was not referring to a tall man in a blue sweater since no such person was present.

(3) Since referents depend on the external world in a way that intentional meanings do not, it is sometimes said that an expression may have a meaning without having a referent. For reasons already given I doubt that this is the best way of putting the matter. Failure to refer to just what one intends to refer to does not entail failure to refer at all. However, the dependence of referents upon the world external to the referential relation does bring about numerous situations in which, while meanings remain what agents intend them to be, referents may be quite different from what agents take them to be. While the meaning of a medieval man's expression for "the earth" was as he intended it to be, the referent of this term was very different from what he took it to be. For an ancient Greek who took current myths literally, "Pegasus" was the winged-horse captured by Bellerophon; but the referent of that expression was not an actual horse of that description but rather a mythological horse of that description. A primitive man may take his word for "demon" to refer to a vicious personal being whereas the actual referent of his term is in one aspect a

figment of the collective imagination of his group and in another
aspect certain natural forces harmful to man. I may take the
referent of my statement about a sea monster to be such a
monster whereas in fact it is no more than a monster of my
dream. I may refer to the next prime number after one billion
while having a quite incorrect notion of what that number is or
even no notion at all what it is.

(4) Since what is referred to exists and has its own character
independently of being referred to, the same referent may be
referred to even within the same utterance by expressions having
very different meanings. This occurs, for example, as has often
been pointed out, when someone says that the morning star is
the evening star. It also occurs when I inform someone that my
wife is the teacher of physics at Northrop Collegiate School or the
mother of my eldest daughter, and in countless other instances of
these and other kinds.

(5) The converse disparity occurs whenever one meaning is
used to refer to many things or events. This happens for example
when one speaks of the "moons of Jupiter," the "wives of King
Solomon," the "citizens of America," the "stars of our Galaxy,"
or the "days of the year." In each case a single complex meaning
is involved, but the referents may be very numerous, so numerous
indeed that in some instances they cannot in practice be counted.
To be sure, the referents referrred to by way of a meaning may
in a given case belong to a class; but this does not alter the fact
of a plurality of reference over against a singularity of meaning
such as entirely precludes the identity of meanings and referents.

(6) As was pointed out in earlier discussion of the ways of
meaning, intentional meanings do not change, not because they
are in some mysterious sense eternal, but just because, being
determined by intentions at the moment of their occurrence, they
do not have the sort of temporal spread that change requires.
Most referents, however, are obviously subject to change. They
come to be, undergo continuous and sometimes dramatic alterations, and eventually cease to exist. Thus the persons we refer to
are born, pass through childhood, youth, maturity, and old age,
and die. The other organisms to which we refer pass through
parallel processes. Artifacts are made, altered, and destroyed.
Even mountain ranges, oceans, planets, suns and stars, come to be,
flourish, and perish. But any such changes in any object to which

one refers leave the intentional meaning of his utterance unaffected. If I say that Jones's face is red, that the face of Jones, as he is now, is of a certain color is what I mean no matter what the color of Jones's face was at some earlier period; and if Jones's face immediately afterward becomes pale, that makes no difference to the intentional meaning of what I said.

(7) Since the distinction between true and false declarative sentences is usually taken to rest upon possible differences between what a declarative sentence means and what it refers to; if meanings and referents were identical, all declarative sentences would presumably be true. Various devices have, as has been seen, adopted to avoid this paradoxical conclusion, but each device succeeds in only relocating the problem. The most plausible of these devices are the attempts, within causal theories of the kinds developed by Ogden and Richards and the General Semanticists, to explain false sentences as misplaced references; but such accounts, besides introducing vast and apparently unnecessary complexities into semantic theory, leave on our hands the unresolved problems of what the misplacing in question consists in and of how it is related to its own referents.

Apart from the foregoing kinds of objections to any assimilation of meanings to referents, each particular version of such assimilation has its own difficulties. Some difficulties of this sort were earlier mentioned in connection with the presentation of each such version with the exception of the last which assimilates some—but not all—aspects of meanings to referents. All of the leading versions of this last mentioned kind of theory, including Mill's account of denotation and connotation, Frege's distinction between sense and reference, and Lewis's and Carnap's accounts of extension and intension, have contributed very substantially to the understanding of the character of meaning by helping to isolate what must eventually be seen to constitute meanings from closely associated referential factors in meaning situations and by throwing significant light on the distinctive character of meanings. But insofar as these accounts have also regarded connotations, references, and extension as parts of meanings, they have been as mistaken as any referential accounts of meanings; for in view of the foregoing kinds of considerations, denotations (in Mill's sense), referents, and extensions can no more be parts of meanings than they can be meanings.

4. Meanings, References, and Referents

The primary purpose of the present chapter is to clarify the roles of references and referents in meaning situations and to disclose, as far as can be done prior to specific inquiry concerning meanings themselves, how meanings are related to referents. In what has been said in the two preceding sections, a number of relevant considerations have been indicated, for example, that most bearers of reference are also bearers of meaning in the intentional way, that most bearers of meaning in the intentional way are also bearers of reference, that the intentional acts that eventually determine intentional meanings and those that eventually determine referents are closely analogous to one another and intimately interwoven with one another, but that neither meanings nor any aspect of meanings are to be assimilated to referents. Two main points bearing directly on the relation of meanings and references and indirectly upon that of meanings and referents remain to be presented in the present section.

a. Whenever references occur, they are achieved in part by way of intentional meanings. To this extent intentional meanings are necessary conditions of references. To be sure objects and events as such do not depend upon the intentional or dispositional meanings of the terms by which they are referred to. The man, the tree, or even the concept to which I refer is likely to be what it is regardless either of my reference to it or of the meanings of the terms in which the reference is made. A respondent's apprehension of a referent also does not depend upon the meaning intended by the agent in referring to the referent. I may get what you refer to even though I fail to understand what you mean and I may fail to get what you refer to even though I get what you mean. Nevertheless, an object's being at a given moment a referent does depend upon someone's intending to refer to it; and that in turn depends upon someone's intending in using a bearer to make apprehensible a meaning through which attention can be focused upon the object. When an agent refers to an object or event, he never refers to a bare particular but always to something having properties and relations some of which can serve as recognizable marks of this referent. In order to refer to an object or event, he uses to bear his reference, terms having meanings that he takes to be linked with recognizable marks of the object or event in such fashion as to direct the attention of his respondent to the object or event as what he refers to.

Apart from the meaning aspects of the expressions we use, we should not only not be able to understand or characterize the objects and events we refer to, but we should not even be able to refer to them; for how else can a thing be referred to save by some relational or qualitative property rendered apprensible by intelligible meaning? The intention meaning aspect of our references is, moreover, abundantly evident in the character of the expressions we use to refer. If the expression is a definite description, such as "the man to my right" or "the lady in the blue dress," the intentionally meaningful character of the bearer of reference is evident in the character and context of the utterance or inscription. A spoken or written sentence affords no other means of referring to a situation than through meanings, and a predicate refers to an aspect of a thing or situation by way of its meaning. If an expression is a demonstrative such as "this" or "that," the intentional meaning of the term, i.e., thing pointed at, looked at, etc., is still such that the agent expects the respondent to recognize the referent by way of it. When the expression is a well known proper name, the agent is guided in his referring by his anticipation of the respondent's readiness to identify the referent through apprehension of intended meanings. Even gestures refer only by virtue of having a certain significance.

The sort of dependence of referents upon intentional meanings involved in the fact that expressions refer by way of their meanings throws significant light on a number of related matters. To begin with, it helps to show that the fact that every bearer of reference is also a bearer of meaning in the intentional way is no mere coincidence but an inevitable product of the basic character of reference; for if intentional meanings are indispensable media of references, references must inevitably be associated with meanings. The sort of dependence of referents on meanings now under consideration also shows that the close analogies and intricate ties between the referential and meaning factors in meaning situations are not accidental but are grounded in the character of the intentions on which referring by way of meaning depends. It suggests in fact that references and meanings arise, not from separate intentional acts, but despite their own inevitable diversity, from the very same intentional acts in which the one is achieved in large measure by way of the other.

A fact of special importance that the dependence of references on meaning helps to explain is that the referents of expressions are, with rare exceptions, not the meanings of these expressions. When someone says, "The cat is on the green mat," the reference of the sentence, if it has one, is a certain situation involving a cat and a mat, not the meaning of the sentence; the reference of "the cat" and "the mat" are a certain animal and a certain mat, not the meaning of these nouns; and the reference of "green," if it has one, is the particular color of this mat, not the meaning of the adjective "green." The situation is similar with respect to nearly all other expressions except perhaps abstract singular terms such as "redness" and "virtue." This extreme rarity of instances in which expressions refer to their own meanings would be enigmatic on the basis of either a stimulus or a referential theory of meaning, but it is just what the dependence of reference on intentional meaning would lead one to expect.

b. Although meanings can not be assimilated to referents, or even properly said to contain referents, many meanings contain referential aspects and can not be adequately characterized without giving due attention to these aspects. The referential aspect of many intentional meanings represents the other side of the fact that intentional meanings are necessary conditions of references. It does not imply that every intentional meaning contains a reference or that even all those intentional meanings purporting to contain references actually do, for in case there is no referent, there is strictly speaking no reference. It certainly does not imply that any dispositional, causal, or implicative meaning contains a reference, for references are achieved only through intentional acts. It does suggest that a great many --perhaps most-- intentional meanings are intended, not just to yield internally coherent conceptual structures, but also to direct attention beyond themselves and to link their bearers with a non-linguistic and transconceptual world, and that due notice of this referential aspect of intentional meanings is essential to any adequate account of intentional meanings. If attempted references isolated from intentional meanings would be senseless and incapable of referring, most attempted meanings would be aimless, unfocused and eventually themselves senseless if they failed altogether to point beyond themselves. When for an attempted reference contained in an intentional meaning, there is an actual referent, the attempted reference becomes an actual reference.

The referential aspect of meanings is most strikingly seen in subject terms of uttered or inscribed declarative sentences though here, as elsewhere, the referent itself lies altogether outside of the meaning. If I say, "My wife is at home," the expression, "my wife," has of course a certain conceptual meaning; but apart from that, to try to explain the meaning of the sentence without explaining that the expression, "my wife," in my statement referred beyond itself to a certain person would be to miss a main point of the statement. The meanings of predicate terms can also be seen to include attempted references which become actual references when there is a referent, though reference is not the major function of such terms. In my statement about my wife, "is at home" includes a reference to a particular place; and the meaning of that part of the statement, though including essential conceptual features, also includes reference to that place. It seems not implausible to hold that even less significant verbal units, such as prepositions, often also point beyond their internal conceptual import and make at least some relational referential contributions to the total intentional import of the sentences in which they occur, though the manner of this contribution may be extremely complex. Certainly, it appears to be in accord both with common usage and good sense to say that sentences usually purport to direct attention beyond themselves and thus to contain attempted references to situations which they describe. The sentence about my wife undertakes to direct attention to a situation regarding the present location of my wife. If someone says that Smith is just, he attempts to refer to a more or less durable situation concerning the character dispositions of Smith. The meanings even of questions, requests, and exclamations can be seen to purport to refer to situations, i.e., situations that are dubious, desired, or remarkable, etc., provided one does not confuse these references with the referents to which their bearers refer or the conceptual aspects through which they are made.

The presence of a referential aspect within meanings themselves helps to explain why all, or nearly all, bearers of meaning in the intentional way also have, or purport to have, referents; for if meanings themselves contain references, their bearers are surely properly said to have, or purport to have, referents. The presence of referential aspects alongside conceptual ones in meanings also helps to explain the temptation to regard meanings and referents as identical; for if there are not only close analogies and intricate ties between the referential and meaning aspects of meaning situations but also purported references within meanings themselves, the suggestion becomes very powerful indeed that meanings and referents are one and the same, and only persistent attention to the existential uniqueness of referents can disentangle the two.

If, as has now been claimed, every bearer of reference is also a bearer of intentional meaning and most bearers of intentional meaning are also bearers of reference, and if every reference is achieved by way of intentional meaning and many intentional meanings include purported references; then one can understand, not only why people often look to referents in the search for meanings, but also why in fact they should. In finding a referent of a bearer of intentional meaning, one finds something which it is intended to refer to, something in the designation of which its meaning plays a vital role. We teach our children the meanings of expressions by indicating the things to which they commonly refer. We explain dark sayings to one another by the same means, and when one gets what something refers to, he usually gets also what is meant. Referents are, moreover, in substantial part specifically designatable, publicly verifiable, and subject to scientific scrutiny as meanings are not. The quest for referents —far from being a needless complication—can then be extremely useful in any sound search for meanings. Nevertheless, one can pick out referents without getting meanings and give examples of what is meant without grasping just what the examples are examples of. To know what the referents of bearers of intentional meanings are is to come very close to apprehending these meanings but, in itself, it is not yet fully to grasp these meanings.

CHAPTER VII

VERIFICATION AND MEANING

Since many utterances, inscriptions, and other expressions are such that what they assert can be seen to be true (or false) by virtue of their relations to certain existing conditions, the conditions of verification, or of discernment of the truth (or falsity), of expressions are likely to be revealing with respect to the meanings of expressions. In this connection, three related but quite different kinds of claims have come to play prominent roles in discussions of meaning in recent years. One consists of claims that the meaningfulness of an expression is determined by the existence of conditions by which its truth (or falsity) can be discerned, its verifiability. A second kind of claim is that the meaning of an expression consists in the operations by which verifying conditions are brought about. The third kind consists of claims that the meaning of an expression is just those conditions by which it can be verified, its truth conditions. In the first section of the present chapter, I shall sketch the views of representative inquirers who have presented each of these kinds of claims. In the remaining sections I shall, in an effort to clairfy the roles of verifying conditions in meaning situations, attempt to comment upon certain excesses, on the one hand, and insights, on the other, of each of the main types of claims presented in the first section.

1. Representative Views Concerning Verifying Conditions and Meanings

The suggestion that the meaning of an expression is closely connected with the conditions of its verification is deeply rooted in British and American empiricism. In 1620, Francis Bacon warned that words consist often of "names of things which have

179

no existence" such as "fortune, the primum mobile, the planetary orbits [and] the element of fire," and sometimes of "confused signs," such as "moist," which are "hastily abstracted . . . . without any due verification."[1]

John Locke deplored all use of words "without clear and distinct ideas"[2] and insisted that even abstract ideas must be rooted in experience. George Berkeley took even Locke's experientially grounded abstract ideas to be too remote from verifying experiences to be meaningful and undertook to limit meaningful language (except as it applied to "notions," such as that of a mind) to terms referring to immediate experiences. Unable to find any verifying experience even for Berkeley's expressions for notions, David Hume excluded even these from the realm of meaningful expression, and admonished his readers as follows: "If we take in our hands any volume.....let us ask, *"Does it contain any abstract reasoning concerning quantity or number? No. Does it contain any experimental reasoning concerning matter of fact and existence?* No. Commit it then to the flames; for it can contain nothing but sophistry and illusion."[3]

In the nineteenth century, J. S. Mill was unable to make sense of words for physical objects save in terms of "permanent possibilities of sensation," and subsequently Ernst Mach found words for atoms and other unobservables of science to be intelligible only as convenient devices for the guidance of experience. C. S. Pierce's formula for making an idea of an object clear was simply to "consider what effects, which might conceivably have practical bearings, we conceive the object of our conception to have."[4] William James, following what he took to be Pierce's thought, declared that "the effective meaning of any philosophic proposition can always be brought down to some particular consequence, in our future practical experience, whether active or

---

[1]Francis Bacon, *Novum Organum* Part I, paragraphs 43-60, in *Great Books of the Western World* (Chicago: Encyclopedia Britannica, Inc., 1952), Vol. 30, pp. 112 f.

[2]John Locke, *An Essay Concerning Human Understanding,* in *Great Books of the Western World,* Vol. 35, pp. 291 f.

[3]David Hume, *Inquiry Concerning Human Understanding,* in *Great Books of the Western World,* Vol. 35, p. 509.

[4]C. S. Peirce, "How to Make Our Ideas Clear," Reprinted in Henry D. Aiken, *Philosophy in the 20th Century* (New York, Random House, 1962), p. 113.

passive; the point lying rather in the fact that the experience must be particular, than in the fact that it must be active."[5]

The empirical tradition which linked meanings closely with the experiential conditions of their verification passed through Bertrand Russell to Ludwig Wittgenstein. Wittgenstein's *Tractatus Logico Philosophicus*, which, following Frege, took sentences rather than words to be the basic units for meaning analysis, became the principal fountainhead of contemporary claims linking verifying conditions and meanings. Building all meaningful propositions upon atomic facts by way of elemental sentences and a purely formal logic, Wittgenstein declared in his *Tractatus* that "to understand a proposition is to know what is the case if it is true" and that a proposition "is understood by anyone who understands its constituents."[6] Wittgenstein himself did not develop from the ideas of the *Tractatus* a verification theory of meaning; indeed, he repudiated the attempt to develop such a theory, on the ground that verification was "just one way of getting clear about the use of a word or sentence."[7] His remarks about the understanding of a proposition were eagerly seized upon by members of the Vienna Circle and others. The ideas of the *Tractatus* have often been referred to in support of all three of the major types of current verification theories. Among these types, I shall discuss first the one that takes verifiability or confirmability to be a criterion of meaningfulness, next the one that takes meanings to be equatable with the operations employed in verifications, and finally the one that takes meanings to be identifiable at least in a large part, with confirming experiences.

a. Since both the central idea and the major developments of the verifiability theory of meaningfulness are well illustrated in the works of Rudolf Carnap, who has been the most influential advocate of that theory, I shall, in presenting the claims of that theory, focus attention largely upon works of Carnap. In order

---

[5]William James, "Philosophical Conceptions and Practical Results," quoted in *Readings in 20th Century Philosophy,* ed. William P. Alston and George Nakhnikian (London and Glencoe, Illinois: Collier-Macmillan Limited and The Free Press, 1963), p. 13.

[6]Ludwig Wittgenstein, *Tractatus Logico Philosophicus,* tr. D. F. Pears and B. F. McGuinness (London and New York: Routledge & Kegan Paul, and The Humanities Press, 1961), p. 41.

[7]Quoted in John Passmore, *A Hundred Years of Philosophy* (London Gerald Duckworth & Co., Ltd., 1957), p. 371.

to broaden the base of subsequent discussion, however, I shall also introduce a few leading ideas of other advocates of the verifiability criterion of meaningfulness. As will be evident in considering Carnap's work, advocates of the view in question were at first disposed to equate verifying conditions and meanings, but subsequently they were for the most part content to insist that verifiability, or even confirmability, was the *criterion of meaningfulness*.

In his earliest well known work, *Der Logische Aufbau der Welt*, Carnap held that all empirically meaningful statements led back to basic empirical statements expressing memory similarities,[8] which were epistemologically basic in that all other statements were dependent upon them. Controversies between realism and idealism were, he thought, rooted in pseudo-questions, as were indeed all other metaphysical claims. All meaningful statements were founded in the end upon statements expressing immediate experiences; and apart from such experiences, nothing could be considered meaningful.

By 1932 Carnap had come, under the influence of Otto Neurath, to regard the basic sentences to which all meaningful sentences must be reduced, not as immediately experiential or phenomenalistic, but as observational or physicalistic. In his essay "The Elimination of Metaphysics Through Logical Analysis,"[9] Carnap contends not only that "the meaning of a statement lies in the method of its verification,"[10] but also that all empirically meaningful sentences are literally translatable into basic or "protocol" sentences formulating observations.[11] Meaningful statements are always either "true solely by virtue of their form [and] say nothing about reality" or they are "self-contradictory.....hence false by virtue of their form" or they are "[true or false] empirical statements and belong to the domain of empirical science." "Any statement one desires to construct which does not fall within these categories becomes automatically meaningless."[12]

---

[8]Rudolf Carnap, *Der Logische Aufbau der Welt* (Berlin-Schlachtemsee: Weltkreis-Verlag, 1928), p. 91.

[9]Rudolf Carnap, "Uberwindung der Metaphysik durch Logische Analyse der Sprache," *Erkenntnis*, Vol. II, 1932; Tr. by A. J. Ayer, in A. J. Ayer, *Logical Positivism* (Glencoe, Illinois: The Free Press 1959), pp. 60-81.

[10]*Op. cit.*, p. 76.

[11]*Op. cit.*, p. 63.

[12]*Ibid.*, p. 76.

To ascertain the meaning of a word that appears in an empirical statement one must first understand its syntax; e.g., "stone" occurs in such expressions as "X is a stone." One has then to determine the sentences from which representative sentences containing the word are deducible, the conditions under which these representative sentences are supposed to be true, and the manner of the verification of such sentences."[13] The sufficient and necessary conditions for an empirical statement's being meaningful are that the empirical criteria of its words be known, that the basic observation sentences from which the sentence is deducible be stipulated, that the truth conditions of the sentence be determined, and that the method of verification of the sentence be known.[14] Metaphysical terms, such as "principle" and "God," and sentences containing them, cannot meet these tests, and are therefore meaningless.[15] They would not even occur in a well constructed language.[16] Indeed all metaphysical terms have to be excluded altogether from meaningful discourse; for "since 'metaphysics' does not want to assert analytic propositions nor to fall within the domains of empirical science, it is compelled to employ words for which no criteria of application are specified and which are therefore devoid of sense."[17] Metaphysics is in fact simply poor art such as is practiced, for example, by "musicians without musical ability."[18]

Not long after the publication of "The Elimination of Metaphysics," Carnap came to see, even while insisting in *The Unity of Science* that the physical language was the basic language of science, that a singular sentence about a metaphysical object could not literally be equated with or translated as a series of observation sentences: "From no collection of protocal statements, however many, can [a physical-object sentence] be deduced."[19]

---

[13]*Ibid.*, p. 62.
[14]*Ibid.*, pp. 64 f.
[15]*Ibid.*, pp. 65 ff.
[16]*Ibid.*, p. 68.
[17]*Ibid.*, p. 76.
[18]*Ibid.*, p. 80.
[19]Rudolf Carnap, *The Unity of Science*, Tr. by Max Black (London: Kegan Paul, Trench, Trubner Co., Ltd.; see also Rudolf Carnap "Philosophy and Logical Syntax," reprinted in W. P. Alston and George Nakhnikian, *Readings on Twentieth Century Philosophy*), pp. 424-460, especially pp. 425 f.

By 1936, Carnap was ready to abandon altogether the attempt to equate meanings with verifying conditions or to translate empirically meaningful sentences into observation sentences. He now sought to show that for a sentence to be empirically meaningful it need only be linked through reduction chains with confirmatory sentences. Thus, in his "Testability and Meaning," Carnap specifically rejects the attempt to equate the meaning of a sentence with observation sentences deducible from it, on the ground that one could never exclude all untested instances or avoid absurdities that would follow from such instances. For example, if saying that something's being soluble in water is equivalent to saying that when immersed in water that thing will dissolve, a match that has never been so immersed will have to be said to be soluble since the falsity of the experimental condition implies the truth of the proposition that if the experimental condition is fulfilled the solution occurs.[20] What Carnap now wishes to do is not to equate the meaning of an empirical sentence with a series of observation sentences deducible from it, but to make the meaningfulness of an empirical sentence dependent on the possibility of deducing *some* such sentence from it. Thus "what gives theoretical meaning to a statement is.....the possibility of deducing from it perceptual statements," and what shows one's assertion to be meaningless is his "inability to give rules according to which we could deduce perceptual statements from his assertion."[21] Meaningful terms may, Carnap at this stage thought, be introduced into scientific discourse, without explicit definitions, by way of reduction sentences. Such sentences introduce empirically meaningful predicates by indicating experimental conditions from which if certain results occur, the predicate applies, and if certain results fail to occur, the predicate does not apply. For example, "solubility in water" may be introduced by saying that if any thing is put into water at any time, then if it dissolves, it is soluble in water, and if it does not dissolve, it is not soluble in water.[22] When, by such reduction sentences, the predicate in question is so introduced as to exclude from consideration cases in which experimental conditions do not occur, the requirement for experi-

---

[20]Rudolf Carnap, "Testability and Meaning" in *Philosophy of Science,* Vol. III (1936), p. 440.
[21]*Philosophy and Logical Syntax,* p. 426.
[22]"Testability and Meaning", pp. 440 f.

mental meaningfulness is not that the application of the predicate be fully confirmable, in the sense that all possibilities of their falsification be excluded, or that such applications could be tested; it is rather only that instances of the application of the predicate should be confirmable in the sense of being linked by reduction chains with observation predicates.[23]

However, even the substitution of disposition terms for observational definitions and of reduction chains for observational equivalents leaves the criterion of meaningfulness still too rigid, and fails to do justice to probabilistic and modal aspects of the relations of expressions and their meanings in the actual work of scientists and men of common sense. Hence, in his latest writings, Carnap undertakes to describe the conditions of meaningfulness in a new way that gives due consideration to these factors. Disposition terms can, Carnap now believes, be used for scientific purposes and they can be introduced by reduction chains, but when they are used, they serve the purpose largely of what are now called "intervening variables," which formulate observable data but are subsequently replacable by more adequate representations.[24] Disposition terms may, moreover, require logical modalities for their adequate representation.[25] The more fundamental terms of scientific inquiry are theoretical concepts introduced by the postulates of a theoretical system, some of whose terms are connected with observation terms by correspondence rules.[26] The criterion of meaningfulness is then that an expression is significant in a given language system if and only if it satisfies formation rules of the language, and every descriptive term in it is such as to lead, directly or indirectly, by the rules of the language, to some observable consequence.[27] Put negatively, the principle is as follows: "If it is in principle impossible for any conceivable observational result to be either

---

[23]*Ibid.*, p. 456 and *op. cit.*, Vol. IV (1937), p. 34.

[24]Rudolf Carnap, "The Methodological Character of Theoretical Concepts," in *The Foundations of Science and the Concepts of Psychology and Psychoanalysis,* Vol. I, *Minnesota Studies in the Philosophy of Science,* ed. Herbert Feigl and Michael Scriven (Minneapolis: University of Minnesota Press, 1956), p. 73.

[25]*Ibid.*, p. 64.

[26]*Ibid.*, pp. 49 ff.

[27]*Ibid.*, p. 60.

confirming or disconfirming evidence for a linguistic expression A, then expression A is devoid of cognitive meaning."[28]

Among other current writers, who urge verifiability criteria of meaningfulness, the first to be mentioned here has advocated formulations similar to those of Carnap. The second, third, and fourth are in basic agreement with the latest phase of Carnap's thought. The fifth stresses the role of falsifiability rather than verifiability in disclosing meaningfulness. The sixth liberalizes verifiability criteria beyond the limits indicated by any of the others.

In the original text of the first edition of the *Language, Truth and Logic*, A. J. Ayer declares that "a sentence is factually significant to any given person, if, and only if, he knows how to verify the proposition which it purports to express—that is, if "he knows what observations would lead him, under certain conditions, to accept the proposition as being true, or reject it as being false."[29] Ayer goes on to reject the demand for practical or actually achievable verifiability in favor of "verifiability in principle," and strong verifiability or probability in favor of weak verifiability or empirical probability, as criteria of meaningfulness in empirical propositions. Accordingly, he says that the mark of a factually meaningful proposition is that "some experiential propositions can be deduced from it in conjunction with certain other premises without being deducible from those other premises alone."[30] Subsequently in the introduction to the second edition of *Language, Truth and Logic*, Ayer undertook, in answer to certain objections, to reformulate his account of verifiability to read as follows. "A statement is directly verifiable if it be either itself an observation statement, or is such that in conjunction with one or more observation-statements it entails at least one observation-statement which is not deducible from these other premises alone; and "a statement is indirectly verifiable if.....in conjunction with certain other premises it entails one or more directly verifiable statements which are not deducible from these

---

[28]Rudolf Carnap, "Replies and Systematic Expositions" in P. A. Schilpp, *The Philosophy of Rudolf Carnap* (LaSalle, Illinois: Open Court, 1963), p. 874.

[29]A. J. Ayer, *Language, Truth and Logic* (London: Victor Gollencz, Ltd., Second edition, 1950), p. 35.

[30]*Ibid.*, p. 39.

other premises alone, and.....these other premises do not include any statement that is not either analytic, or directly verifiable, or capable of being independently established or indirectly verifiable."[31]

Otto Neurath was largely responsible for persuading Carnap and most of the other members of the Vienna Circle to exchange the conception of coherence with patterns of physicalistic observation sentences for that of reducibility to direct expressions of experience as a criterion of meaningfulness. Thus in his essay on "Protocol Sentences,"[32] Neurath argues that it is impossible to get back to pure expressions of experience in that there can be no private language,[33] that any of several possible bases for meaningful language will do, but that in fact a physicalistic language representing things in the ordinary macrocosmic way is on the whole most suitable. He recommends the use of such basic sentences as the following: "Otto's protocol at 3:17 o'clock: [at 3:16 o'clock Otto said to himself: (at 3:15 o'clock there was a table in the room perceived by Otto)]."[34] To attempt to get beyond a base of the coherence of observation sentences concerning physical objects was, Neurath held, to fail to recognize our situation in the world: "We are like sailors who must rebuild their ship on the open sea, never able to dismantle it in dry-dock and to reconstruct it there out of the best materials."[35]

Hans Reichenbach was apparently never willing to equate the meaning of a statement with expressions of immediate experience into which the statement could be translated or even to regard the deducibility of such expressions as criteria of meaningfulness. His questions were from the outset, not those concerning meaning as such, but those concerning "the conditions under which a sentence has meaning and the conditions under which two sentences have the same meaning."[36] Reichenbach holds that the basic sentences of the verifiability theory are best con-

---

[31]*Ibid.*, p. 13.
[32]Otto Neurath, "Protocol Sentences," in A. J. Ayer, *Logical Positivism*, pp. 199-208, from *Erkenntnis*, Vol. III, 1932/33.
[33]*Op. cit.*, p. 205.
[34]*Ibid.*, p. 202.
[35]*Op. cit.*, p. 201.
[36]Hans Reichenbach, "The Verifiability Theory of Meaning" in *Contributions to the Analysis and Synthesis of Knowledge, Proceedings of the American Academy of Arts and Science*, Vol. 80, 1951, p. 47.

ceived in physicalistic terms but that special rules are required to link the concepts of quantum mechanics with such sentences.[37] While agreeing fully with the members of the Vienna Circle that scientifically meaningful statements should be distinguished from metaphysical statements on the one hand and *a priori* statements on the other, Karl Popper holds that no sharp distinction can be drawn between meaningful statement and statements that are not meaningful and that in any case, metaphysical statements are by no means meaningless.[38] Scientifically meaningful statements are not, however, to be distinguished by their verifiability, for verifiability depends upon induction, which, as Hume showed, can never be carried through and, in fact, is not the method of science.[39] The demarcation is rather to be conceived in terms of falsifiability. In general *"it must be possible for an empirical scientific system to be refuted by experience."*[40] *"Testability is the same as refutability, and can therefore likewise be taken as a criterion of demarcation."*[41] It may, of course, be objected that there are always ways of avoiding refutation, but the core of scientific method lies in the endeavor to achieve refutation in order to ascertain what theories can survive. The point in science is to achieve not maximal probability but maximal content, and this can be done only by making hypotheses sufficiently detailed to be subject to refutation.[42]

In two essays, "Problems and Changes in the Empiricist Criterion of Meaning,"[43] and "The Concept of Cognitive Significance,"[44] which have been widely accepted as significant summaries of the earlier achievements and shortcomings of the verifiability criterion of meaningfulness, Carl Hempel has set forth and evalu-

---

[37] *Ibid.*, pp. 55 ff.

[38] Karl Popper, "The Demarcation Between Science and Metaphysics" in P. A. Schilpp, *The Philosophy of Rudolf Carnap*, p. 183. See also Karl Popper, *The Logic of Scientific Discovery* (London: Hutchinson, 1959), pp. 34 ff.

[39] *Ibid.*, p. 40.

[40] *Ibid.*, p. 41.

[41] "The Demarcation Between Science and Metaphysics," p. 186.

[42] *Ibid.*, pp. 220 ff.

[43] *Revue Internationale de Philosophie*, Vol. IV (1950), Reprinted in A. J. Ayer, *Logical Positivism*, pp. 108-129.

[44] "*Contributions to the Analysis and Synthesis of Knowledge*," Vol. 80 (1951, pp. 661-677, *Proceeding of the American Academy of Arts and Sciences*).

ated such phases of the development of verifiability criteria of meaningfulness as those indicated in the foregoing account of the thought of Carnap and others. His criticisms are in general that virtually all criteria proposed up to the time of his writing were, in some respects, so wide as to allow nonsensical statements and, in others, so narrow as to exclude scientific ones. His own conclusions are that the criteria of cognitive significance can be best applied "to sentences forming theoretical systems" or even "to such systems as wholes" rather than to isolated systems, that in any case the distinction between what is meaningful and what is not is no sharp dichotomy but "a matter of degree," and that systems must be judged, not by one criterion alone, but by their "clarity and precision,.....explanatory and predictive power,...... and the extent to which....[they].....have been confirmed."[45]

b. Although the immediate source of operationalism as an account of meaning was the reflection of a physicist upon the manner in which inquiry in physics is conducted,[46] the initial operationalist way of construing meaning had a good deal in common with the verifiability criterion of meaningfulness and was welcomed by the advocates of such a criterion as significant support. The founder and principal spokesman of operationalism was the physicist P. W. Bridgman.

The main ideas concerning meaning that Bridgman presents in his book, *The Logic of Modern Physics*, are somewhat as follows. Instead of trying to equate concepts or meanings of terms with properties, which are at best all too difficult to identify, we should equate them with the operations by which we determine the applicability of the terms. Thus, "the concept of length involves as much as and nothing more than the set of operations by which length is determined." Indeed, in general, we mean by any concept nothing more than a set of operations; "*the concept is synonymous with the corresponding set of operations.*"[47] After all, "the meaning of a term is to be found by observing what a man does with it, not what he says about

---

[45]"The Concept of Cognitive Significance", p. 74.
[46]See P. W. Bridgman, *Reflections of a Physicist* (New York: The Philosophical Library, 1955), pp. 2 ff.
[47]P. W. Bridgman, *The Logic of Modern Physics* (New York: The Macmillan Company, 1927), p. 5.

it;"[48] and the actual procedures of great scientists, such as Einstein, have been operational. Very often, when we construe a term by means of a variety of operations, the results coincide sufficiently, within normal ranges of applications, to permit such construction. For example, length measured by cords and length measured by triangulation are ordinarily the same. However, that such varied operations yield the same results is known only by experience, and we have no way of knowing that the coincidences will be preserved when the concepts are applied beyond their normal ranges. Hence, to avoid confusion and to forestall such shocks as came to us in Einstein's discoveries, we should, when precision is necessary, define each concept by reference to a single type of operation and recognize that where there are different operations, there are different concepts. Thus, for example, "in *principle* the operations by which length is measured should be *uniquely* specified."[49] Although mental operations are by no means to be ruled out, "the operations to which a physical concept is equivalent are actual physical operations."[50] Among the principal merits of the application of operational analysis is its disclosure of the meaninglessness of such problems as those of the absoluteness of space and time and the boundaries of space and time.[51]

In his later writings, Bridgman insists that he has intended to propound no new dogma and that he deplores the word "operationalism." Thus, he points out that the operational criterion is designed to be a necessary but not a sufficient condition of meaningfulness,[52] and that his earlier claim "that meanings are *synonymous with operations*" was excessive.[53] "A term," he comes to hold, "is defined when the conditions are stated under which I may use the term and when I may infer from the use of the term by my neighbor that the same conditions prevailed."[54] Operations are not so much meanings as ways of checking the applicability of definitions. They, rather than properties, are chosen for this purpose for the reasons that one can

---

[48]*Ibid.*, p. 7.
[49]*Ibid.*, p. 10
[50]*Ibid.*, p. 7.
[51]*Ibid.*, pp. 39 ff.
[52]*Ibid.*, p. 5.
[53]*Ibid.*
[54]*Ibid.*, p. 77.

readily grasp operations but not properties, and that operations used for checking applicability tend to remain constant even when properties change.[55] Although Bridgman was always disposed to prefer overt operations to pencil and paper ones, he came to have a high regard for the usefulness, and even indispensability, of the latter.[56] While his writings have often been used in support of rigidly physicalistic theories, Bridgman always insisted that the foundations of science are in the end subjective and that failure to distinguish between mine and thine is one of of the most serious mistakes of modern culture.[57]

c. Many of the current advocates of verifiability criteria of meaningfulness, including Carnap, were in the initial phases of their inquiries interested, not only in criteria of meaningfulness, but also in the character of meanings. Moreover, some writers favorably disposed to verifiability criteria of meaningfulness have continued throughout their careers interested in the character of meanings and have in fact presented verification or confirmation theories of meaning. Since such views of meaning involve a good deal more than verifiability criteria of meaningfulness, I shall sketch the relevant views of two such writers.

(1) Although Moritz Schlick died before the retreat of the members of the Vienna Circle from their original identification of meanings with verifying experiences was complete, he resisted the earlier phases of this retreat and continued until the end of his life to identify empirical meanings with experiential truth conditions. Schlick may accordingly be appropriately regarded as representative of largely unqualified identification of empirical meanings with confirmatory experiences.

Like most of the members of the Vienna Circle, Schlick drew a sharp distinction between logical and mathematical propositions, on the one hand, which he took to be formal and devoid of empirical content, and empirical propositions, on the other hand, which he took to be the substance of common sense and scientific knowledge. He hailed the discovery by Frege, Russell, and Wittgenstein of the purely formal character of logic

---

[55]*Ibid.*, pp. 128 ff.

[56]*Ibid.*, pp. 71 ff.

[57]*Ibid.*, pp. 43 ff. See also P. W. Bridgman, *The Intelligent Individual and Society* (New York: The Macmillan Company, 1938), pp. 148 ff., 153 and 158.

as a sort of "turning point" in philosophy, which at last removed
the final barrier that had long prevented the identification of the
meanings of all substantive statements with their verifying conditions.[58] As a result of this discovery, one could, he thought, see
that "wherever there is a meaningful problem one can in theory
always give the path that leads to its solution" and that "giving
this path coincides with giving its meaning."[59]

The meaning of an empirical statement was always for
Schlick just the conditions under which it could be verified.
"The statement of the conditions under which a proposition is
true is the same as the statement of its meaning."[60] To describe
the meaning of a sentence is to give the rules that "will tell us
exactly in what circumstances the sentence is to be used."[61] Thus,
when one asks for the meaning of a sentence, what he expects is
"instruction as to the circumstances in which the sentence is to be
used,.....description of the conditions under which the sentence
will form a *true* proposition, and of those which will make it false,"
i.e., the "method of its verification."[62] Such an account of meaning
is sometimes called "the experimental theory of meaning" but in
fact it is no mere theory at all but "a simple statement of the way
in which meaning is *actually* assigned to propositions."[63]

That upon which the verification of an empirical sentence
rests is not, as even some positivists want to say, mere coherence
with other sentences or any system of sentences, for even "fairy
stories" may be quite coherent.[64] The desired basis is also not
merely one of economy of formulation, for the most economical
base may still be an incorrect one.[65] The basis cannot consist of
so-called protocol statements reporting someone's alleged observation, for regarding such statements "the possibilities of error are
innumerable."[66] Rather the basic statements upon which verifica-

---

[58]Moritz Schlick, "The Turning Point in Philosophy," in A. J. Ayer,
Logical Positivism, pp. 55 ff.
[59]*Ibid.,* p. 56.
[60]Moritz Schlick, "Positivism and Realism" in *Ibid.,* p. 87.
[61]Moritz Schlick, "Meaning and Verification" in Herbert Feigl and
Wilfrid Sellars, *Op. cit.,* pp. 146 f.
[62]*Ibid.,* pp. 147 f.
[63]*Ibid.*
[64]Moritz Schlick, "The Foundation of Knowledge," in Ayer *Op. cit.,*
p. 215.
[65]*Ibid.,* pp. 216 ff.
[66]*Ibid.,* p. 212.

tion must in the end rest are statements "that express facts of one's own perceptions." "What I see I see."[67] Such statements are "absolutely certain."[68] In the end they depend on "paintings or gestures" and can never be fully put into words. To be sure they pass away as quickly as they come, but it is in the satisfaction that they yield that the fruit of knowledge is attained. "Like a flame, cognition as it were licks out to them, reaching each but for a moment, and then at once consuming it..... These moments of fulfillment and combustion are what is essential. All knowledge comes from them. And it is for the source of this light the philosopher is really inquiring when he seeks the ultimate basis of knowledge."[69]

The possibility of verification in terms of which meaning is defined is not, as it is sometimes taken to be, either technical possibility or physical possibility; it is rather the logical possibility of perceptual experience. "The empirical circumstances are all important when you want to know if a proposition is *true*...., but they can have no influence on the *meaning* of the proposition."[70] For something to be logically possible in the requisite sense is for it to be such that it can be *described*.[71] Thus, ruled out are such sentences as "My friend died the day after tomorrow." "The campanile is 100 feet and 150 feet high" and "The child was naked, but wore a long white nightgown."[72] However, statements to the effect that the other side of the moon has a certain character, that the soul of man survives death, or that the earth will, after all organisms have died, have certain properties are logically in order and clearly meaningful in that one can say what their verifying conditions would be like even if in fact they are never tested.[73]

(2) Like Schlick and Carnap, Gustav Bergmann was a member of the Vienna Circle and has always wished to confine the meaningful largely to the experienceable. However, he is by no means

---

[67]*Ibid.*, pp. 218 f.
[68]*Ibid.*, p. 223.
[69]*Ibid.*, p. 227. See also M. Schlick, "Facts and Propositions" in Margaret Macdonald, *Philosophy and Analyses* (Oxford: Basil Blackwell, 1954), pp. 232-239.
[70]Moritz Schlick, "Meaning and Verification," p. 154.
[71]*Ibid.* p. 154.
[72]*Ibid.*, p. 154.
[73]*Ibid.*, pp. 153 ff.

confident that the meaningfulness of a statement in ordinary
language can always be clearly determined.[74] For those statements
whose meaningfulness and verifiability can be determined, Bergmann makes no claim that their verifiability has to be established
before their meaningfulness can be recognized.[75] He is rather concerned initially with the meaningfulness of particular terms, and
regarding these, he modifies the stringency of the usual verificationist's demands by recognizing certain special predicates not
strictly empirical, such as predicates referring to mental acts,
evaluative characters, and semantic properties.[76] In general, what,
for him, determines the meaningfulness, and in the end also the
meaning, of a particular term is its experiential applicability in
some sentence or other; and what determines the meaningfulness,
and eventually the meaning, of a sentence is its formulatability in
an ideal language so construed as to be capable of expressing all
that ordinary language expresses without including any substantive
terms other than experiential ones. In such an ideal language,
Bergmann insists, "a particular is to occur in a statement only if its
referent is immediately apprehended—in perception, memory, or
imagination—by a speaker, and....an undefined predicate is to
occur in a statement only if at least one exemplification of it is
known to the speaker."[77] Such a language needs no reduction
chains or counterfactuals and quite properly adheres to the basic
insights of Hume.[78] Its principle of acquaintance has the same
status as all principles of its kind in philosophical thought, namely,
that of a part of an informal commentary on the ideal language.[79]

  (3) In view of the difficulties that kept cropping up in early
attempts to identify meanings with experiential verifying conditions, and indeed even in verifiability criteria of meaningfulness,
unqualified identification of meanings with verifying conditions

---

[74]Gustav Bergmann, "Comments on Professor Hempel's 'The Concept
of Cognitive Significance' " in *Contributions to the Analysis and Synthesis
of Knowledge,* pp. 81 f.
  [75]Gustav Bergmann, *The Metaphysics of Logical Positivism* (New York:
Longman, Green & Co., Inc., 1964), pp. 156 ff.
  [76]*Ibid.,* pp. 16 and 243 f.; and "Comments on Professor Hempel's 'The
Concept of Cognitive Significance,' " pp. 80 f.
  [77]*The Metaphysics of Logical Positivism,* p. 158.
  [78]"Comments on Professor Hempel's 'The Concept of Cognitive Significance,' " p. 83.
  [79]*Ibid.,* pp. 83 f.

has become increasingly untenable and certainly would not have been attempted by such a thinker as C. I. Lewis. Lewis was in fact one of the severest critics of a narrow verifiability criterion of meaningfulness; he pointed out that such a criterion trapped its advocates in a "here and now" predicament which if consistently followed through would preclude such clearly meaningful expressions as statements about the other side of the moon, the external world, and immortality.[80] However, what could still be held with reference to the verifying conditions of an expression was that they constituted at any rate a very important aspect of meaning; and this Lewis, influenced more by the pragmatist movement of James and Dewey than by the analytic one of Russell and Carnap, did hold.

As has been noted in an earlier chapter, Lewis took every significant expression to have four modes of meaning. One of these—the denotational mode—has already been explored in connection with reference theories of meaning. The most important of the modes of meaning in Lewis's way of thinking is, however, not the denotational one but the connotational or intensional one. It is in connection with his account of the meanings of empirical expressions in this latter mode that the verificational aspect of Lewis's view of meaning comes principally to light. The connotation or intension of a term in its formal or linguistic aspect is, according to Lewis, "the conjunction of all other terms each of which must be applicable to anything to which the given term would be correctly applicable."[81] In the same formal aspect, the intension of a proposition is "whatever the proposition entails." However, this formal linguistic aspect of intension is only a derivative aspect; what is basic is rather the sense meaning of terms and propositions. In this "simplest and most frequent sense which is the original meaning of meaning," the meaning of A is "what we have in mind in using 'A',....the concept of A,....the criterion in mind by which it is determined whether the term in question applies or fails to apply in any particular instance."[82] In the same

---

[80]C. I. Lewis, "Experience and Meaning" in Herbert Feigl and Wilfrid Sellers, *Readings in Philosophical Analysis* (New York: Appleton-Century-Crofts, Inc., 1949), pp. 128 ff.

[81]C. I. Lewis, *An Analysis of Knowledge and Valuation* (LaSalle: Open Court Press, 1946), p. 39.

[82]*Ibid.*, p. 43.

fundamental sense, the intension of a proposition is its "deducible consequences" or alternatively "whatever must be true of any possible world in order that this proposition should be true or apply to it."[83]

Subsequently delineating what is meant by a criterion in mind, Lewis indicates that such a criterion has nothing to do with a picture or an image but is rather a sort of Kantian schema. The presence of such schemata is indicated by our evident ability to distinguish, for example, between a polygon having 999 sides and one having 1000 sides, not indeed by means of a picture, but by means of a rule serving as a criterion in mind.[84] In further explanation of the interpretation of propositions in terms of implications, Lewis stresses the roles alike of possible operations and possible observations and calls attention to the incompleteness of all empirical confirmations, hence also, of all formulatable meanings. Thus, the meaning of any statement about a physical object, for example that here is a door knob, is an endless series of what Lewis calls "terminating judgments," e.g., to the effect that if I were seen to look in a certain direction I would have certain visual impressions; if I were to seem to move forward and reach out my hand, I would have certain tactile impressions, etc. Each such terminating judgment is in principle fully verifiable; and while the totality of such terminating judgments can never, even for a single statement, be fully traversed, the confirmations of a few suitably chosen ones is often sufficient to give fairly strong confirmation to the statement in question. In any case, in the conjuncts of such propositions the basic meaning of any physical object statement, whether of common sense or of science, is to be found.

2. *Limitations and Achievements of Verifiability Criteria of Meaningfulness*

Although verifiability criteria have been presented for the most part as crucial tests for meaningfulness rather than as meanings or any other ingredients in meaning situations, they

---

[83]*Ibid.*, p. 56.
[84]*Ibid.*, p. 134.

are designed to show the presence or absence of meanings and accordingly may, within limits, have significant uses in helping to disclose the character of meanings. I shall endeavor now to ascertain what some of these limits and uses are.

Early proposals concerning verifiability criteria, such as that every meaningful statement could be translated into statements reporting sensory experience or observations or that from any meaningful statement such statements could always be deduced, have now been largely discredited, not just by opponents of verifiability criteria, but most convincingly by writers who formerly advocated just such proposals and by other writers who continue to advocate verifiability criteria. Explicit recognitions by Carnap and Hempel that the criteria at first proposed would, on the one hand, exclude from the meaningful many of the scientific statements that they wished to include and, on the other hand, include many of the metaphysical statements they wished to exclude are striking cases in point. The verifiability criteria that would then seem mainly to merit careful consideration would be liberalized criteria of the sort suggested in the later writings of Hempel and Carnap and in general to the following effect: that a meaningful sentence is one that belongs to a system of sentences connected at various points with possible sensory or observational experiences that tend to confirm the truth or falsity of that sentence. In considering the limitations and achievements of verifiability criteria of meaningfulness I shall focus attention mainly upon these liberalized criteria. Sometimes the proponents of verifiability criteria have been careful to say that they were concerned with criteria of meaningfulness in science only, but some of them have occasionally written as though this were the only sort of meaningfulness worth being concerned with. In any case, the problem of the present inquiry insofar as it concerns criteria is the problem of criteria of meaningfulness generally. Accordingly, I shall undertake here to indicate from the point of view of that broadly conceived problem first some inadequacies and then some significant insights of the kind of liberalized verifiability criteria under consideration.

a. One limitation of the sort of verifiability criteria under consideration for the disclosure of the character of meanings involves no criticism of advocates of such criteria who know what they are doing but none the less represents a deficiency in such criteria, namely, that of limiting the meaningful to verbal expression. In our daily experience multitudes of things and events are regularly and unobjectionably taken to be meaningful that can in no way be construed as verbal expressions. Included among these are, as has been previously noted, bodily attitudes and motions, emotions, impulses, desires of many kinds, and non-verbal artifacts, not to speak of historical events, life, and even the universe. Verifiability criteria are not applicable to the meaningfulness of any of these bearers of meaning for the simple reason that none of these bearers of meaning makes any truth claims. One does not test truth claims of bodily attitudes, feeling, or life; still less can he test the meaningfulness of a ritual dance, a mountain, or a thunderbolt by checking its truth claims.

A second, and more serious, limitation attaching the sort of verifiability criteria of meaningfulness now primarily under consideration is that, having unjustifiably restricted the meaningful to verbal expressions, they also tend unwarrantedly to restrict the meaningful to sentential expressions. For practical purposes, meaningful sentences consist largely of sentences actually uttered or inscribed, together with often repeated short sentences that may be thought of as standard sentences; for while many combinations of words can become sentences, only those effectively do so which come to be uttered or inscribed. However, it is quite plain that many verbal expressions, including phrases of various sorts as well as separate words that are not sentences, are meaningful and that apart from the meanings of such expressions, the formation of most meaningful sentences would itself not be possible. "Here," "is" and "book" have meanings in English apart from which my statement "Here is a book" would have no meaning; and "is meaningful" has a meaning apart from which " 'Here is a book' is meaningful" would not be meaningful. Actually, not only may non-sentential words and phrases be meaningful, but they may be fully empirically meaningful. When the notion of truth is stretched to cover something's being true of something, words may even, in a very loose fashion, be said to fall under verifiability criteria. However, verifiability and confirmability apply primarily to sentences; and by concentrating on these most advocates of verifiability criteria have—inadvertently but none the less effectively—tended to neglect the meanings of non-sentential words and phrases. In

so doing, not only do they underemphasize an enormously important range of verbal bearers of meaning, but they also tend to
narrow unduly the range of meaningful sentences; for many a
sentence is meaningful when its substantive terms are meaningful
and its grammar is in order even when no way of verifying it is in
sight.

A third limitation of verifiability criteria of meaningfulness
in the form under discussion is that, having incorrectly confined
the meaningful largely to sentences, they also tend unjustifiably
to restrict the meaningful to sentences that can be either true or
false. Not only are many things and events that are not verbal
expressions and many verbal expressions that are not sentences
meaningful, but many sentences that neither are nor are to be
expected to be either true or false are also meaningful. Requests,
petitions, prayers, expressions of surprise, grief, fear or hope,
jokes, promises, agreements, contracts, and commands are almost
invariably treated as meaningful but none of them either is or
claims to be either true or false. Moreover, while each of them
requires a certain kind of context, none of them either does or
can be expected to indicate the kind of confirmatory conditions
demanded by even the most liberal verifiability criteria of
meaningfulness.

A fourth limitation of verifiability criteria of meaningfulness
is that of failing to include in the meaningful any true or
false sentences except those that are confirmable in some degree
by sensory or observational experiences and of construing all
other non-tautological declarative sentences as merely expressions
of emotion. The fact is that many different kinds of declarative
sentences not confirmable by sensory and observational experiences
alone are repeatedly uttered and inscribed in ways that, though
not identical with verifiability criteria, indicate full cognitive
meaningfulness. One important class of such sentences consists
of statements in which we directly report our intentions, beliefs,
desires, feelings, and emotions. To be sure there are many instances
in which the existence of such experiences can be confirmed by
observation of associated phychological and behavioral factors;
but there are many others in which they cannot and concerning
which it is at least theoretically possible that we shall never know
how to confirm them in sensory or observational ways. Yet with
regard to these latter sentences we already know perfectly well

what we mean by them. A second class of apparently cognitively meaningful but not sensorily or observationally confirmable sentences consists of presumably factual sentences which seem neither to be quite tautologous nor quite dependent upon particular sensory experience or observation yet scarcely require more than to be understood in order to be accepted, for example, such statements as that "no two objects can occupy the same place at the same time," that "all colored things are extended," and that "no area that is red all over can also be green." A third class consists of philosophical statements such as that "chairs are physical objects," that "there are other minds," that "generalizations cannot be reduced to singular statements," and that "physical objects cannot be reduced to sensory experiences;" for while it is by no means clear just what such statements mean, it does now seem clear that more is involved in them than is to be found in corresponding "syntactical statements" and that they do, as John Wisdom and others have shown, make points that are worth making. Regarding sentences in logic and mathematics, however clear it seemed in the early days of logical positivism that mathematics could be reduced to logic and tautologies, even this is by no means so clear today; and good reasons can be given for thinking that many sentences of mathematics and some of those of logic may be cognitively meaningful without being either tautological or empirically confirmable. Other classes of sentences that seem to be meaningful without being empirically confirmable are ethical, evaluative, and theological ones. Just what such sentences may mean is very difficult indeed to show, but for no statements are people more ready to give reasons than for these, and to claim that they only express feelings and say nothing is in the end an obvious travesty of the intentions from which they arise. Finally, as has often been pointed out and acknowledged, formulations of verifiability criteria themselves are cognitively meaningful without being subject to confirmation by sensory or observational experiences.

A fifth limitation of verifiability criteria is that they obscure the fact that confirmation conditions depend upon meanings rather than meanings upon confirmation conditions, and accordingly that even when sensory and observational confirmation conditions are relevant to meanings, confirmation conditions can often not be determined until meanings are known. For a sentence to the confirmation of which sensory and observational experiences are relevant, to be confirmable requires, to be sure, that confirmation conditions be in some sense in what the sentence means, but always the meaning is logically prior to the confirmation conditions.

In the instance of some simple standard sentences, truth conditions seem indeed to be given with the meaning—e.g., "The sky is blue," "Fire burns," "Ice is cold"—though even here one asks for the meaning before asking for the truth conditions. However, in the instances of the vast majority of uttered and spoken sentences, the meaning, instead of being given as a whole already linked with truth conditions, is a composite creation dependent upon the meanings of the terms used, the grammar of the language, and the intent of an agent or agents; and only after the composition is carried through, does the question of truth conditions for the whole arise at all. This is evident even for such ordinary sentences as "The book on my right is larger than the one on my left" and "Dogs are troublesome animals to keep in a city." It is even more obviously true of complex scientific statements. Whenever truth conditions are associated with the understanding of complex sentences, they follow, and are often not recognized until sometime after the meanings of the sentences have emerged from the grammatical vocabulary and contextual components of the relevant situations. Besides, as will presently become clear, the confirmatory conditions of a sentence may depend upon implications that are quite remote from its intentional (or dispositional) meaning and derivable from that meaning only by way of empirical generalizations and scientific laws that are admittedly no part of the meaning. Thus, when Newton first suggested that the motion of the tides was caused by the gravitational pull of the sun and the moon, his meaning was readily apparent, but only after he had drawn out elaborate mathematical inferences based on previously established laws was he able to work out detailed confirmatory conditions. Actually, for virtually any empirical sentence, the confirmatory conditions deducible from it together with established laws are virtually or actually infinite, but one can know its meaning without knowing all these conditions and must know its meaning before he can begin to work them out.[85]

One more limitation of the verifiability criteria under consideration is that they rest in part upon a confusion of intentional and dispositional meaning, on the one hand, and implicative meaning on the other. To be sure every significant sentence has complex implicative meanings, and the intentional and dispositional meanings of many sentences involve complexities in themselves that are difficult to distinguish from implications. Moreover, the implications of sentences depend upon the intentional and dispositional meanings of these sentences and are highly relevant to the confirmation of the truth or falsity of these sentences. However, none of these considerations in any way justifies the equating of implications the fulfillment of which in some degree confirms a sentence, with the intentional or dispositional meaning of that sentence. In order that a sentence should have implications or implicative meaning, it must first have intentional or dispositional meaning. To conflate the two obscures the distinctive character of each. It also confuses the character of scientific inference, which draws out implications from intentional and dispositional meanings rather than equating implications with such meanings. That here is a cube implies but does not intentionally or dispositionally mean that here is a twelve edged figure, and that here is a man implies but does not intentionally mean that here is one who could under certain conditions learn to read. Implications of sentences may yield criteria of the truth of these sentences and constitute implicative meanings of these sentences, but they do not constitute intentional or dispositional meanings of these sentences.

Nevertheless, whatever may be the limitations of the verifiability criteria under consideration or of the theories that advocate them, the advocacy of such criteria has served to bring to light at least one insight sufficiently important to overshadow many mistakes. This insight may be formulated in the following manner. Whatever may be the meanings of other things, the

---

[85]For a detailed presentation of consequences of this sort of principle relative to the requirements of modern scientific inquiry, see J. O. Wisdom, "Metamorphoses of the Verifiability Theory of Meaning," *Mind*, Vol. 72 (1963), pp. 335-347.

meanings of sentences belonging to that limited class of sentences the truth or falsity of which can be confirmed by sensory and observational experiences consist in part of possible patterns of experience the fulfillment of which would help to confirm the truth or falsity of these sentences. Such an insight makes no claim concerning the meaning or lack of meaning of anything other than special classes of publically confirmable sentences. It offers no suggestion that the experience patterns mentioned constitute the whole of the meanings of the sentences in question. Nor does it indicate that every sensory or observational experience that could help to confirm a sentence is a part of its meaning. What it does recognize is just that for the class of sentences in question, their meanings consist at least partly in possible patterns of sensory or observational experience the fulfillment of which would help to show the truth or falsity of these sentences, and this recognition can be readily seen to be both significant and sound.

Stimulus and response theories of meaning have been concerned with physical, physiological and psychological conditions closely connected with meanings but without ever quite getting at meanings themselves. Referential theories have been concerned with referents that some bearers of meaning are focused upon but without ever quite getting at the meanings that focus upon these referents. Verifiability theories lead at once to patterns of possible experience in which the meanings of the sentences to which these theories are applicable must in part consist. That the meanings of the sentences in question must in part consist of just such patterns is subsequently to be argued at some length in a larger context, but the essential truth of this contention already becomes apparent as soon as one begins to reflect seriously upon the relation of the meaning and truth of sentences to which sensory and observational experiences are relevant. The truth of such sentences must inevitably be construed as in some sense agreement of facts with what is meant by the sentences. But what the facts can thus agree with can in the end only be conditions included in the meanings of these sentences, and these conditions include the very sorts of patterns of possible experience in which the meanings of the sentences in question are being said to consist. The requisite conditions must in some sense be experiential else they would not be intelligible, but they must be possible experiential conditions rather than actual experiences since the sentences under consideration are meaningful prior to their verification and even if they turn out to be false. Thus if someone says there's an apple on the table, a part, at any rate, of what is meant is that if some sentient being were in a favorable situation, he would have certain sensations of touching, tasting, etc., or that he would see, touch, taste, etc., an apple. If someone says that Jones is ill, a part of what is meant is that some sentient being favorably placed would have sensory or observational experiences of certain symptoms. And a part of what is meant by saying that bodies gravitate is that favorably placed observers would have suitable experiences of certain movements of bodies. Whatever else the meanings of these sentences include, they include at least these patterns of possible experiences.

3. Operations and Meanings

As in the case of verifiability theories of meaningfulness, so in the case of operational theories of meaning, initial versions of the theories proved to be far too severe, and more moderate versions were soon adopted by the leading advocates though not by all their disciples. Among the modifications of operationalism adopted by leading operationalists were a readiness to recognize a plurality or relevant operations formulatable as contrary to fact conditionals, and an acknowledgement of paper-and-pencil operations. However, even a liberalized operationalism that retains any distinctive character remains a view that meanings are to be taken as operations employed in verification, and the operations remain sensible and observable. It is mainly with reference to the operations involved in a liberalized version of operationalism that I wish to comment upon the role of operations in disclosing the character of meanings.

Although the operations put forward by operationalists are different from the criteria put forward by the verificationists, the former, like the latter, are designed to clarify meanings by reference to conditions involved in the verification of empirical declarative sentences. Largely for this reason, the operations emphasized by operationalists have many of the same limitations as the criteria emphasized by verificationists with reference to the disclosure of the character of meanings. Thus, for example, the attempt to regard "operations" as meanings, or even as criteria of meanings, unjustifiably excludes from the meaningful, things that are not verbal expressions, all verbal expressions that are not either true or false, and all true or false sentences that cannot be tested by observable operations. Such a procedure also often confuses implications that are valid and useful for confirmations with intentional and dispositional meanings through which such implications can be inferred and tested but which themselves have a different logical status.

However, the operations stressed by operationalists are not as has been noted, the same as the criteria stressed by the verificationists. They constitute rather only a part of these criteria. Hence, whatever advantages they may have with respect to specificity, operations may be expected to be even more excessively restrictive with respect to meanings than are the verificationists' criteria.

One special limitation of operations with respect to the disclosure of the character of meanings is that any attempt to equate meanings with operations tends to obscure what Friedrich Waismann has called the "open texture" of most scientific and common sense concepts. The criteria of the meaningfulness of a sentence appealed to by liberal verificationists were any conditions tending to confirm the sentences; but in order to avoid surprises, strict operationists defined every term by a single operation and even liberal operationists confined their definitions to limited sets of operations. In fact, however, the terms that we commonly employ, though often reasonably precise, remain open to new discoveries and new decisions. Being a man is being rational or having a capacity to speak or to laugh or to do any of a number of other things. No one operational test claims exclusive right, and there are always things that may happen that are not fully covered by previous operational accounts. Even length may be determined either by rods or by tapes or by triangulations or by time intervals required for traversing or in any of many other ways; and some questions concerning what happens in measurement are yet to be determined. The applicability of a term depends, not merely on one or a few tests, but on an "unlimited number of tests;" and with reference to new experiences and possible new discoveries, the applicability of a term may not have been determined at all. Thus, no definite number of tests can determine fully whether or not an object is made of iron; and for a conceivable creature that looks and acts like a dog in other ways but talks, there is as yet no way of knowing whether or not the term "dog" applies.[86]

A second special limitation of operations with respect to the disclosure of the character of meanings is that attempts to equate them with meanings tend to obscure a systematic character of meanings that is amply recognized in the application of liberal verifiability criteria of meaningfulness. Most of the important terms in science, and many of those of ordinary language, are intricately interwoven with other terms in systems that are tied to observational experience, not by way of single concepts definable by specific operations, but by way of groups of concepts linked to observation at various points. Thus, in physics, "molecule," "atom," "electron," "proton," "neutron," and even "mass" and velocity," far from being definable each by its own operation, belong to clusters of concepts in which each depends on the others; and it is the whole cluster rather than any one concept by itself that is to be linked with observational experience. Similarly, one cannot make clear sense in psychology of "ego," "id," "super-ego," "libido," or even "perception," "emotion," or "behavior" apart from the clusters of related concepts to which they belong. Such ordinary terms as "dollar," "cent," "cost," "major," "colonel," or "capitol" can in no way be understood or explained apart from the clusters of concepts, and indeed the way of life, to which each belongs; and any attempt to equate the meaning of any of these words with a separate set of operations is futile. Operations may vastly assist the clarification of some such meanings but they are not equatable with any of them.

A third special limitation of operations with respect to the discernment of the character of meanings is that the attempt to equate operations with meanings obscures the role, in certain meanings, of possible sensory and observational experiences. Whenever the applicability of a term is properly tested by way of operations, the process involves two distinct phases. One is

---

[86]Friedrich Weismann, "Verifiability," *Proceedings of the Aristotelian Society,* Supplementary, Vol. 19 (1945), p. Reprinted in A. G. N. Flew, *Logic and Language,* first series, 1951, and in Ernest Nagel and Richard Brandt, *Meaning and Knowledge* (New York: Harcourt Brace and World, Inc., 1965), pp. 38-46.

the performance of the operation. The other is the making of observations or noting the results of the operation. The equating of operations with meanings themselves so emphasized the first of these phases as to obscure the second, which is at least as important. Thus, to test the length of a rail is not only repeatedly to apply a rod to it but to notice the number of times the rod has been applied. To determine how cold a liquid is, is not only to introduce a thermometer, but also to notice the reading. And even to determine whether or not a locomotive is approaching is not only to stop, look, and listen but also to notice what is seen and heard. Likely enough operationists have not been unmindful of this sort of consideration, but this consideration has for the most part not been present in their operational formulae; and the lack of it has worried such empirically minded philosophers as C. I. Lewis, who declared himself ready to accept operationalism only if to its operations be added the empirical results of operations as also vital parts of meanings.

Nevertheless, however limited operations are with respect to the disclosure of meanings and however unbalanced the accounts of meanings that attempt to equate operations with meanings, operations have an important role with respect to the meanings of the sorts of sentences to which verifiability criteria are relevant. Indeed, with respect to such sentences, operational conditions are properly included in their meanings. That experiential conditions are included in the meanings of sentences to the confirmation which sensory and observational experiences are relevant has already been established. For example, that "Here is an apple" means in part that in a favorable situation someone would have certain sensations and could make certain observations. That "Jones is ill" means in part that, favorably placed, someone could observe certain symptoms. But experiential conditions always include operational conditions that make sensory and operational experiences possible even though these operational conditions be no more than looking or listening. An adequate account of the meaning of "Here is an apple" will include such statements as that if one were to look he would see....., if he were to reach out his hand he would feel......, if he were to sniff he would smell....., etc. Similar sorts of operational conditions need to be indicated for other formulations of experiential conditions. Hence since operational conditions are included in experiential conditions and experiential conditions are included in the meanings of the kinds of sentences in question, operational conditions are also included in these meanings. Operational and experienceable consequences always go together; neither occurs or would be of much use alone. Verificationists were not unaware of operational conditions but stressed experiential results. Operationalists were not unaware of experiential results but stressed operations. Each of the two sorts of factors constitutes a coordinate part of the meaning of an empirical declarative sentence, and each must be mentioned in any adequate account of this aspect of the meaning of any such sentences.

4. Experiential Truth Conditions and Meanings

Experiential truth conditions of an uttered, inscribed, or standard sentence are possible patterns of experience the fulfillment of which contributes to the justification of the claim that the sentence is true. For example, for the spoken sentence, "Here is a sheet of paper," experiential truth conditions include such conditions as the following: if in certain circumstances one should look in a certain direction he would have such and such visual experiences, if in certain circumstances one should reach out his hand he would have specifiable tactile experiences, if one should draw a pencil across what was before him he would upon looking see a mark, etc. Experiential truth conditions may be identified with the sort of sensory and observational conditions pointed out by verificationists as criteria of meaningfulness; but they may also, as will presently appear, be given wider interpretations. In discussing the relation of truth conditions to meanings, I shall first point out some mistakes involved in attempts to equate the two and then offer some constructive suggestions concerning how truth conditions can throw light upon, and even be equated with, parts of meanings in certain kinds of instances.

A difficulty involved in attempts in general to equate meanings and truth conditions of any kind is that such attempts obscure the fact that many truth conditions of declarative sentences lie altogether outside the crucial intentional and dispositional meanings of these sentences. Failure to notice this is perhaps due to failure to distinguish clearly between intentional and dispositional meanings, on the one hand, and implicative ones, on the other. Every confirmable implication of a sentence belongs to its truth conditions, and the range of such conditions for almost any empirical sentence is vast; but only a small proportion of these implications are included in the intentional or dispositional meanings of such a sentence. The intentional meaning of a sentence depends upon the intentions of an agent and includes just those truth conditions he intends his respondents to apprehend as his meaning, and the dispositional meaning of a sentence depends on the dispositions of agents and includes those truth conditions these agents are disposed to intend in using the sentence. Apart from the intentional and dispositional meanings of a sentence, the sentence would have no implicative meanings; and while all of the implications of what is intentionally or dispositionally meant by a sentence are to be included in its truth conditions, only those of them that can be said to be intended, or are such that agents are disposed to intend them, can be included in the basic intentional or dispositional meanings of the sentence. If a man relatively innocent of formal geometry says that here is a triangle, what he says implies that here is a plane closed figure the sum of whose angles is 180 degrees; but although this implication is included in the truth conditions of his statement, it is not included in his meaning. If a prospector says that here is a bit of sulphur, what he says implies, in the light of established scientific knowledge, that here is a substance that will yield certain characteristic spectroscopic lines; but unless he happens to be a chemist, these truth conditions are no part of what he means and even then they may not be. Moreover, the fact that triangles have angles equal to 180 degrees is no part of the meaning of "triangle" in English. Similarly, the fact that sulphur yields characteristic spectroscopic lines is no part of the meaning of "sulphur" in English, no matter how useful this fact may be in locating samples of sulphur.

A mistake involved in attempts specifically to equate meanings with truth conditions consisting of sensory and observational experiences is that such attempts obscure the fact that many different kinds of things clearly have meanings to which the truth conditions in questions are not relevant. For example, sensory and observational truth conditions are, for reasons previously indicated, not relevant to the meanings of non-verbal bearers of

meaning, to non-sentential verbal ones, to non-declarative sentential ones, or to sentential ones not confirmable by sensory or
observational experience. They are only indirectly relevant to the
meanings of many expressions and statements about feelings and
impulses; by themselves, they throw little light upon the inductive
import of generalizations and predictions; and they are uninformative with reference to the crucial phases of the meanings of
evaluative statements.

Nevertheless, within the limits of their applicability, i.e.,
with reference to declarative sentences that are confirmable by
way of sensory and observational experiences, the truth conditions put forward by verificationists, i.e., possible patterns of
sensory or observational experience, are not only relevant to
meanings but those of them which agents and groups intend, or
are disposed to intend, their respondents to apprehend are parts
of these meanings. Thus if someone says that here is a piece of
paper, he intends his respondent to understand, among other
things, that if a person of normal vision were to look at the
object indicated he would have a certain sort of visual experience.
If one says that the sky is blue today, at least an important
part of what he means is that in looking up one will see an
expanse of blue. If one says that the dog is in the next room,
at least an important part of what is meant is that if one were
to enter that room he would observe a certain familiar vivacious
barking animal; and if one says that thunder always follows lightning, an import part of what he means is that if one recalls conditions preceding the observed instances of thunder, he normally
finds among them observed flashings of lightning.

The experiential truth conditions indicated by the criteria
put forward by verificationists are, moreover, by no means the
only experiential truth conditions that are pertinent to meanings.
As most of the writers referred to in the third part of the first
section of this chapter as advocates of truth-conditional views
as well as some verificationists have pointed out, the class of truth
conditions pertinent to meanings can be enlarged in several ways
beyond the limits suggested by verification criteria. Each of these
enlargements discloses experiential truth conditions that are pertinent to the meanings of a larger group of bearers of meaning.

One enlargement suggested by the writers under consideration
is the inclusion of experiences neither actually nor technically

possible but still possible in principle. On the basis of such an enlargement, kinds of experiences than an observer would have even at the most distant and inaccessible parts of the universe, or at the farthest reaches of the past or the future, may come to be included in the meanings of statements about events at such places and times; and nothing of which there could conceivably be any sensory or observational experience would be excluded from the meaningful or such that at least a part of its meaning could not be characterized.

A second expansion of the class of experiential truth conditions relevant to meanings, proposed by experiential-truth-conditional theories such as those of Bergmann and Lewis, consists of the inclusion of truth conditions of words or phrases that may apply to or be *true* of something. This extention of the applicability of truth conditions to words and phrases, avoids objections to verifiability criteria to the effect that they tell us nothing of the meanings of non-sentential expressions and that they mistakenly require us to know the truth conditions of sentences before we know the meanings of sentences. If experiential truth conditions are applicable to words and phrases as well as to sentences, the meanings of the words and phrases composing a sentence can be at least partially ascertained by way of their experiential truth conditions before the question of the truth conditions of the sentence is raised; and by considering these meanings within the patterns of grammar and the contexts in which they occur, one may arrive at the meaning of a sentence without raising the question of its truth conditions. To be sure, in arriving at the meaning of a sentence one may have also arrived at certain of the truth conditions of the sentence, but the latter will be dependent on the former and not conversely. The enlargement of the class of truth conditions to include those of words and phrases also helps one to see how sentence involving logical confusions and even self-contradictions, and hence being inapplicable in any state of affairs, can none the less have meanings. Moreover, it also shows us how questions, commands, requests, and all manner of other non-declarative sentences can be empirically meaningful without needing to be verifiable sentences.

A third, and more important, expansion of experiential truth conditions suggested by verification criteria, proposed especially by Lewis and to a more limited extent by Bergmann, is to the effect that experiential truth conditions relevant to meanings are to include a considerable variety of cognitive, emotional, and valuational conditions not properly regarded as either sensory or observational. As Lewis plausibly argues, the experiential conditions relevant to the meanings of some expressions cannot be limited to observations or sensory experiences but must include feelings; and even logic must in the end rest upon intimations that are not sensory. A sound empiricism must recognize the whole range of experience, each part in its appropriate place. This sort of expansion of the experiential truth conditions of expressions enables a view that equates truth conditions with meanings to claim that experiential truth conditions can form substantial parts of the meanings of many expressions from which they would otherwise be excluded. Thus, affective and conative experience patterns now become parts of the meanings of statements concerning all manner of feeling, impulse, and thought which otherwise—on older verificationist principles—would have had to be regarded as entirely dependent for their meanings upon behavioral criteria. Similarly, meanings of statements and terms involving scientific generalizations come to include those inductive acceptances of certain ways of putting data together as reasonable that are characteristic of everyday inference and scientific thought. Mathematical relations are seen to be less vacuous than they otherwise would appear. Inklings of incompatibilities of colors, the impossibility of two things occupying the same space at the same time, and many other similar intimations that are neither quite logical truths, nor empirical discoveries come to be incorporated in the experiential truth conditions of statements and terms that are relevant to the meanings of these statements and terms. If someone says that it can't rain today because it's never rained when there were no clouds, the pattern of assurance of the continuity of past, present, and future is relevant to his meaning; and when one reminds someone that the box can't be blue because it's red, the patterns of his experiential, but not strictly sensory, assurance of the incompatibility of colors is involved in his meaning. When I say I have a pain in my hand or that I am sad, a part of what I mean includes the patterns of my own experience of my pain or sadness, and my meaning is not wholly dependent, if indeed it is dependent at all, upon observable criteria.

In sum, one seems to be justified in saying something like the following about the role or truth conditions in meanings. Declarative sentences to the confirmation of which sensory and observational conditions are relevant have such conditions as parts of their meanings. A great many more declarative sentences to the confirmation of which a wider range of experiences are relevant have experiential conditions as parts of their meanings. Most substantive terms have dispositional meanings in terms of experiential conditions that would obtain if they should be true of something. Accordingly, many discursive sentences concerning matters which cannot be tested are still meaningful by way of experiential truth conditions implicit in the arrangement of their terms in their contexts. But apart from some experiential truth conditions no sentence can be meaningful.

To say that experiential truth conditions are included in the meanings of most substantive words and virtually all sentences is, however, not to say that meanings are to be thought of as exclusively or even necessarily primarily experiential truth conditions. Meanings often clearly include other factors such as referential and affective patterns. Moreover, even the experiential truth conditions that enter into meanings are not meanings merely because they are truth conditions. They are rather truth conditions because they are meanings. Truth conditions are useful criteria of meanings and are sometimes coincident with meanings; but even when they are identical with meanings, their meaning aspect remains prior to their truth conditional one. A speaker intends what he does in speaking primarily as his meaning and only secondarily as a set of truth conditions; and a hearer gets what a speaker intends first as a meaning and only on the basis of that as a set of truth conditions. A word means what speakers intend in using it and only by way of speaker's intentions does it involve truth conditions.

CHAPTER VIII

USES AND MEANINGS

The suggestion that meaning is in some fundamental way connected with use goes back at least as far as Socrates who, whatever he took meaning to be, sought out the meanings of words by inquiring into ways in which people used words. This sort of search has been in some measure continued by almost all subsequent philosophers. In the works of the American philosophers Peirce, James, and Dewey, a notion of meaning as function became explicit. However, it was in the "ordinary language" philosophy, centered first in Cambridge and then in Oxford, that the notion that use either is meaning or is the primary clue to the discernment of meaning came to occupy a central role in philosophical method. In discussing use and meaning I proposed first to sketch some leading ideas of certain representative and highly influential advocates of use approaches to meaning. I shall then set forth the major features of three different kinds of use approaches to meaning and go on to indicate some principal merits and deficiencies of each of these approaches.

1. Some Recent Advocates of Use Approaches to Meaning

a. Not long after the publication of his *Tractatus Logico Philosophicus*, Ludwig Wittgenstein began a devastating attack upon the logical atomism of his own earlier view and of other then current atomistic accounts of meaning. As an alternative to all such views, he urged that inquiry be focused upon use rather than meaning but developed no systematic account of the character of use. Both his criticism of other views and his alternative proposals have had far-reaching effects upon current accounts of meaning.

According to Wittgenstein's earlier view of meaning as

216   THE CONCEPT OF MEANING

presented in the *Tractatus*, in an ideal language designed to
avoid the inaccuracies and ambiguities of ordinary language and
to reveal the basic character of language, atomic sentences
picture connections of simple objects, refer to atomic facts, are
truth-functionally combined to form complex sentences, and
enter into inferences only through a calculus of tautologies. In
Wittgenstein's later thought, with which the present account is
primarily concerned, ordinary language, instead of being an
inferior instrument to be replaced by a better one, is in the end
the only workable instrument we have and is quite adequate
both for ordinary and philosophical purposes. Thus "when I talk
about language... I must speak the language of everyday. Is this
language too coarse and material for what we cant to say? Then
how is another one to be constructed?....In giving explanations I
already have to use language full-blown (not some sort of pre-
paratory, provisional one.)"[1] One may be inclined to think that
an unanalyzed sentence loses much of the meaning of an analyzed
one, but the converse is equally true.[2]

    The search for simplicity is after all a vain search, and to
suppose that sentences picture their meanings is a serious mistake.
We can represent some words by pictures, but any picture can
be used in a variety of different ways.[3] Indeed, it is in large
measure by the pictures which we tend to force upon words that
we are misled in the interpretation of language, for our pictures
merely trace "the frame through which we look at" a thing, not
the "thing's nature."[4] The expressions that we use instead of being
crystal clear are often quite properly indefinite in varying degrees.[5]
The logic in terms of which we draw inferences, instead of being a
smooth calculus of tautologies, is a wide diversity of principles
agreed upon by virtue of our ways of life and our common
characteristics as human beings. It is built, not for smooth surfaces, but to take hold upon the "rough ground" upon which it
must operate. "We want to walk; so we need friction."[6]

---

[1]Ludwig Wittgenstein, *Philosophical Investigations,* Tr. By G. E. M.
Anscombe (New York: The Macmillan Company, 1953), p. 48b.
    [2]*Ibid.,* pp. 30e ff.
    [3]*Ibid.,* p. 54e.
    [4]*Ibid.,* pp. 48e and 127e.
    [5]*Ibid.,* pp. 45e ff.
    [6]*Ibid.,* p. 46e.

The notion that what an expression means is always something that can be pointed out or defined ostensively is, Wittgenstein holds, obviously false; for "an ostensive definition can be
variously interpreted in *every* case"[7] and, in any event, always
requires substantial prior understanding of language. To suppose,
as Augustine did, that meanings are commonly things or events
that can be referred to is a crude mistake. Such a view may
work for the most primitive sort of language, but it will not do
for the sort of language we use.[8] Naming belongs primarily to
the teaching and learning of language not to the using of language. To equate meaning with some sort of experience is by
no means unnatural but nearly always misleading, for "the meaning of a word is not the experience one has in saying or hearing
it."[9] Images may often be associated with meaningful experiences
but are by no means essential to them. "The same thing can come
before our minds when we hear the word and the application will
still be different."[10] No such "criterion for the sameness of two
images" can be found as is required for sameness of meaning.[11]
Actually, "it is no more essential to the understanding of a proposition that one should imagine anything in connection with it,
than that one should make a sketch of it."[12] Feelings, like images,
are often found with meaningful experiences, but they do not give
the individual words their meanings.[13] "Nothing is more wrong-
headed than calling meaning a mental activity."[14] "When we
want to know if someone can play chess we aren't interested in anything that goes on inside him" or in "a particular feeling," we are
interested rather in the criteria which would demonstrate his
ability.[15]

The principal constructive theme of Wittgenstein's thought
concerning meaning is its emphasis upon use as the key to
understanding. Wittgenstein's repeated counsel is that one should
look not for meaning but for use, and his counsel has become a

[7]*Ibid.*, p. 14e.
[8]*Ibid.*, p. 3e.
[9]*Ibid.*, p. 181e.
[10]*Ibid.*, p. 55e.
[11]*Ibid.*, p. 117e.
[12]*Ibid.*, p. 120e.
[13]*Ibid.*, p. 146e.
[14]*Ibid.*, p. 172e.
[15]*Ibid.*, p. 181e.

working slogan for a large group of philosophers in England and America. Wittgenstein is careful not to say that all meanings are to be equated with uses. Nevertheless, he does say that "for a large class of cases......in which we employ the word 'meaning' it can be defined thus: the meaning of a word is its use in the language."[16] Moreover, in view of the explanations of meanings that Wittgenstein actually gives, it seems not unlikely that he was inclined to think of the meanings of most words largely in terms of their uses. Instead of being regarded primarily as names, pictures and descriptions, words should be thought of largely as tools each of which has its own use.[17]

A major difficulty in the thinking of most philosophers about the meanings of words is that these philosophers have limited themselves to a narrow range of examples. The number of kinds of uses of words is very great. Just as "the hammer, pliers, saw, screw-driver, rule, glue-pot, nails and screws" in the tool box have diverse functions, so have the words in a language. Verbal expressions may be used not only in describing but also in "giving orders, and obeying them,....constructing an object.... from a description, reporting an event, speculating about an event, forming and testing a hypothesis, presenting the results of an experiment in tables and diagrams, making up a story and reading it, play-acting, singing catches, guessing riddles, making a joke.... solving a problem in practical arithmetic, translating from one language into another, asking, thanking, cursing, greeting, praying."[18] Within each of these and other broad kinds of uses of expressions are to be found the specific uses of particular words and expressions, and much of Wittgenstein's work consists of efforts to clarify uses of expressions that are especially likely to be confusing. One must not, however, expect to find, even for a single word, just one meaning or even a class of meanings having a common property. Meanings of words are rather like families in that each involves "a complicated network of similarities overlapping and criss-crossing."[19]

To speak of the meaning of a term as its use is of course to

---

[16]*Ibid.*, p. 20e.
[17]*Ibid.*, p. 6e.
[18]*Ibid.*, pp. 11e f.
[19]*Ibid.*, p. 32e.

speak in rather general terms. Wittgenstein makes what he has in mind more specific in a number of different ways. For one thing, the use of an expression is never an isolated function but is always an integral part of an entire way of life. Thus the agreement of mathematicians depends upon agreement in language, which is in the end "not agreement in opinions but in form of life."[20] In like manner, the uses of "belief," "hope," and "grief" are integral to "the weave of our lives."[21] Pretending depends upon a mode of life in which animals do not share,[22] and "if a lion could talk, we could not understand him." More specifically, the use of any particular expression depends upon the language system to which it belongs. There can be no private language including, for example, terms for one's own pains known only to oneself; for even the naming of pains requires a prior language system and the recognition of pains requires criteria dependent upon such a system.[23] It is impossible to intend to play chess unless there is already a game of chess,[24] or to tell anyone what the chess king is unless he knows the rules of chess.[25] To raise intelligent questions about words or to give explanations, "I already have to use language fullblown."[26]

The uses of words must be construed in terms, not only of general ways of life and language systems, but also of particular settings and purposes. Thus whether or not an expression is a word or a proposition "depends on the situation in which it is uttered or written."[27] To determine whether or not an apparently self-evident sentence such as "I am here" makes sense, one "should ask himself in what special circumstances this sentence is actually used.[28] Similarly, to determine whether or not an odd statement, e.g., to the effect that a pot talks, makes sense we should need to "have a clear picture of the circumstances."[29] Repeatedly, one must ask "under what circumstances does it make

---

[20]*Ibid.*, p. 88e.
[21]*Ibid.*, p. 174e.
[22]*Ibid.*, p. 90e and *Ibid.*, p. 223e.
[23]*Ibid.*, pp. 88e ff.
[24]*Ibid.*, p. 82e.
[25]*Ibid.*, p. 15e.
[26]*Ibid.*, p. 49e.
[27]*Ibid.*, p. 24e.
[28]*Ibid.*, p. 48e.
[29]*Ibid.*, p. 97e.

sense to say 'I meant'," and "what circumstances justify me in saying 'He means . . . .'?"[30] Questions of understanding are questions of application rather than questions of feeling,[31] and application is often best determined by behavior[32] and demonstrated capacity to "go on." Only when he has learned to continue beyond a given number does a child understand natural numbers.[33]

Wittgenstein often represents the use in which a meaning consists as a purpose of an expression. Thus when a child hears an utterance, what counts is not his getting a picture but his grasping the purpose of the utterance;[34] and to clarify the meaning of a statement, one must ask "for what purpose do we say this?"[35]

One is often disposed to think of the apprehension of the meaning of an expression as an interpretation that is subsequent to the hearing or reading of the expression. But the apprehension of a meaning is more intimately related to the expression than that. It is rather like seeing something in a certain way, as when one sees a set of lines now as a solid cube and now as a hollow inverted one, or a drawing, now as a duck and now as a rabbit.[36] It requires no intermediate entities and can occur at once and without being subject to rational control.

b. Like Wittgenstein, John Austin held that the bearers of meaning most worthy of investigation consisted of expressions of ordinary language. To be sure such expressions may be imperfect and one may even "be compelled to straighten them out to some extent."[37] However, instead of being inferior to invented languages, they are likely to include distinctions far more refined and complex than any individual is "likely to think up."[38] They are the tools with which we must work, and to have clean tools whose uses are well understood, is a prime requisite of good workmanship.[39]

---

[30]*Ibid.*, p. 149e.
[31]*Ibid.*, pp. 58e and 126e.
[32]*Ibid.*, p. 417e.
[33]*Ibid.*, pp. 57e ff.
[34]*Ibid.*, p. 4e, see also pp. 91e f.
[35]*Ibid.*, p. 137e.
[36]*Ibid.*, pp. 194e ff.
[37]John Austin, *Philosophical Papers* (Oxford: Clarendon Press 1961), p. 181.
[38]*Ibid.*, p. 130.

In an early essay on "The Meaning of a Word," Austin rejects the notions of concepts and propositions as meanings of words and sentences, renounces the quest for anything like meaning in general, and points out that there are many different reasons for people's using the same word for different things that require no doctrine of universals. In his subsequent essay on "How to Talk," he partly withdraws the nominalism of this early essay,[40] and in "A Plea for Excuses" he speaks diffidently of 'meanings,' whatever they may be."[41] Austin never simply equates meanings with uses and in his *How to Do Things with Words* repeatedly suggests, but without explanation, that meaning as such is to be identified with sense and reference, which are distinguishable from the speech acts with which he is primarily concerned.[42] Meanings are, however, for him, revealed only by detailed investigation of uses.[43]

The main focus of Austin's attention is the uses of expressions thought of as speech acts. The discipline through which uses are thus sought requires us to look "not merely at words.....but also at the realities we use words to talk about."[44] It is best referred to not as "linguistic' or 'analytic' philosophy" but as "linguistic phenomenology."[45] Such inquiry has at its disposal the wealth of data found in dictionaries, the impressive body of the law, and findings of psychologists.[46] Given ample patience, it should enable us to sketch out in considerable detail the patterns of use of a great variety of words.

Statements are, Austin holds, either constantive or performative. Constantive statements are "strightforward statements of fact," which are either true or false.[47] Performative utterances as such "do not 'describe' or 'report' or constate anything at all,

---

[39]*Ibid.*, p. 129 f.
[40]Roderick Chisholm, "Austin's *Philosophical Papers*," *Mind,* Vol. LXXIII (January, 1964), pp. 1-26.
[41]*Philosophical Papers,* p. 130.
[42]J. L. Austin, *How to Do Things with Words* (Cambridge: Harvard University Press, 1962), pp. 95 ff, 108, and 147. See also *Philosophical Studies,* pp. 181 ff.
[43]*Ibid.*, pp. 25 ff.
[44]*Ibid.*, p. 130.
[45]*Ibid.*, p. 131.
[46]*Ibid.*, pp. 134 f.
[47]*How to Do Things With Words,* p. 3.

are not 'true or false'; and" "the uttering of the sentence is, or is a part of, the doing of an action, which.....would not normally be described as saying something."⁴⁸ They include such expressions as "I do...." as uttered in the course of the marriage ceremony; " 'I name this ship the *Queen Elizabeth*' as uttered when smashing the bottle against the stem" and "I bet you a six-pence it will rain tomorrow."⁴⁹ All such expressions can, without being either true or false, be felicitous or infelicitous depending upon whether or not the words, circumstances, procedures, and persons are appropriate to the performance undertaken.

Careful reflection reveals, however, that even the making of a constative statement is, like the making of a performative statement, a verbal act. Thus analysis of the kinds of verbal acts becomes a sort of comprehensive analysis of linguistic activity both interesting in its own broad character and among the best ways of getting at more specific uses and meanings. Verbal acts are of three main kinds or levels: the "locutionary," "illocutionary," and "perlocutionary." A locutionary act is in general the uttering of a certain sentence "with a certain 'meaning,'....i.e., with a certain sense and with a certain reference."⁵⁰ It is "saying something in.....(the) full normal sense."⁵¹ It involves a "phonetic act," that is, making a noise; a "phatic act," that is, the "uttering of certain vocables.....as belonging to a certain vocabulary ... and as conforming to a certain grammar;" and a "rhetic act," that is, "using vocables with a certain more-or-less definite sense and reference."⁵² Performance of a locutionary act is also performance of an illocutionary act. It is an act *in* saying something as opposed to performance of an act *of* saying something.⁵³ It is an act such as informing, ordering, warning, suggesting, or promising in its own character and in abstraction from its normal consequences. Special consequences sometimes required for the happy or successful completion of an illocutionary act are that what is said be understood, that certain effects inconsistent with intended ones (e.g., calling a ship by a name different from the one to be given)

⁴⁸*Ibid.*, p. 5; see also *Philosophical Studies*, p. 222.
⁴⁹*How to Do Things With Words*, p. 5.
⁵⁰*Ibid.*, p. 94.
⁵¹*Ibid.*
⁵²*Ibid.*, pp. 95 ff.
⁵³*Ibid.*, p. 99.

be excluded, and leading by conventions to certain types of responses such as answers to questions.[54] Perlocutionary acts are acts of bringing about the normal consequences of what we say. They are "what we achieve by saying something" and accordingly include "convincing, persuading, deterring, and....surprising or misleading."[55]

The force of an expression, which is at least as important as its meaning, can be understood only in the light of the character of the illocutionary and perlocutionary acts to which it belongs; and even the meaning of an expression, though specifically belonging to the locutionary act, is adequately seen only in the light of the full range of speech acts to which it belongs. What specifically the understanding of the meaning requires is, however, understanding of syntax and circumstances of utterance. According to one simplified model commonly and properly used, major expressions consist, in simple instances, of item words and type words, the former having references or indicating objects or events and the latter having senses or suggesting patterns.[56] "That is a daphnia" would be a case in point, the first term being an item word and the last a type word.[57] Even this sort of simplified model, as it is actually exemplified, yields at least four different kinds of speech acts, and each of these may involve a variety of meanings depending upon the circumstances of utterance. With regard to a certain flower, as I say, "That is a daphnia," I may be calling the flower a daphnia, describing it as a daphnia, exemplifying "daphnia," or classifying it as a daphnia.[58]

In order to get more specifically at the aspect of the uses of an expression that are closely related to its meaning, one must examine the precise syntax and the particular circumstances of its utterance in detail and point out what one would say under various conditions. Thus, for example, an adequate account of the meaning of the verb "to know" involves recognizing that one appropriately asks "How do you know?" never "Why do you

---

[54]*Ibid.*, pp. 115 f.
[55]*Ibid.*, p. 108.
[56]*Philosophical Studies*, pp. 181 ff.
[57]*Ibid.*, p. 189.
[58]*Ibid.*, p. 194.

know?" and "Why do you believe?" never "How do you believe?"[59]
It also requires recognizing that properly saying that one knows
something includes being sure, being in a position to be sure, having
come to be in such a position, being able to distinguish the kind of
thing one is sure about, having a suitable method for so doing,
and taking a pledge of commitment beyond merely stating a
fact.[60] Similarly, an adequate understanding of pretending involves recognizing that "pretend" is a verb so used that one can
properly be said to be pretending only if, e.g., one is not actually
doing the thing he is said to be pretending to do, is "present and
active," and publicly behaves so as "to disguise some reality."[61]

c. The principal target of the polemical part of Gilbert Ryle's
essay, "The theory of Meaning," is the view that meaning is
naming and that meanings are basically entities named, as Fido
is named "Fido." The origin of this view in modern philosophy
is to be found, Ryle thinks, in J. S. Mill's treatment of all words
as names.[62] Although Mill himself saw clearly enough that certain
terms basic to logic were not names and that proper names had no
meanings and were to be distinguished from common names, which
had connotations as well was denotations; his followers lost sight
of the more refined aspects of his theory and stressed the denotational side of his view exclusively. They were thus misled into
supposing that platonistically conceived classes and properties
must be posited as entities named by predicate terms. Such a
supposition, however, inevitably brought about its own collapse;
for, as Russell saw, the concept of classes leads to such self-contradictory notions as that of the class of classes not members of
themselves. In any case, the view that meaning is naming is from
the outset an implausible account and must be rejected on the
following grounds: that sentences are not, as it would imply, mere
lists of words; that descriptive phrases having different meanings
can apply to the same object; that there are "descriptive phrases
to which nothing at all answers;"[63] "that meanings are not born

[59]*Philosophical Studies*, pp. 45 ff.
[60]*Ibid.*, pp. 47 ff.
[61]*Ibid.*, pp. 210 f.
[62]Gilbert Ryle, "The Theory of Meaning" in C. A. Mace, *British Philosophy in the Mid-Century* (London: George Allen and Unwin Ltd. 1957),
pp. 240 f.
[63]*Ibid.*, p. 245.

and do not die"[64] as things named do; and that most words are not nouns.

Through the efforts of Wittgenstein and others philosophy has now been in considerable part freed from the "Fido-Fido" fallacy. Meaning can now be properly equated with use. Thus, "considering the meaning...of an expression is considering what can be said with it, [and] the meaning of....a word or phrase is a functional factor or a range of possible assertions, questions, commands, and the rest."[65] One must see words not as independent entities but in the framework of sentences. "Word meanings do not stand to sentence-meanings as atoms to molecules or as letters of the alphabet to the spellings of words, but more nearly as the tennis racquet stands to the strokes that are made with it."[66] The meaning of a term is basically the rules of its use. Thus, "the notion of meaning [is] composed of rules."[67] And "to know what an expression means involves knowing what can (logically) be said with it, ... the rules of the employment of that expression."[68] Thus meanings are like the pieces of a chess game in that they consist in what can and cannot be done with the thing in question.[69] A meaning of an expression is "a style of operation performed with it, not a nominee but a role."[70]

Professor Ryle is particularly concerned that use should not be confused with certain related notions. For one thing, use should not be confused with language. "A language....is a stock, fund or deposit of words, constructions, intonations, cliche phrases and so on."[71] Speech, on the other hand, to which use belongs is "the activity.....of saying things."[72] People may, of course, make mistakes in grammar, but these are not the sorts of mistakes of use with which philosophers are concerned and the saying "Don't ask for the meaning; ask for the use" is directed

---

[64]*Ibid.*, p. 245.
[65]*Ibid.*, p. 248.
[66]*Ibid.*, p. 249.
[67]*Ibid.*, p. 254.
[68]*Ibid.*
[69]*Ibid.*, p. 255.
[70]*Ibid.*, p. 262.
[71]Gilbert Ryle, "Use Usage and Meaning" in *Aristotelian Society, Supplementary Volume* 35 (1961), p. 223.
[72]*Ibid.*

"to philosophers and not to lexicographers or translators."[73] "Logical grammar" is quite different from the grammar of a language. Use is also, and for similar reasons, to be distinguished from usage. "A usage is a custom, practice, fashion or vogue. It can be local or widespread, obsolete or current, rural or urban, vulgar or academic." "Use, by contrast, is a technique, knack, or method."[74] It presupposes language and usage and, given these, it is essentially determined. One can go wrong regarding it and either one has it or not. It is quite distinct from style, which builds upon it.[75] Use is also to be distinguished from "utility." questions."[76]

Two other characteristic ideas of Ryle's require mention in passing. The first is Ryle's claim that that which has use consists of words rather than sentences. Ryle holds that to a word belongs "a body of unwritten rules"[77] and that one who has gotten these rules understands the word; but that there is no such body of rules for a sentence. When one has gotten his words and the rules of grammar, one can construct his own sentences; so that if a sentence has meaning, it does so in a manner quite different from that in which a word does. "Sentences and clauses make sense or make no sense, where words neither make sense nor do not make sense but only have meanings."[78] The remaining characteristic claim of Ryle requiring mention here is the claim that whereas philosophers who equate meaning with use often insist that philosophy requires the use of ordinary expressions only and must express itself in ordinary language, philosophy may in fact properly inquire concerning extraordinary uses and express itself in technical terms. The focus of philosophy upon ordinary use and non-technical explanatory terms is, Ryle thinks, guided, not by any *a priori* restrictions, but by the practical considerations that inquiry concerning stock uses is more fruitful than inquiry concerning extraordinary uses and that explanation in non-technical terms is usually more enlightening than explanation in technical ones.

---

[73]*Ibid.*, p. 230.
[74]Gilbert Ryle, "Ordinary Language" in V. C. Chappell, *Ordinary Language* (Englewood Cliffs: Prentice-Hall, 1964), p. 31.
[75]*Ibid.*, p. 40.
[76]*Ibid.*, p. 30.
[77]*Ibid.*, p. 35.
[78]*Ibid.*, p. 35.

2. Principal Varieties of Use Approaches to Meaning

As the foregoing accounts will already have suggested use can be construed in a number of different ways giving rise to a number of different use approaches to meaning. Thus the use of an expression may be construed either as circumstances regularly accompanying occurrences of the expression, as rules for the employment of the expression, or as functions of the expression. Approaches to meaning corresponding to each of these constructions of use have been frequently developed in recent years both by the writers already considered and by other writers as well. None of the writers considered has stressed any one of these approaches to meaning to the exclusion of the others. However, even these writers tend from time to time to stress one or another of these approaches more than the others; and other writers, now to be mentioned alongside those previously considered are much more disposed to stress one approach in preference to the others.

a. The approach to meanings of expressions by way of use construed as circumstances regularly accompanying occurrences of these expressions is to be found in certain parts of the works of all of the writers so far considered.

Wittgenstein in his *Philosophical Investigations* admonishes anyone endeavoring to understand an expression to ask such questions as these following: "Have we a clear picture of the circumstances in which we should say that....."[79] In what situations do we say.....?" "In what circumstances should I say.....?"[80] "What circumstances justify me in saying....?[81] "In what sort of context does.....occur?"[82] In a somewhat similar vein, Austin, in his essay, "The Meaning of a Word," suggests for clarifying meanings of words, the expedient of "getting the questioner to *imagine*, or even actually *experience*, situations which we should describe correctly by sentences containing the words."[83] Austin's

---

[79]*Op. cit.*, p. 97e.
[80]*Ibid.*, p. 125e f.
[81]*Ibid.*, p. 149e.
[82]*Ibid.*, p. 188e.
[83]*Philosophical Essays*, p. 25.

own penetrating analyses of the meanings of the words he selects for special study consist of detailed accounts of just such situations. Although Ryle regards regularities in the conditions of employment of terms as merely "usages" with which philosophical inquiry into meanings is not directly concerned, even he regards inquiry into such regularities as having a place in inquiry into meanings, and a good many of his own accounts of meanings of particular words are in large measure accounts of circumstances in which words are regularly employed.

Oxford philosopher Jonathan Cohen stresses interpretation of use as regularity of circumstances more than any of the writers thus far considered. He regards the opposing *de jure*, or rule-of-use interpretation, which he ascribes to many of his Oxford colleagues, as suited rather to the school-room than to the serious study of language. Much better for purposes of serious study is, he thinks, the interpretation in terms of "regularity of use," a *de facto* view that holds "that most statements about meanings are, or should be, construed as statements about occurrences, states, situations, or habits of certain sorts and their observable or introspectable relations to one another."[84] Cohen's account of use and meaning does not, however, exclude other phases of use. The facts with which the uses pertinent to the meanings of a sentence are to be equated can, Cohen thinks, be interpreted either causally or purposively without affecting the basic semantic considerations.[85] Moreover, the meaning of a word is fully shown not merely by "descriptions of the ends that its use achieves or of the occasions that evoke its exclamation...but by indicating what it contributes to the meaning of those whole utterances in which it occurs."[86]

An American writer Paul Ziff has undertaken to show in careful detail how meanings can be discerned by tracing out nonsyntactic semantic regularities."[87] Basic meanings are, according to Ziff, to be found through noting regularities actually found

---

[84]Jonathan Cohen, *The Diversity of Meaning* (London: Methuen and Co. Ltd. 1962), p. 24.
[85]*Ibid.*, pp. 25 ff.
[86]*Ibid.*, pp. 45 f.
[87]Paul Ziff, *Semantic Analysis* (Ithaca: Cornell University Press, 1960), p. 42.

in occurrences of expressions. Thus if someone says, "The door is open," then usually "some" "situationally determined door is open." When someone says, "Look at that swine;" generally there is a swine present in the context of the utterance.[88] "If 'Hello' is uttered, then generally one person is greeting one or more others."[89] Indeed "generally speaking, a metalinguistic statement of a regularity pertaining to U_i will have the form 'If U_i is uttered then generally such and such.' "[90] Projections of basic meanings, may be discerned by pairing expressions for which specific regularity conditions are not yet given with those for which such conditions are available. Thus while "There is a purple gila monster on my lap staring at me" has no specific conditions for utterance, it can be paired with sentences that do and so achieve meaning.[91] In this manner statements of non-repeatable facts, such as Caesar's crossing the Rubicon at a specific time, can also be handled. So also can statements about the past and about dreams.[92] A full formulation of the meaning of any term will include what may be called the distributive set for that word, i.e., the set of contexts in which it occurs. Such a set for the word "good" will include for example: "That is good," "What good is that?" and "She is good to me." A full formulation of the meaning of a word will also include its "contrastive" set, i.e., the set of words that could be put in place of the word is the contexts in which the word occurs. The contrastive set of the term "good" include for example "That is fine," "That is pleasant," and "She is mean to me."[93] In order to achieve a satisfactory account of the meaning of a term, one must form an hypothesis grounded in the relevant distributive and contrastive sets and then test this hypothesis to see if it works for varied cases and explains the deviations.[94]

Another American writer William P. Alston places the regularity account of use within a quasi normative framework. Thus, for Alston, the use of an expression that is relevant to its

[88]*Ibid.*, pp. 125 and 45.
[89]*Ibid.*, p. 46.
[90]*Ibid.*, p. 46.
[91]*Ibid.*, p. 67.
[92]*Ibid.*, pp. 142 ff.
[93]*Ibid.*, p. 147.
[94]*Ibid.*, pp. 146-149.

meaning consists of those conditions which would regularly be taken to be necessary to what Austin has called the illocutionary force of the expression. For example, the meaning of the expression "to serve," as in tennis, is given by mentioning conditions such that if one were in a given instance "to admit as certain that one of these conditions did not hold," he could not use the expression to perform the illocutionary act normally performed by the verb "to serve."[95]

b. Although the approach to meanings of expressions by way of use construed as rules for the employment of these expressions is different from, and more complex than, the approach to meanings of expressions by way of use construed as circumstances regularly accompanying these expressions, the former approach as well as the latter is present in the works of all of the writers considered in the first section of this chapter. This approach is suggested in Wittgenstein's concept of language as consisting of games constituted by rules. Many different games, Wittgenstein thinks, make up a language, and a language is made up largely of its rules. Among the language games constituting a language, the naming game is likely to be a relatively small and unimportant part, if, indeed, it can really be said to be a part at all. Understanding a word is, Wittgenstein thinks, somewhat like understanding what the king is in chess, dependent in a large part upon knowing the rules.[96] Rules are not, however, for Wittgenstein, all there is to use; for, in his thought, the use of idea is prior to the rule-of-the-game idea, and even in chess the use of the king can sometimes be learned by observation without learning the rules.[97] Moreover, the rules can be changed and even made up as one goes along.[98]

In the thought of Ryle the rule aspect of use tends to take precedence over the others. While use may, for Ryle, be built upon usage, it consists not of those mere regularities which constitute usage but of those rules and capacities that grow out of regularities. Use, and meaning, are for Ryle "compact of rules," so that "to know what an expression means involves knowing what can

---

[95]*Ibid.*, p. 43.
[96]*Philosophical Investigations*, p. 14e.
[97]*Ibid.*, pp. 14e and 27e.
[98]*Ibid.*, p. 37e.

(logically) be said with it and what cannot (logically) be said with it. It involves knowing a set of bans, fiats, and obligations, or, in a word, it is to know the rules of the employment of that expression."[99]

Although John Austin was, for reasons that will subsequently appear, less concerned with rules directly governing meanings than with rules concerning the performing of certain aspects of speech acts; he was much concerned with these latter, and these latter have important indirect bearings on meanings. Thus, in his paper on "Performative Utterances," Austin writes of the uses of such expressions as "I do take this woman to be my lawful wedded wife" and "I name this ship the *Queen Elizabeth*," as used in the acts of marrying a wife and christening a ship, that to perform the acts in question at all, the use of these expressions must conform to the rules that "the convention invoked must exist and be accepted.....[and] that the circumstances in which we purport to invoke the procedure must be appropriate for its invocation." He then goes on to indicate a number of less rigorous requirements not always necessary for the performance of the acts in question but required for the felicitous performance of these acts, for example, that the ceremony be carried through "correctly and completely," that the agent "have certain feelings and intentions," that there be no serious misunderstanding," and that there be no "duress."[100]

Whereas rules of use have been discussed informally and unsystematically for particular expressions by Wittgenstein, Ryle, Austin and other "ordinary language" philosophers, Noam Chomsky, Jarrold Katz and other linguistically oriented philosophers at M.I.T. have undertaken to work out a formal system of rules of grammar and word meaning that will constitute a theory of language capable of predicting what any competent user of a language will use any expression in that language to mean or will understand by that expression. A language, these writers contend, in the tradition of Humboldt, is a vast interrelated system of terms and structures such that every part of it affects every other and that if one part is activated "the whole system will

---

[99]Gilbert Ryle, "The Theory of Meaning," p. 254.
[100]J. L. Austin, *Philosophical Papers,* pp. 224 ff.

resonate."[101] The sentences, in which alone fully developed meanings are expressed, far from acquiring meanings by mere conjunctions of meanings of collection of words, become meaningful only as meanings are built up from the meanings of the constituent words through a complex rule-constituted grammar mastered by competent users of a language. Substantial parts of this grammar are universal and depend upon innate tendencies common to human beings.[102] When a child is confronted with speech data of his cultural setting, he progressively formulates, in the light of his shared innate tendencies, increasingly successful hypotheses regarding the syntax of his language, until at a fairly early age he has essentially mastered and internalized a system of rules constituting the syntactical aspect of his language. Alongside this syntactical knowledge he also comes to develop formal and substantive meaning rules. Thus, when a competent user of a language speaks, he produces meaningful sounds that, in line with internalized syntactical rules, build up the expression of his full meaning.[103] By taking not of the internal system of syntactical and meaning rules employed by competent users of a language, one may work out a precise theory of a language such as will enable one to ascertain the meaning of any given expression in the language. To apply such a theory to a sentence, one needs to trace out the structure of the sentence according to the syntactical part of the theory and then to apply to the ascertained structure a carefully formulated dictionary of meaning rules that supplies both formal features of the terms and appropriate substantive meaning markers. In so doing, one may learn that a sentence is anomalous if some of the various parts will not fit together, that it is analytic if its subject includes its predicate, or that two sentences are synonymous if their structures and markers are alike. If the theory is correct, the meaning discerned through its application will conform to the meaning intuitively assigned to a sentence by fluent speakers of the language.

---

[101]Noam Chomsky, "Current Issues in Linguistic Theory" in Jerry Fodor and Jerrold J. Katz, *The Structure of Language* (Englewood Cliffs: Prentice-Hall, Inc., 1964), p. 58.

[102]Noam Chomsky, *Aspects of the Theory of Syntax* (Cambridge: The M.I.T. Press, 1965), pp. 47 ff. and Jerrold J. Katz, *The Philosophy of Language*, pp. 240 ff.

[103]*Ibid.*, Chap. IV.

c. Perhaps the most natural way to construe the notion of the use of an expression is to think of it as the function, role, job, or purpose of the expression. The approach to meaning by way of use construed in this way has had a considerable place in current thought concerning meaning.

Thus, in considering a picture account of the meanings of a word, Wittgenstein invites us to consider "the purpose of the word" and notes that its function is not calling pictures to mind.[104] Similarly, in considering an explanation of obedience to an order, he asks us to inquire: "For what purpose do we say this? What kinds of actions accompany these words? In what scenes will they be used and what for?"[105] He is, moreover, very fond of representing words as tools and of each of the many varieties of language as "a part of an activity, or form of life."[106] The uses with which he equates many meanings seem indeed to be in large measure equatable with functions in a form of life.[107]

Although Ryle is careful to point out that "questions of the use of an expression are "How-questions not What-for-questions,"[108] he wishes to think of the meanings of expressions largely in terms of functions or roles. Thus, "the significance of an expression and the powers or functions in chess of a pawn, or the queen have much in common. To know where the knight can and cannot be, one must know the rules of chess."[109] The meaning of a word he suggests is its role," "the way of wielding" it.[110] Thus, "to know what an expression means is to know how it may and may not be employed,"[111] and "learning the meaning of an expression is..... learning to operate with an expression and with any other expression equivalent with it."[112] Meanings are not things but "powers," "jobs" and "values." "The meaning of an expression is not an entity denoted by it, but a style of operation performed with it not a nominee but a role."

104*Philosophical Investigations,* p. 4e.
105*Ibid.,* p. 137e.
106*Ibid.,* p. 11e.
107Cf. *Ibid.,* p. 20e.
108"Ordinary Language," p. 30.
109"The Theory of Meaning," p. 255.
110*Ibid.*
111*Ibid.*
112*Ibid.,* pp. 256 f.

The Danish philosopher, Niels Christensen, is in essential agreement with Ryle and others that meanings are jobs; but he makes a distinction within the notion of a job between the job to be done and the doing of the job, between function and functioning, or, as he prefers to put it, between an office and the performing of the duties of an office. For Christensen a sign or symbol is analogous to an office holder or official, and a meaning is analogous to an office.[114] The office constituting a meaning consists of the functions that an official occupying that office is to perform. To perform the functions of an indicative sentence is specifically to inform or to state a truth,[115] and to perform the functions of other expressions, such as commands, is to inform for special purposes. When expressions are not performing their functions they may still be said to "have meanings much as officials off duty have office."[116]

The most influential of recent formulations of functions of expressions are to be found in Austin's accounts of various kinds of acts. Thus Austin distinguishes between "locutionary," "illocutionary," and "perlocutionary" acts. A locutionary act is an "act of saying something" ....in the full normal sense,.....which includes the utterance of certain noises, the utterance of certain words in a certain construction, and the utterance of them with a certain "meaning" in the favorite philosophical sense of that word, i.e., with a certain sense and with a certain reference."[117] An illocutionary act is a locutionary act performed in "asking or answering a question, giving some information or an assurance or a warning, announcing a verdict or an intention, pronouncing sentence, making an appointment or an appeal or criticism, making an identification or giving a description, and the numerous like."[118] And a perlocutionary act is a speech act designed to achieve "certain consequences" beyond the "conventional" ones, including, for example, "persuading, rousing, or alarming"[119] persons to whom it is addressed.

---

[113]*Ibid.*, p. 263.
[114]Niels Egmont Christensen, *On the Nature of Meanings* (Copenhagen: Munksgaard, 1965), p. 38.
[115]*Ibid.*, pp. 57 f.
[116]*Ibid.*, p. 58.
[117]*How to Do Things with Words*, p. 94.
[118]*Ibid.*, p. 98 f.
[119]*Ibid.*, p. 103.

3. Principal Achievements and Limitations of Use Approaches to Meaning

Current approaches to meaning by way of use have been widely acclaimed as the most significant advances in theory of meaning for many centuries. If achievement of clarifications of intentional and cultural meanings that people actually attach to expressions is to be taken as a test, as in some measure it must be, then there are good reasons for thinking that this acclamation may be justified. Instead of attempting to force encountered meanings into preconceived molds, use approaches to meaning endeavor to explicate such meaning as they find them. The actual clarifications worked out in detail by way of such approaches to meaning, though scarcely spectacular, are impressive and promising. Wittgenstein has supplied new insights, for example, concerning meanings of expressions referring to actions, perceptions, and pains. John Austin has called attention to previously neglected aspects of meanings of such terms as "real," "see," "immediately see," "know," "excuses," "pretending," "if," and "can." Gilbert Ryle has appropriately focused upon previously insufficiently emphasized aspects of meanings of such terms as "mind," "intelligence," "sensation," "thought" and "observation." H. L. A. Hart and others have illuminated a number of puzzling legal terms. R. M. Hare, Stephen Toulmin and others have placed inquiry concerning ethical questions in fresh perspectives. Anthony Flew and others have disclosed neglected meanings of such well-known expressions as "free will." And a considerable number of essayists have brought to light a previously unsuspected wealth of meanings in theological and political terms earlier regarded by positivistically inclined writers as merely emotive.

Nevertheless, use approaches to meaning have some limitations even with respect to the intentional and cultural meanings to which they are designed to apply, and these limitations are currently coming increasingly to be recognized even by advocates of these approaches. Perhaps the best way to bring both the achievements and limitations of use approaches to meaning into proper perspective will be to consider successively the achievements and limitations of each of the three main types of use approaches to meaning indicated in the preceding section.

a. That circumstances in which expressions are regularly

employed can be revealing with respect to meanings of these expressions has earlier been noticed in what has been said concerning the roles of contexts, stimuli and referents in meaning situations. But contextual features can be quite remote from meanings, and stimuli and referents can be misleading with respect to meanings. The major achievement of advocates of the use approach to meaning by way of regularly recurring circumstances is to show specifically how attention to circumstances regularly recurring with expressions, and not necessarily stimuli or referents, may lead directly or indirectly to apprehensions of meanings of these expressions.

Thus, it seems clearly to be the case, as advocates of a regularity approach to meaning claim, that by comparisons even of non-linguistic circumstances in which a given expression of a language system occurs, one can progressively rule out what is unessential and focus attention upon circumstances that are crucial to the meaning of the expression. By comparing various circumstances in which the English word "red" is used, one may eliminate all manner of factors such as sizes, shapes, and weights that which are not essential to the meaning of the word, and focus upon the factor of hue that is essential. By comparing circumstances in which the word "oxygen" occurs, one may eliminate such incidental circumstances as association with nitrogen and being breathed, and focus upon crucial physical and chemical properties.

It seems even more clearly to be the case, as advocates of regularity approaches to meaning hold, that by considering the grammatical and verbal circumstances in which an expression regularly occurs, one can, within an established language system, approximate the meaning of an expression with considerable accuracy. Thus one may, in the manner of Austin, describe various verbal contexts in which the expression "know" is regularly used and, in so doing, not only eliminate circumstances that are largely irrelevant, but also distinguish varieties of meanings of the expression depending on varieties of contexts. One may also, in the manner of Ziff, systematically compare the various grammatical contexts in which an established expression occurs and, in so doing, so map out the grammatical relations of the expression as to indicate clearly the scope and character of its mesaning. One may also compare the terms that may be substituted in the contexts in which an expression may occur without apparent alteration of the meaning of that expression and the terms that may be substituted in the expression with various resulting alterations in the meaning of the expression and, in so doing, increasingly approximate the location of the expression within the system of terms that constitutes the vocabulary of a language. The actual achievements of advocates of regularity approaches to meanings are significant testimony to the essential soundness of their methods within established language systems; and that such achievements have been possible should not have been surprising; for children have always been taught and learned meanings of expressions by having their attention called to circumstances in which these expressions regularly occur, and aliens have always been able to learn new languages by similar techniques.

To be sure, one cannot directly trace out regularities of the circumstances of a token expression actually occurring in a particular verbal context, for that token expression occurs only once. However, one can follow up the regularities of instances of the type to which the token expression belongs and, in so doing, arrive at a highly plausible account of the meaning of the token expression itself. Thus, while a person may not know what my request to "go away" means just by hearing that utterance, he may by noticing circumstances accompanying similar utterances surmise the meaning of my utterance; and, in fact, it is in large measure by doing just this sort of thing that my respondents are likely to have been prepared to grasp the meaning of my spoken request.

Not only may circumstances in which bearers of meaning are regularly used be revealing with reference to the discernment of the meanings of expressions, but characteristics of these circumstances are often characteristics meant in the cultural and intentional meanings of these expressions. Situations in which one speaks of something's being "green" are very often situations in which a crucial circumstance is something's greenness; and situations in which one speaks of something's being "elliptical" are often situations in which a prominent circumstance is something's being elliptical. One is also most likely to say, "The cat is on the mat," when among present circumstances is the cat's being on the mat.

However, just because circumstances regularly associated with the uses of expressions can be enormously helpful guides to the discernment of cultural and intentional meanings of these expressions, it is important to keep in mind some major obstacles to attempts to equate these regularly recurring circumstances with these meanings or even to regard such circumstances as in themselves adequate guides to these meanings.

One reason that circumstances regularly accompanying occurrences of expressions cannot be equated with meanings of these expressions, or even regarded as in themselves adequate guides to these meanings, is that such circumstances inevitably include circumstances that have comparatively little relevance to the meanings in question and that cannot be distinguished from circumstances that are specifically relevant, by reference merely to their character as associated circumstances. Circumstances regularly accompanying the use of any word or sentence include an enormous range of chemical, physical, astronomical, geological, physiological, sociological and psychological factors that in no significant way distinguish meanings of one expression from those of another and have relatively little bearing on the meaning of any expression. Circumstances not only regularly associated with occurrences of particular expressions but peculiar to these occurrences are notoriously difficult to locate; but even when they can be found, they seem to contain factors largely unilluminating with reference to the meanings of these expressions. Thus, for example, circumstances regularly accompanying the uses of the words "purple," "ugly," and "lonely" seem clearly to include various complexes of physiological and electronic events, as well as psychological ones which are quite distinct from the cultural and intentional meanings of these expressions and at present, at any rate, throw little light upon these meanings.

Not only do circumstances regularly accompanying occurrences of expressions include circumstances relatively unilluminating with regard to intentional and cultural meanings of these expressions, but circumstances regularly accompanying occurrences of expressions also fail to include certain circumstances that are highly illuminating with regard to intentional and cultural meanings of these expressions, namely, circumstances not yet instantiated but such that if ever they were to be instantiated the expressions in question would be applicable. When a child who understands the term "man" has as yet encountered only members of his own race, possible encounters with persons of other races are highly relevant to the meaning of the term "man" in his vocabulary in that if they should be instantiated he would be ready to apply them. Even before people had encountered black swans, such a possible encounter was relevant to the meaning of the term swan in that people were ready to apply the term swan in such circumstances when these circumstances occurred. Presumably human beings more than sixteen feet tall have not yet been encountered, but circumstances in which they might be encountered are relevant to the meaning of the term "human" in that people are prepared to apply the term in case these circumstances occur. Moreover, since at any given stage of the development of an individual the range of circumstances actually encountered is limited, a very important test of the meanings of the terms in a person's vocabulary consists in the manner in which that person is prepared to apply these terms in possible, as well as actual, circumstances; and at a different level, the same sort of thing is true with respect to the terms in the vocabulary of any given group of language users.

A third reason why circumstances regularly accompanying expressions cannot be equated with, or regarded as in themselves adequate guides to meanings of, these expressions is that such circumstances afford no explanation for the capacity of competent users of a language to use and understand novel expressions. For any given individual at any given time, the proportion of the expressions he could use and understand to those he has actually used or encountered at all, not to speak of regularly encountered in specifiable circumstances, is a very small fraction. All that an individual requires to use and understand vast ranges of expressions is an initial vocabulary and certain principles of syntax by which vocabulary items may be intelligibly combined. Armed with these basic elements, he is ready to form and understand novel intelligible combinations of expressions virtually without limit. With respect to most living languages, the number of possible intelligible expressions is unimaginably large; but only a relatively small fraction of these expressions have ever been formed, and only a much smaller fraction has regularly recurred in specifiable circumstances. Capacity readily to yield novel intelligible expressions that can by no means be accounted for as regularities of actual occurrences is an evident feature of the ordered dispositions both of individuals and of groups of language users.

A further reason that circumstances in which expressions regularly occur cannot be equated with meanings of these expressions is that the relations of expressions and accompanying circumstances do not, as such, carry the sort of normative force that attaches to the relations of expressions and their meanings in an established language. Although cultural meanings come to be linked with word types by way of regular use, once the resulting usages are established, these usages come to constitute standards within language groups. Individuals tend to look to these standard usages to guide their own speech; and while usages are subject to continuous change, departures from them without good reasons are open not only to misunderstanding but also to some censure. Thus the word "horse" is not merely regularly used to mean animal of a certain sort but is such that while an individual may arbitrarily use it in a radically different way, and in the end perhaps even establish a new usage, he is in so using it likely needlessly to mislead his respondents and to be in some degree blameworthy for so doing.

One more reason why circumstances regularly accompanying expressions cannot, as such, constitute intentional or cultural meanings of these expressions is that, no matter how close their characters are to characters involved in intentional and dispositional meanings, these circumstances do not, as such, stand in certain relations essential for intentional and dispositional meanings. As was seen in earlier discussion of the ways of meaning, whatever is an intentional meaning of an expression is so by virtue of its being intended to be apprehended as intended, and whatever is a dispositional meaning of an expression is so by virtue of its being that such people are disposed to intend it to be apprehended as intended. Circumstances regularly accompanying expressions do not, as such, stand in these relations and for this reason, even if for no other, cannot, as such, constitute intentional or cultural meanings of expressions.

"Purple" culturally means purple only if people are disposed in using "purple" to mean purple, and "The cat is on the mat" means that the cat is on the mat only if that is what people are disposed in using that expression to mean. Some circumstances regularly accompanying expressions can be useful

in clarifying meanings of these expressions; but only as circumstances are linked with intentions and dispositions to convey
meanings, can circumstances that are highly relevant to meanings
be distinguished from others that are not. It is interesting to
note in this connection that even such a writer as William Alston,
who stresses the role of circumstances in meanings, implicitly
acknowledges the role of an intentional framework for intentional
and cultural meanings by equating such meanings of expression,
not with circumstances actually accompanying the uses of these
expressions, but with the conditions that one would take to be
necessary to his performing the speech acts that he performs in
using these expressions.[120]

b. Rules of use are intimately connected with circumstances
regularly accompanying expressions in that, embodied in dispositions of users of language, they select the circumstances in
which expressions are regularly used and in that they can often
be ascertained by attention to these circumstances. Accordingly,
it should scarcely be surprising to find that the approach to
meaning by way of use construed as rules of use has most of the
advantages that the approach by way of use construed as circumstantial regularities has over all previously considered approaches
to meaning. In addition, the rule-of-use approach has other advantages of its own that largely free it from the difficulties that
plague the regularity view and that render it a major step forward
in the endeavor to ascertain the character of meaning.

Rules of use, though intimately related to circumstantial
regularities, are not bound by circumstantial regularities. Hence
the approach to meaning by way of rules of use is able to avoid
being misled, as the regularity approach sometimes is, by
regularities largely unilluminating with regard to meanings but is
free to focus upon what is directly pertinent to meanings as the
regularity approach is not. The rule-of-use approach to meaning
is also, unlike the circumstantial-regularity approach, not limited
to actually occurring circumstances, but is able to give ample
weight to circumstances in which an expression would under
certain conditions be used as well as to circumstances in which
it is actually used. The circumstances in which an expression
would under specifiable conditions be used but has not yet been

---

[120]William Alston, *Philosophy of Language,* p. 43.

used are, moreover, often vital for the understanding of the expression. Thus, for example, rules of the use of "pentagonal," as embodied in the dispositions of contemporary speakers of English, determine, not only the circumstances of actual utterances of the term, but also circumstances in which the term would be used in specifiable conditions; and tests for the current meaning of the expression will inevitably have to be determined not merely in terms of how the expression has been used but more importantly in terms of how it would be used given the requisite conditions.

A further advantage of the rule-of-use approach to meaning is that it is capable, as most of the approaches previously considered are not, of doing justice to the systematic character of meanings. Few if any meanings of expressions are intelligible alone. Almost all such meanings are integral parts of whole systems of meanings. They are intricately interwoven in relations of inclusion, exclusion, implication, contradiction, comparison, and contrast, with other meanings. If meanings are regarded as stimuli, responses, referents, truth conditions, or recurring circumstances, these relations are likely to appear enigmatic; but it is of the very nature both of rules in general and of rules of meaning in particular to be related to one another in systematic order, and the relations among meanings that are actually encountered are clearly of the sorts that one should expect if meanings were constituted by rules of use.

The principal merit of the rule-of-use approach to meanings is closely connected with the one just mentioned and consists in the capacity of this approach to give a coherent account of how expressions encountered for the first time can have meanings. The significant fact involved in this consideration is not just that new expressions with news meanings can be introduced into a language by laying down adequate rules for their uses, but the much more important fact that, given a list of meaningful rule-governed linguistic expressions, the addition of relatively few further rules concerning how these expressions can be meaningfully combined can permit a user of the language to form and understand a vast range of expressions never before encountered. Thus, whereas when a child understands only single word sentences, he can say or understand little; when he masters the basic rules of the syntax of his language, he can, even with a very limited vocabulary, produce and understand a vast variety of expressions. Similarly, by the use of more complex rules of vocabulary and syntax, a competent speaker of a language becomes capable of using and understanding a virtually infinite variety of expressions. Specific rules by which this sort of achievement is possible are formulated in traditional grammars and expanded and clarified in modern generative grammars; but prior to any explicit formulation, they are rooted, as advocates of rule-of-use accounts of meaning insist, in the capacities of competent users of language.

One more merit of the rule-of-use approach to meanings is the fact that it recognizes, as no other approach so far considered does, the normative character of the relations between expressions and their cultural meanings. Cultural meanings of expressions are, to be sure, not decreed by anyone but remain closely connected with regular usages and subject to change with changes in usage. However, so long as a usage remains in force in a given language, the rules formulating it are binding upon users of that language and constitute a standard to which such users are expected to adhere except when there are good and sufficient reasons for deviations. Thus children are taught that they ought to speak and write in certain ways, and departures from standard usage-- if not of a language in general then at any rate of the dialect in force--tend to elicit uneasiness both in speakers and hearers. These considerations, which remain unrecognized in other approaches to meaning, are amply recognized in rule approaches, for to be in some sense normative is of the essence of a rule.

However, despite the very substantive theoretical and practical merits of the rule-of-use approach to meaning, the following considerations would seem to preclude any attempt to equate intentional and cultural meanings of expressions with rules of use or to regard such rules as by themselves adequate guides to these meanings.

First, although rules of use do not include circumstances entirely unilluminating regarding meanings, they do include varieties of rules that remain largely unilluminating for this purpose and that cannot, merely by way of the notion of rule-of-use, be distinguished from rules that are relevant to meanings. Such rules-of-use include, for example, rules of rhyme, meter, rhythm, and rhetoric. They also include rules for effective advertising, rules for successful propaganda, and many other kinds of rules only indirectly related to meaning rules but just as much rules of use as are meaning rules themselves. At best then, the notion of a rule-of-use requires considerable further qualification before it can be thought of as affording adequate clues to meanings, not to speak of defining them.

Second, although the cultural meanings of expressions seem always to be covered by rules of use, this is by no means always true of the intentional meanings of expressions. To be sure, in producing the utterances and inscriptions that convey intentional meanings, we are generally guided by the rules of use for these expressions. But it sometimes happens that a philosopher, a poet, or even a common man wants to express a thought or feeling for which there is no established verbal practice and no adequate rule. In such a case, he must depend upon whatever insights into causal relations and analogies he takes to be useful to supplement the available verbal expressions and hope that what he wants to say may be understood. Actually, it often happens that the accepted rules, though extremely useful, are not adequate to the meanings we wish to express, so that in speaking or writing we strive, through new arrangements and whatever other means are available, to convey fresh meanings by established words. Were it not for such efforts to reach beyond accepted rules, the basic novelties in expression that are constantly occurring would not be achievable, and languages would tend to become fixed systems capable indeed of patterns never before formulated but of no fundamental changes.

Third, no matter how closely linked to meanings rules of use may be, their logical status is so different from that of meanings that to attempt to equate the two becomes a fundamental mistake. The contents of rules and meanings stand in radically different frames. If one wished to press the connections of rules of use and meanings beyond the point to which most advocates of rule-of-use approaches to meaning wish to press it, one could make rules of use actually include meanings by saying, e.g., that a rule for the use of "x" is that "x" is to be used when one wishes to say "y" (what x means). But even then the meaning and the content of the rule lie in different logical frames. The one is something prescribed; the other, something intended or disposed to be intended. Rules of use are prescriptions for use, formulations of how to speak, direction as to how to write. Meanings are intended to be made apprehensible or disposed to be so intended. We say of rules of use, but not of meanings, that they prescribe how words are to be used, tell us under what conditions words are to be used, indicate what words are to be used when, that they are regulative, indicate how we ought to speak, that they are binding, and that they are to be obeyed but can be disobeyed. On the other hand, we say of meanings, but not of rules of use, that they are what terms, utterances and inscriptions mean; that they are what people intend to lead respondents to apprehend in producing utterances and inscriptions; that words and other expressions have them and that some of our utterances and inscriptions adequately express them while others do not. Only as one sees intentional and cultural meanings within the intentional and dispositional frames that thus sharply distinguish them from the prescriptive frames of rules does one begin to appreciate the distinctive character of such meanings; and indeed only then can one distinguish those rules that are highly relevant to intentional and cultural meanings from those who are not.

Not only are rules of use logically distinct from meanings, they seem to presuppose meanings. If rules of use consisted of prescriptions concerning how expressions are to be used in order to yield certain meanings—e.g., " '...' is to be used to say '....' "— then that they presupposed meanings would be obvious. However, even when rules of use are construed, as most advocates of the rule-of-use approach to meaning wish to construe them, as prescriptions concerning the introduction of expressions into various kinds of settings, they still seem clearly either to presuppose meanings or else to obscure meanings in a senseless regress. Every rule of use by its very nature is formulatable in words, and these words must have meanings. The meanings in question may to be sure be formulatable in further rules of use; but if any of the rules involved are to be intelligible, the process must presumably come somewhere to rest in apprehensions of meanings of words in which rules are expressed. Not only must separate words in which the rules are formulated have meanings, but the rules as wholes must have meanings. These meanings too may be construed as further rules; but rules as mere forms tell us nothing, and sooner or later apprehensions of meanings of rules as more than sentenial expressions must be achieved. Apparently then the rule of use account of meaning, helpful as it is, in the end pushes the problem of meaning a step farther back rather than resolving it.

c. One major advantage of the approach to intentional and cultural meanings by way of uses construed as functions is shared to some extent by other use approaches but is achieved more fully by this one, namely, the capacity of the function-approach to embrace and illuminate the whole range of meaningful expressions. Actually nearly all utterances and inscriptions, just by virtue of being produced with intentions to lead respondents to apprehend something as intended, have intentional meanings; and nearly all culturally accepted expressions, just by virtue of being such that people are disposed in using them in suitable contexts to apprehend something as intended, have cultural meanings. The basic question about such expressions is not whether or not they have meanings but what meanings they have. Theories of meaning often obscure these considerations, in part by focusing predominantly upon certain types of expressions to the exclusion of others, and in part by specifically ruling out certain types of expressions as nonsense. Thus, stimulus, response, and referent theories tend to exclude all expressions save those for which specific stimuli, responses and references can be found; and verification theories sometimes rule out all expressions for which no confirmations can be found. Function theories reverse this trend and specifically recognize and seek to find meanings for all expressions for which any functions whatever can be found in human speech and language. They formally attend to and inquire concerning all manner of expressions that have been taken all the while by common sense to be meaningful but that have often been obscured by other theories. Thus, not only declarative sentences subject to sensory confirmation, but other indicative sentences and all manner of questions, requests, petitions, commands, jokes, suggestions, hints, exclamations, and the like are clearly seen to be meaningful and are examined with utmost seriousness and precision.

A second significant advantage of the approach to meaning by way of use construed as function is that, in focusing upon the functions of expressions, it largely avoids the temptation, to which many accounts of meaning succumb, to classify expressions by attending only to the forms of these expressions and that, in grouping expressions in other ways, it throws a larger light upon their meanings. For example, the expression "I know that there's a bittern in the garden" is formally similar to multitudes of indicative statements, but by attending to the kind of speech act involved, Austin shows that it is also a personal certification of endorsement; and apart from recognition of this fact, the meaning of the statement cannot be fully appreciated. Similarly, the expression "He raised his arm" is formally similar to the "He hurt his arm;" but, by attending to the functions of expressions, H. L. A. Hart has succeeded in disclosing that the former kind of expression ascribes responsibility to the agent while the latter does not. Again, whereas "That is good" is formally similar to "That is blue," it has in actuality, as R. M. Hare has shown, marked affinities with "I commend that," which is relevant to its meaning. By thus mapping expressions not so much by their forms as by their functions, advocates of the function version of the use approach to meaning help to eliminate old errors, to bring about new insights, and to resolve some long-standing philosophical problems.

A third significant merit of the approach to intentional and cultural meanings of expressions by way of the uses of these expressions construed as their functions is an implicit recognition of the central roles of intentions and dispositions to intend with reference to such meanings. To be sure, most advocates of a function approach to meaning do not explicitly emphasize intentions; but one can not emphasize functions, purposes, roles, jobs, and offices of expressions, as speech acts accomplished through expressions, without implicitly recognizing the crucial character of the intentions and dispositions to intend that underlie the production of expressions; and indeed, the whole current concern with the functions of expressions is, in part at any rate, a concern with these intentions and dispositions to intend. Thus in the function version of the use account of meaning, there emerges an account of intentional and cultural meanings oriented to the intentions and dispositions that, as has been repeatedly seen, inevitably prove to be determinative of such meanings.

One more merit worthy of special mention in the approach to the intentional and cultural meanings of expressions by way of their uses construed as functions of these expressions consists in the consideration that when the functions of expressions are fully specified, they may be said actually to include the meanings of these expressions. To be sure, discussions of functions of expressions may take place either on a level of broad generalization, as when one inquires whether an expression functions as a locutionary, illocutionary or perlocutionary speech act, or on a level of more restricted generalization, as when one asks whether an illocutionary speech act is a stating or an inquiring or a requesting, etc. But ultimately we wish to specify functions of expressions more fully, and the sort of specification we seek to achieve must include reference to specific meanings; for whatever other functions an expression may have, it must exercise these functions by way of leading respondents to apprehend meanings or being suited to doing so. Thus the function, job, or role of "The dog is in the basement" is, very generally, to say something meaningful, but specifically to convey the information that the dog is in the basement; and to do this job the utterance must carry the meaning that the dog is in the basement. Similarly, the function, job, or role of "I promise that I will come" is to make a certain promise, and to this end it must convey some meaning; but to perform its specific role it must convey the meaning not only that I hereby make a promise, but that what I promise is to come. The case is similar with all other speech acts; they perform their functions, jobs, or roles by way of the meanings they are designed to convey, in such fashion that their functions, jobs, or roles cannot be specified without reference to some meanings or be fully specified apart from reference to their specific meanings. In the light of this consideration, one can see why inquiries for the uses of expressions as the functions of expressions should nearly always be rewarding in the course of quests for intentional and cultural meanings of expressions. To discern the specific job of an expression, one must have some understanding of that part of the job which consists in the conveying of a meaning through which the remainder of the job is done.

However, whether functions, jobs, or roles of expressions are described as broad types of speech acts or as quite specific speech acts including specific meanings, they can scarcely be thought of as identical with intentional or cultural meanings or as completely satisfactory guides either to particular meanings or to the character of meaning. To this extent, despite its marked successes, the approach to meaning by way of use construed as function has, like use approaches, serious limitations.

On the one hand, accounts of the functions, jobs, or roles

of expressions construed as general types of speech acts contain no specific meanings and, while supplying some general information about these meanings and environs in which they occur, tell us too little in particular about what they are or how they can be ascertained. Thus, to say that Jones's statement that "Smith may be in error" is an illocutionary statemental act involved in the perlocutionary act of persuading Brown not to trust Smith, gives considerable information about the setting and general character of the meaning of the statement but leaves the particular meaning of the statement still indeterminate and yields no adequate clue to what a meaning is. Similarly, if someone explains that "I wish you would go" is an expression that can be used for commanding, requesting, or stating depending upon specifiable types of situations, he will have laid out important facts concerning the setting of the expression and suggested significant boundaries within which its meaning lies, but he will have told us far too little concerning what the particular meaning is or what any meaning consists in.

On the other hand, if functions, jobs or roles of expressions are construed as quite specific speech acts, the meanings of the locutions employed are clearly included in them, but they are included along with a great many other features of the functions of these expressions and without any adequate indication of how to single them out or to determine what they are. Thus when Austin tells us that a statement that "I know that there is a bittern in the garden" is a speech act in which I give my personal pledge to the statement that there's a bittern in the garden on the basis of having "been trained in an environment where I could become familiar with bitterns, had certain opportunity in the current case, learned to recognize or tell bitterns, [and] succeeded in recognizing or telling this is a bittern,"[121] he has no doubt given considerable information about the meaning of the expression; and if he had described the speech act involved fully, he would no doubt have included full information about its meaning. However, the information in question does, and would, remain embedded in a multitude of others aspects of the speech act without affording any means of separating out what the meaning of the expression consists of.

---

[121]J. L. Austin, *Philosophical Papers*, p. 48.

The situation is similar when Hart characterizes the speech act involved in saying "He did it," or when Hare characterizes the speech act involved in saying "This is good." Indeed, while full characterization of the jobs of any expressions or of the speech acts involved in using them includes characterizations of meanings of these expressions, it includes, along with these characterizations many other items, about forms and modes of speech and about their intended and actual accomplishments, without supplying any method for distinguishing or showing what the meanings are or what manner of concepts they embrace. To distinguish meanings from factors closely associated with them is a task that remains to be done, and some matters concerning how it is to be done will be discussed in the two concluding chapters.

CHAPTER IX

EXPERIENCE PATTERNS AND MEANINGS

The foregoing survey of major features of meaning situations has disclosed a number of important features of such situations that must be duly recognized in any adequate account of the concept of meaning. It has shown that meanings are always meanings of bearers; that meanings may be meant by being intended to be apprehended, by being disposed to be so intended, by being causally inferable, or by being logically implied; and that bearers of meaning occur in various kinds of contextual settings that significantly affect their meanings. It has also shown that while meanings cannot be identified with either stimuli, responses, referents, confirmatory conditions, or uses, factors of these kinds are often closely related to, and significantly help to disclose, meanings, for example: that stimuli, not only prompt intentions issuing in utterances and inscriptions, but often also manifest the character of meanings intended; that responses often contain apprehensions of meanings that come to light in overt behavior; that referents are referred to by way of meanings and hence often display characters of meanings; that possible confirmatory conditions are often included in meanings; and that uses, regarded as regularities, rules, and functions, are on the whole the most revealing guides to meanings.

What has now to be undertaken is the crucial task of working out a clarification of the central concept of meaning itself. To this end I shall endeavor to present a set of sufficient and necessary conditions for the applicability of the substantive term "meaning" that will be in accord with such characteristics of meaning situations as have been disclosed—or may be disclosed by further reference to examples—and that will at the same time be as illuminating as possible concerning the character of meanings, the major differences among kinds of meanings, and the common features—if any—of meanings.

251

Since a conjunctive set of sufficient and necessary conditions for a concept, or for the applicability of corresponding terms, is likely to be more revealing than a disjunctive set, it would be desirable, if possible, to disclose such a conjunctive set for the concept of meaning. And since a set of conditions that is empirically operational is likely to be more helpful in providing a basis for the employment of a concept than one that is not, it would be desirable, if possible, to disclose a set of sufficient and necessary conditions for the concept of meaning that is thus operational. However, limits to what can be achieved are obviously involved in the character of the data and the state of present knowledge; and what is to be attempted will have to depend more on the character of the data and the level of present inquiry than upon what one might otherwise desire to accomplish.

1. Meanings as Satisfying Major Meaning Functions

If any set of sufficient and necessary conditions for the concept of meaning is to be obtained, it will presumably be disclosed at least in part by noticing the way in which meanings are had or meant, i.e., the manner in which the various factors that enter into meanings are eventually so focused as to determine something that may justifiably be called a meaning. However, examination of the manner in which meanings are meant has disclosed that, instead of there being just one way of meaning yielding a single kind of meaning, there are at least four ways of meaning resting on four distinct meaning functions and yielding varieties of meaning so different from one another that to ascribe a meaning in one way is to say something very different from what would be said in ascribing a meaning in another way. Apparently there are no meanings in general but intentional, dispositional, causal, and implicative meanings, each defined by its own function and tested by methods different from those involved in testing other kinds of meaning. If this be so, there is little prospect of arriving at any conjunctive set of sufficient and necessary conditions for all meanings. Accordingly, without claiming that a single conjunctive set of sufficient and necessary conditions for all meanings is logically impossible, I shall forego any quest for such a set of conditions as very unlikely to succeed and be content to search for more restricted sets of conditions that can be more readily found.

Fortunately, the same meaning functions that distinguish ways of meaning and apparently preclude any single conjunctive set of sufficient and necessary conditions for all meanings seem to afford a basis for what may be regarded as a disjunctive set at least of sufficient conditions for the concept of meaning. The functions in question are, as will be recalled, as follows: (1) X is a meaning of a given bearer in the intentional way if and only if someone, in producing that bearer, intends to lead a respondent to apprehend X as what he intends his respondent to apprehend; (2) X is a meaning of a given bearer in the dispositional way if and only if, were someone to produce that bearer to lead a respondent to apprehend something as what he intended his respondent to apprehend, he would in all probability intend his respondent to apprehend X as what he intended his respondent to apprehend; (3) X is a meaning in the causal way if and only if there is something such that X can be correctly inferred through its causal connections; (4) X is a meaning in the implicative way if and only if there is a Y such that Y implies X. Since these functions have been delineated without using the term "meaning" or its equivalents and without presupposing a concept of meaning, to employ them in specifying conditions for the correct use of the term "meaning" and the characterization of the concept of meaning involves no damaging circularity.

In order actually to show that the disjunction of four functions in question represented a sufficient condition for the applicability of the substantive "meaning," one would have to examine every situation in which one of these functions was satisfied in order to make sure that what satisfied the function was indeed properly called a "meaning." Instead of undertaking any such prodigious task, I shall have to be content to offer a few brief remarks on the point in question, which is in any case hardly likely to be highly controversial. The four functions under consideration were arrived at, not to fulfill theoretical requirements, but in a quest for functions that actually determined meanings. Nowhere in this quest was an instance encountered of anything satisfying one of the functions that one would not readily refer to as a meaning. Nor was any such instance encountered in the extensive inquiries concerning various factors in meaning situations that followed the formulation of these functions. No such instance is encountered in the examination of cases that follows the present chapter. Indeed, to such an extent does what we require in calling anything a meaning seem to be fulfilled by anything that satisfies one of the functions under consideration that it appears extremely unlikely that anything could satisfy any of the functions under consideration and not be properly referred to as a meaning of the kind indicated by that function. Accordingly, though without claiming to have demonstrated the point, I suggest that one may safely make the modest, though relatively uninformative, assumption that the four indicated meaning functions constitute a disjunctive set of sufficient conditions for the concept of meaning in the sense that, given an appropriate bearer of meaning, whatever satisfies any one of these functions, relative to that bearer is a meaning of that bearer in the way of meaning defined by that function.

If, as earlier discussion of the ways of meaning suggested, the indicated meaning functions are such that, not only is everything that satisfies one of them a meaning, but nothing that does not satisfy one of them is a meaning, i.e., there are no other functions that determine meanings, or any other ways of meaning, then the four major meaning functions may be said to supply a disjunctive set of conditions for the concept of meaning that is, not only sufficient, but also necessary. The suggestion that the four major meaning functions furnish a disjunctive set of necessary conditions for the concept of meaning is, however, less obviously plausible than the suggestion that these conditions constitute a set of sufficient conditions for that concept; and hence, it requires somewhat more discussion. Certainly, I would not want to say that there are no possible subdivisions or arrangements or meaning functions other than those involved in the four indicated meaning functions; but I do suggest that, by and large, the four major meaning functions cover the main manners in which meanings are eventually determined and that in this sense there are no other significant ways of meaning. This suggestion is not, to be sure, of a sort that can be proved to be correct, but considerations can be called to mind that tend to indicate that it is plausible.

One such consideration is that while each of the functions in question has its limits, the disjunction of the four of them has a scope so broad that it would be extremely difficult to conceive of anything at all that did not fall under one or the other of them. Some meanings are meant by way of the intentions of agents; and these meanings include meanings of every utterance, every inscription, every gesture, every production of any kind by which any human being, or any other being capable of intending to convey a meaning, has ever intended, or will ever, intend to convey any meaning. Other meanings are meant by way of dispositions of individuals or groups to intend to convey meanings; and these meanings embrace meanings of every word, phrase, sentence, emblem, insignia, sign or symbol belonging to the stock of available bearers of meaning of every human being. Some meanings are meant by way of being causally inferable; and because every object and every event in the universe stands in causal relations, these meanings include meanings of everything that actually exists. Finally, some meanings are meant by way of being implied; these include everything implied by everything that any one has ever said, or thought or ever could say or think. Indeed, so comprehensive is the scope of what is meant through all the ways of meaning together that, if the crucial question concerning an alleged meaning were the question whether or not in fact it was a meaning, the disjunction of the major meaning functions would fail to draw any very useful distinction between what is and what is not a meaning. Actually, the crucial question concerning anything said to be meaning is, not whether or not it is a meaning, but in what way, or in virtue of what function, it is a meaning and what its character as a meaning is; and the apparent comprehensiveness of the disjunction of the indicated major ways of meaning remains as presumptive evidence against the likelihood of there being any other significant ways of meaning.

Aside from calling attention to the apparent comprehensiveness of the domain of the major ways of meaning, about all that can be done to show that there are no other significant ways of meaning is to inquire into the other functions that seem most likely to define such ways of meaning, to determine whether or not they give evidence of so doing. Already some such inquiry into functions that could conceivably be thought to define ways of meaning has been carried out in inquiring into factors in meaning situations sometimes equated with meanings, and no such inquiry has disclosed any way of meaning other than the four previously discussed. However, since some explicit inquiry of the sort in question seems to be called for, I have chosen for special consideration, six functions which seem to contain more promise of defining additional ways of meaning than any others. If even these functions fail to indicate significant ways in which anything is eventually determined that we are justified in calling a meaning, the case for the comprehensiveness of the ways of meaning previously discussed may be considered sufficiently strong for present purposes. The six functions chosen may be roughly characterized as those of: being referred to, being denoted (in the sense of belonging to a class to which a term applies), being suggested, being an emotion prompting, or prompted by, a bearer of meaning, being verbally equivalent to a bearer of meaning, and being taken to be a meaning. Some of these functions have already been considered in other connections while others have not. I shall, even at the cost of some repetition, briefly examine the claims of each to constitute a function justifying the ascription of the term "meaning" to that which satisfies it.

a. Bearers of meaning in the intentional way often refer to some object or event, and being referred to by such a bearer is sometimes thought of as a way of a meaning that justifies us in calling referents meanings. The claim that being referred to is a function defining a way of meaning acquires some initial plausibility by virtue of the fact that things referred to are often properly said to be meant. However, by no means everything that is properly said to be meant is properly called a meaning. More specifically things meant in the sense of being referred to are not properly called meanings, and were it not that referring expressions also have meanings distinct from their referents, they could scarcely refer at all. Thus, in "He meant the boy on the left," the particular boy in question is not his meaning; and if the expression "the boy on the left" did not have a meaning quite distinct from that particular boy, it would be of no use in referring to that particular boy. Even in "I meant John," John, though referred to, is not my meaning; and if the expression had no meaning distinguishable from John himself, it could not serve the purpose of referring to John. Being referred to is indeed an important function closely akin to being intentionally meant, but it yields no meaning and does not constitute a way of meaning.

b. Type words and other expressions often stand ready to

be used upon demand to refer to, or in the previously indicated sense *denote*, any member of a class of objects or events called its denotation; and being thus denoted is sometimes thought of as a function defining a way of meaning akin to, but distinguishable from the dispositional way. The suggestion that being denoted in this sense yields a distinct way of meaning derives some initial plausibility from the consideration that we sometimes say that a term means *particular* objects or events to which it stands ready to *refer*. However, even to say that a term means these particular objects or events is stretching the verb "to mean" considerably; and to go on to say that the *class* of objects or events to which a term stands ready to refer is its meaning, or any part of its meaning, is to pass beyond the limits of the term "meaning" altogether. No one's meaning is ever, as has been seen, an object or event referred to, and of no word is the meaning a class of objects or events. What types of expression stand ready to refer to can no more be the meanings of such expressions than particular objects referred to can be meanings of the token expressions that manifest type expressions; for only if the token expressions that manifest type expressions could have referents as their meanings could type expressions have classes of referents, or denotations, as their meanings. Being denoted and denotation are important concepts in analysis of meaning situations; but being denoted is not a way of meaning, and denotation, whatever else it is, is not a kind of meaning.

c. Another way of meaning that could be proposed is indicated by the consideration that expressions often suggest much more than is included in their primary meanings. For example, "bureaucratic" suggests, or connotes (in the ordinary sense), but does not include in its primary meaning, being authoritarian, unimaginative, and rigid; and "The Senator is a smooth character" may well suggest much more duplicity on the part of the senator than one who utters this sentence may intend specifically to attribute to the senator. Such facts as these are of course familiar, but what they indicate with reference to meaning is, not the existence of a special way of meaning, but rather that the meanings of expressions may be construed more strictly or less strictly depending upon the purposes in hand without in any sense implying that all that is suggested by an expression should be included in the meaning of that expression. To attempt to confine the intentional or dispositional meaning of every expression to the strict primary meaning of the expression would be to rule out much that the expression is intended, or disposed to be intended, to lead respondents to apprehend; but to attempt to include in the meaning of an expression all that the expression suggests to anyone would be to break down the useful distinction between meaning and what is suggested but not meant and to rob the term "meaning" of a large measure of its usefulness. Hence, however important it is to recognize that intentional and dispositional meanings often include far more than is strictly stated or primarily meant, no distinct suggestive or connotative (in the ordinary sense) meaning function or way of meaning is either called for or can be without undue confusion, admitted.

d. An additional way of meaning may be suggested by the facts that people are often prompted by emotions to speak or write and intend in speaking or writing to prompt emotions in others, and that expressions are often disposed either to be prompted by emotions or to prompt emotions in respondents. Thus one might wish to say that an expression's being prompted by, or being intended to prompt an emotion, or being disposed to do either, represents a meaning function and a corresponding way of meaning. Actually, the patterns of the emotions that prompt, or are disposed to prompt, speakers or writers to speak or write may well be a part of what the speakers or writers intend, or are disposed to intend, to lead their respondents to apprehend; and the patterns of the emotions that speakers or writers intend, or are disposed to intend, to lead respondents to feel may be patterns of emotions that speakers or writers intend, or are disposed to intend, their respondents to apprehend. Hence, patterns of emotion often quite clearly belong to the intentional and dispositional meanings of the expressions used by speakers or writers. However, on the one hand, patterns as such, whether of emotions or anything else, do not eventually determine either meanings or anything else. And, on the other hand, however much the particular emotions that prompt intentions to speak may influence the intentions that shape meanings of utterances, and however much the classes of emotions may affect the dispositions that shape meanings of words, it is eventuating dispositions that in the end determine the meanings of type words. Whatever, then, may be the role of emotions in meaning situations, it scarcely seems to be that of indicating a special meaning function or way of meaning.

e. Since the quest for verbal equivalents may be an important part of a quest for the meaning of an expression, and since one may say of a given expression that it means certain verbal equivalents, as "occulist" means "eye doctor," the supposition may seem plausible that there is, alongside the dispositional way of meaning, but distinguishable from it as well as from the other ways, what may be called a "lexical" way of meaning. However, since to say that one verbal expression means another verbal expression is merely to mention rather than to use the expressions in question; the meaning of neither is involved. To say that one expression means another is merely to give a rule for finding the meaning of the first expression; that meaning itself comes to light, if at all, not in the second verbal expression but in the meaning of the second expression. To say that one verbal expression means another is in effect to say that the second expression has the same meaning as the first; but to have the same meaning as an expression can scarcely be to be the meaning of that expression unless—as seem very unlikely—an expression can be the very meaning which it has. Hence, being verbally equivalent to a bearer of meaning, however important a function it may be, can scarcely justify one in calling an expression a meaning or properly be said to represent a way of meaning.

f. Correlated with meanings of bearers in each of the major ways of meaning, but quite distinct from these meanings, are what people take or interpret these bearers to mean. Hence the suggestion comes to mind that there may be, in addition to the ways of meaning already indicated, what may be called an interpretative way of meaning. People do in fact often speak of "hearer's meaning;" and were it not that people perceive and interpret, or take, bearers of meanings to mean something, no bearer of intentional meaning would ever be produced, no language would ever develop, and no one would become aware of any meaning at all. Moreover, that a distinction of considerable importance is involved in referring to interpretative meanings is indicated by the manner and frequency of our references to what things mean *to* people. Thus one may say that your statement that you were not guilty meant, to me, that you didn't do it; that "not guilty" means, to most people, fully innocent; that the

meaning of a red evening sky, to the ignorant, is that rain is
likely; or that a meaning of a double negative, to many people,
is a strong negative. Nevertheless, in mentioning what people take
or interpret bearers of meaning to mean, we are talking, not
about what these bearers mean, but about what they are taken,
or interpreted, to mean; and what bearers are taken, or interpreted,
to mean may be quite different from what they do mean. The
differences between the two concepts, and the possible differences
between their referents, require little more than mention to be
recognized. These differences are further confirmed by the ways in
which we refer to hearer's meanings. When we refer to hearer's
meanings we ordinarily refer, not unconditionally to "the meaning"
of a bearer, but to its meaning "to me," "to us," "to them," or to
what it means "to me," "to us," etc.; and even when we do not
introduce the qualifying expressions, what we say implies them.
What the hearer understands the speaker's utterance to mean,
its meaning to him, may be interesting; but what the hearer seeks
to get at is the meaning that the speaker himself means. What
hearers are disposed to understand a word to mean is usually an
important clue to what people are disposed to intend in using
the word, and because speakers and hearers constantly adapt to
one another, the clue is likely to be accurate; but what is basic
concerning the word is what meaning people are disposed to use
it to convey. What people take to be causally inferable from
something and what they take to be implied by something are
valuable clues to what is so inferable or implied, but people may
be mistaken about what is causally inferable or implied by
something, and it is what is actually inferable or implied by
something rather than what is only taken to be so that determines
the causal or implicative meaning of anything. Hence, however
important interpretation and interpretative processes may be in
meaning situations, and however harmless it may be to speak of
hearer's or interpretative meanings, neither these nor any other
facts seem to justify the notion of a separate interpretative
meaning function or way of meaning over against the four major
meaning functions or ways of meaning.

     If, as now seems highly probable, the functions defining the
intentional, dispositional, causal and implicative ways of meaning
not only determine meanings but are essentially the only sorts
of functions that do, then they indicate not only sufficient

conditions for meanings but necessary ones as well. I suggest then that these functions may be taken to supply initial definitions of all of the main varieties of meaning. If this suggestion is sound, anything is a meaning if and only if it satisfies one or more of the indicated meaning functions. Roughly, whatever an agent intends in producing a bearer to lead a respondent to apprehend is an intentional meaning, whatever one or more agents is disposed so to intend is a dispositional meaning, whatever is correctly inferable through its causal relations is a causal meaning, whatever is implied is an implicative meaning, and presumably there are no meanings that are not meant in one or more of these ways.

This suggestion is not in itself, however, very illuminating. One reason is that the set of sufficient and necessary conditions indicated is disjunctive rather than conjunctive. A more important reason is that nothing at all has yet been said about what it is that satisfies any one of the indicated meaning functions. It may well be that such satisfying factors can be found; and it is even possible that some one kind of factor entering into whatever satisfies any one of the four major meaning functions can be found. If such factors, or such a factor, can be found, the pedestrian results so far attained may prove to be more illuminating than they at first appear. In any case, in the next section I shall endeavor to delineate a concept of a factor that seems to hold some promise for the purpose in hand.

2. The Concept of Experience Patterns

The accounts in the preceding chapters of factors in meaning situations that are sometimes equated with meanings may be thought of as accounts of quests for factors that satisfy major meaning functions but that reveal more about meanings than just that meanings are either intended to be apprehended, disposed to be so apprehended, causally inferable, or implied. In some measure these quests have been successful, for they have helped to disclose important conditions which any adequate account of meaning must meet. But they have all failed to disclose any factor equatable with meanings in all the major ways of meaning or even with meanings in any such way.

However, running as a prominent thread through traditional

theories of meaning and clearly present in the backgrounds of
some of the contemporary theories previously considered is a
concept, which, though often mingled with other concepts that
obscure it, seems capable of being clarified and shows some
promise of helping to disclose the sort of factors now being
sought. The concept in question is not a concept of any sort of
particular events or objects; it is rather a concept of repeatable
patterns that I shall refer to as "experience patterns." These experience patterns may indeed be patterns of stimuli, responses,
or referents; but they may also be patterns of many sorts of
sensations, feeling, thoughts and the like, and they may be instantiated in many varieties of the objects and events.

Before attempting to delineate the concept of experience
patterns in detail or to show how it applies to the quest for the
crucial factors in meaning situations, I wish to call attention to a
few of many possible examples of the manner in which this concept
has been prominently present, though often confusedly, both in
the history of thought concerning meaning and in recent thought
upon that subject.

Plato's notions of justice, temperance, courage, wisdom,
beauty and the like, though intermingled with dubious ontological
accompaniments, are in considerable part notions of patterns
capable of manifestation in human experiences and instantiable in
objects, events, and situations of various kinds. The contents of
"mental experience" with which Aristotle identifies the meanings
of "spoken words" are also patterns of possible experience.[1] The
content of the "intellectual conception" with which St. Thomas is
disposed to equate the meaning of a word is, in like manner, a
pattern of possible experience.[2] While the ideas with which Locke
equates meanings are often represented as subjective, their contents are patterns of experience; and Locke often speaks of his
ideas in ways which show him to be from time to time more
concerned with contents than with actual occurrences of ideas.
J. S. Mill insists that a name "connotes.....attributes" and that
"whenever (names) have properly any meaning, the meaning

---

[1]Aristotle "On Interpretation," Tr. by E. M. Edgehill, in *Great Books
of the Western World* (Chicago: Encyclopedia Britannica, Inc., 1962), p. 25.
[2]Thomas Aquinas, "Suma Theologica," in *Great Books of the Western
World*, Vol. 19, p. 62.

resides in what they connote."[3] Excluding from the patterns constituting meanings the psychological factors accompanying them in most earlier representations, Gottlob Frege takes the "sense" of a term to be a "mode of presentation,.....what may be a common property of many and therefore is not a part or mode of the individual mind,"[4] and the meaning of a proposition to be a thought, which being a content of consciousness nevertheless "can be recognized by others just as much as by me,....does not belong to the contents of my consciousness, and can be true without being apprehended."[5]

In more recent years even Quine, who is especially eager to preserve the observable basis of meanings, represents his fundamental stimulus meanings, not as actual events, but as "repeatable event forms." Verificationists, in treating meanings, as confirmatory conditions, implicitly at any rate, are treating meanings as patterns of possible experience. C. I. Lewis is quite explicit in regarding the crucial intentional sense meaning of an expression as a "criterion in mind, by reference to which one is able to apply or refuse to apply the expression in question."[6] J. L. Austin often takes one aspect of meaning of an expression to be its sense, and sometimes represents the meaning of an expression as a "type or pattern." The rules and roles of which Ryle speaks may well be construed as patterns that may or may not be fulfilled. W. P. Alston's "conditions" that one would be prepared to recognize in using an expression can scarcely be regarded in any other way than as patterns of possible events. Finally, in regarding language as "an instrument of communication of thoughts and ideas" and meanings as "representations of classes of thoughts or ideas"[7] Jerrold Katz specifically, though perhaps excessively psychologically, links meanings with patterns of possible experience.

---

[3]J. S. Mill, *A System of Logic* (London: Longmans, Green and Co. Ltd. New Impressions, 1961), pp. 20 f.

[4]Gottlob Frege, "Our Sense and Reference," in Peter Geach and Max Black, *Translations from the Philosophical Writings of Frege* (Oxford: Basic Blacksmith, 1952), p. 59.

[5]Gottlob Frege, "The Thought," First published in *Beitrage zur Philosophie des Deutschen Idealismus,* 1918, Tr. by A. M. and Marcelle Quinton, *Mind,* LXV (1956), pp. 301 and 311.

[6]C. I. Lewis, *An Analysis of Knowledge and Valuation* (La Salle, Ill.: The Open Court Publishing Co., 1946), p. 133.

[7]Jerrold Katz, *The Philosophy of Language* (New York: Harper and Row, 1966), pp. 176 f.

In attempting in the pages that follow to render the concept of experience patterns as clear as possible, I shall be concerned with the definition and principal characteristics of experience patterns, the principal varieties of such patterns, the relations of such patterns to experiences, and the relations of such patterns to things and events.

One sometimes speaks of his having the same thought, feeling, or purpose that he had yesterday or of two or more people's having the same idea, sensation or impulse. More generally, one may speak of his repeatedly having the same experience or of several people's having the same experience. When people speak in these ways, they seem often not to be speaking of actually occurring physical or mental events; for one person's thoughts now and later are necessarily different events, and so are one person's feelings and another person's feelings. They seem rather to be speaking of repeatable and sharable contents or patterns of their own and other people's experiences. Such contents or patterns of actual or possible repeatable and sharable experience, I shall call experience patterns.

Essential to any experience pattern is the character of being a recognizable content of a possible experience, the notion of experience being broadly conceived to include not merely sensible experience, but also thinking, desiring, hoping, loving, hating, and whatever else experience can consist in. Experience patterns inevitability involve structural aspects. The relevant structures may be relatively simple as is, for example, that of the experience pattern exemplified by an idea of an equilateral triangle. They may also be very complex as is the sort of pattern recognizable in an idea of justice. The upper limit of the complexity of experience patterns is the limit of the capacity of mentality itself to apprehend complexity. The lower limit of the structural complexity of experience patterns is the character of a simple qualitative element which might still be recognized though its internal structural complexity was zero. However, it may be doubted if any actual experience is ever altogether devoid of distinguishable features, and even if any were, it would still stand, as will subsequently appear, in enormously complex relations.

Now it will, I think, be readily apparent that experience patterns construed in the manner indicated are of virtually infinite variety. Every change—no matter how slight—in the quality of a content of experience, every alteration in feeling tone, every variation in intensity of associated impulse can be regarded as making an experience pattern different from another one otherwise similar to it; and there is no ascertainable limit to the possible differences. Every pattern in any way sensible, thinkable, feelable, or experienceable in any other way, whether actually experienced or not, is to be included among experience patterns. Every experienceable pattern of every object or event and every content of every imaginative flight—no matter how related or unrelated to any object—is an experience pattern.

The apparently chaotic and evidently boundless variety of experience patterns is, however, by no means as unmanageable as might at first appear. For one thing, much of it need not concern us at all. For another, regarding the part that does concern us, we are free to take it in segments of any size we wish. For example, the patterns of the experiences of a fleeting moment are as much or as little experience patterns as are those of a long span of time, and the patterns of small areas of our perceptual fields are as genuinely experience patterns as are those of larger areas. While the entire pattern of one's experience of a symphony may be taken together to constitute an experience pattern, the pattern of one's experience of one movement of the symphony may also constitute an experience pattern, and so also may that of a fragment of that movement. The whole pattern of one's experience in solving a problem is one experience pattern; that of one's experience in some part of the process is another. One's whole sensory field at a given moment constitutes one experience pattern, his visual field another, and his auditory one another; so also does any experienceable part of any one of these fields.

Even more important for the management and use of experience patterns than the fact that experience patterns can be taken in larger or smaller segments is the fact that they can be abstracted in varying degrees and that the abstractions remain as much experience patterns as the patterns from which they are abstracted. On the other hand, experience patterns may consist of minutely detailed patterns of individual experiences and, on the other hand, they may be the barest abstractions from considerable ranges of experience. They may be full patterns of all aspects of an experience or almost vacuous patterns of one selected aspect. When an artist is looking at a vase of flowers, that pattern upon which he focuses may well embrace a wealth of detail not commonly noticed, but when a botanist looks at the same flowers, the pattern on which he focuses may be that of a single feature of shapes of the petals. The detailed color and shape patterns of my visual image as I look at a self-portrait of Cezanne constitute an experience pattern, but so also does the barest outline of the face or even of the frame. When one listens to a Beethoven sonata, he may select out for attention the patterns of the rhythm, the melody, the harmony, the sound qualities, or the flow of his own thoughts and feelings. As I talk about my latest visit to Chicago, I may have before me the pattern of vivid experiences of some part of the city or I may have before me no more than a schema suited for bare identification of that part of the city. When language is the medium of our thought or expression, the experience patterns that tend to be crucial are likely to be rather criterial schemata than detailed experience patterns. Thus, for example, when I think or speak of something's being a stone, the determinative experience pattern is much less likely to be a detailed image of a stone than a schema in terms of which I would recognize a stone if I saw one. When I speak of wisdom, there is no image that could represent what I intend, and the burden of what I am getting at must be carried by a schema that would permit me to recognize a wise man, given sufficient opportunity to notice what he says and does.

Another feature of experience patterns that tends to make them more manageable than they otherwise would be is that they are related to one another in a number of ascertainable and illuminating ways. For example, some experience patterns are so related that in no instance can the one be instantiated without the other. For example, nothing can be scarlet without being red or red without being colored, and nothing can be square without being rectangular or rectangular without being four-sided. Again, nothing can be a square box without being square and red, and nothing can be human without being animal. Other experience patterns are so related that their instances are always mutually exclusive. Such a relationship holds, for example, between the experience patterns involved in being red all over and green all over at the same time or in being both rectilinear and curved.

Still other experience patterns are so related that the instantiation of the one determines a certain order of the instantiation of the other. For example, when one thing is greater than another, the other must be less than the first; and when one thing is ancestor to a second, and a third is ancestor to the first, the third must be ancestor to the second.

Although some experience patterns are simpler than others and a point is sometimes reached at which no way can be found to find simpler components for an experienced pattern, every experience pattern has at very least the complexity of belonging to a complex relational field, i.e., stands in a vast complex of relations which enter into the determination of its character. Thus, the experience pattern *being red*, though apparently relatively simple, belongs to an enormously varied pattern of relations of hues, shades, intensities, principles concerning shaped surfaces, and principles of refraction and reflection of light waves of different wave lengths. Elaborate orders of experience patterns have been selected out and symbolized in mathematical and logical systems; and no small part of the work of theoretical science consists in the selection, explication, and symbolization of experience patterns whose character and ramifications reflect the course of events that concern us and facilitate the formulation of useful predictions. A great many other less systematic relations among experience patterns are reflected in the logic of ordinary language.

The linking of experience patterns with symbols substantially facilitates not only the communication of experience patterns but also the selection, recognition, synthesis, analysis, and application of such patterns. This consideration obviously represents another important factor that helps to render the otherwise bewildering chaos of experience patterns intelligible and useful. Indeed, so vital is the employment of symbols to the recognition, organization, and communication of experience patterns that one is sometimes disposed to think that the occurrence and order of such patterns is altogether dependent upon the use of symbols. This does not, however, seem to be the case. Many children and primitives show capacity to group and draw out the import of highly complex experience patterns with a minimum of symbolization. Aphasics often lose their capacities to use words while retaining their systems of concepts largely intact. All of us find ourselves groping for words to communicate the patterns of our experiences, and even when our words come to us smoothly, we often find them capable of expressing only fragments of the patterns of experience we would like to communicate.

Although the variety of experience patterns is so vast as to exclude altogether any possibility of complete analysis, at least some main varieties of such patterns can be indicated and should be noticed. Presumably, the earliest recognized experience patterns came dimly to focus out of a chaotic welter of elements of primordial sensation, feeling, and impulse initially too transient and confused to permit clear recognition. Those earliest experience patterns are presumably many-sided chunks of experience that are for one reason or another especially vivid. For primitive men, they may well have been patterns of joyful sights, smells, and sounds of the feast that followed the horde's successful hunt or patterns of the elated sensations, emotions, and impulses of the conquest of some animal or human enemy that had threatened the life of the tribe. For infants, they may well be patterns of such chunks of experience as the splashing, gurgling sound and the warm caressing feel of the bath or the sudden, sharp sound of a parent's warning voice together with the tug of his restraining hand. Such experience patterns as these not only tend to be singled out of the total flow of experience patterns and recognized when they occur, they are also often recalled and sometimes symbolized, e.g., by events that re-enact at least fragments of them, as for example, the ceremonial feast, the song and dance of the victory celebration, or the child's re-enactment in play of the bath or the parental restraint.

Within the patterns even of primitive chunks of experience, as well as in many other experiences, one finds patterns of experience factors that belong primarily to one or another of three commonly distinguished phases of experience, namely, the cognitive, the affective, and the conative. Experience patterns of the first of these kinds include experience patterns of sensations, perceptions, memories, imaginations, conceptions, and thoughts of various sorts. Among experience patterns of the second kind are to be found patterns of all manner of pleasures, pains, loves, hates, joys, sorrows, hopes, fears, faint feeling tones, strong passions, and all else that goes into the affective life of sentient beings. Among experience patterns of the third kind are to be found endlessly varied patterns of tensions and relaxation, of striving and restraining, of impulse and inhibition. None of the phases of experience exemplifying such patterns is likely to be found often in isolation from the others; but in some experiences, one phase is likely to be predominant and in others, other phases. Moreover, with respect to any complex experience, patterns of one kind or another can be abstracted for special consideration.

Many experience patterns of all the indicated varieties, at all levels of sophistication, are non-discursive in the sense that they are not of such kinds that their expressions in any way predicate properties or relations to things by way of them. The patterns of the primitive's images of the successful hunt or of the baby's images of his bath generally yield no predications and are never exhausted by sentences; the same thing is in lesser degree true of most of our images, percepts, feelings, and impulses. The primitive hunter may trace his way through the forest by experience patterns that involve no propositions; the child may act, think, achieve, and understand at a high level of intelligence before he has a command of language; the common man may think, feel and behave consciously and intelligently in many moments of his walking hours without formulating propositions; the musician, the painter, or the sculptor may express his most significant experience patterns in ways that have their own principles but include no predications.

Nevertheless, a substantial part of human experience, especially when it occurs in conjunction with verbal symbols, tends to take the form of discursive experience patterns which bring together what may be called designative experience patterns on the one hand and predicative ones on the other in what may be called propositional experience patterns. By designative experience patterns, I mean patterns exemplified in the sorts of experience in which people use signs and symbols to direct attention to something that they intend to characterize, for example, patterns shared by people who point to the same object concerning which they are about to say something, or who describe the same event to which they are about to attribute properties. By a predicative experience pattern, I mean the sort of pattern exemplified in one's experience in ascribing a property or relation to something. The experience patterns by way of which one identifies the book before him, Benjamin Brogadus Bradshaw, Paris, or an instance of courage are designative experience patterns. Those by way of which one thinks, speaks, or writes about something's being red or tall or populous or a virtue or between Chicago and somewhere else are predicative experience patterns.

Propositional experience patterns are those by the mastery of which we are able at the same time to designate things and to ascribe properties or relations to these things. They are not propositions, at any rate as propositions are equated with sentences or with sentences and meanings or even with ideal sentences or classes of synonymous sentences. Rather they are the kinds of patterns by which one can recognize that a thing has a certain property or stands in a certain relation and by which he is able to formulate a proposition concerning a thing. They are patterns instantiatable in facts, in something's being red or to the right of something else. They are patterns exemplifiable in the contents of experiences of seeing, thinking, or believing that something is red or square or doubting or wondering if it is. The experience patterns by way of which one thinks, speaks, or writes of the book before him's being red, of Benjamin Brogadus Bradshaw's being tall, of Paris's being large, or of courage's being a virtue are propositional experience patterns.

Although for special purposes propositional experience patterns can be abstracted from the attitudinal experience patterns in which they characteristically occur, the experiences which exemplify them never in fact occur alone but occur always in the frameworks of propositional attitudes of asserting, questioning, supposing, doubting, believing and the like. These propositional attitudes, however, inevitably involve assertive, inquisitive, suppositional, "dubitative" and other like experience patterns within which propositional experience patterns are exemplified and apart from which neither propositional attitudes nor the sorts of speech acts within which they occur would be conceivable.

Experience patterns are not only of varied kinds, they are also variously related to experiences. They may, for example, be exemplified by experiences, dispositionally available for experiences, or adumbrated in experiences.

Experience patterns are exemplified by experiences when they are patterns of states of awareness of sentient beings. Thus they may be patterns of sensations, percepts, feelings, and impulses of animals or men. They may also be patterns of recollections, fancies, visions, concepts, judgments, or reasonings of human beings. They may be exemplified in states of awareness representing all sorts of combinations of the foregoing and other kinds of experiences simultaneously as well as in experiences in which different varieties of experience succeed one another in time. In order that experience patterns be exemplified in experiences, they need not be specifically recognized; all that is required is that experiences of which they are patterns occur.

However, experience patterns may in fact be recognized; and indeed when the same experience pattern recurs repeatedly in circumstances that make it especially vivid or for some reason attach special importance to it, it is very likely to be specifically recognized. For example, the infant soon learns to recognize the pattern of its mother's face or the school boy that of the letters of his own name. Experience patterns can often also be called to mind upon demand as a primitive hunter calls to mind the pattern of the forest when he needs to find his way. Experience patterns can usually be recalled and used with vastly increased facility when they come to be symbolized as when, for example, patterns of some objects, properties, and relations are symbolized in words.

Because they can be recognized and recalled, experience patterns—especially those associated with symbols—may often correctly be said to be dispositionally available. That is to say, experience patterns may be such that one or more agents have capacities either to experience or to recognize them upon suitable occasions. If the occasions in question are infrequent events in nature, the dispositional availability of experience patterns is, of course, very limited. If however, an agent has developed a capacity to produce signs or symbols that reliably elicit certain experience patterns, he may create occasions for the occurrence of those patterns almost at will. In this manner the dispositional availability of these patterns comes to be substantially enhanced. If the agent's society has developed a system of symbols in which symbols with associated experience patterns can be used discursively, and if an agent has mastered this system, then the dispositional availability and usefulness of these experience patterns is enormously expanded. Thus, for example, if a boy recognizes a pigeon when he happens to see one, a pigeon experience pattern is to some extent dispositionally available to him. If he has a symbol by which he can call to mind the pattern at will, the pattern is much more fully dispositionally available to him. And if he has mastered the socially conditioned use of the word "pigeon," the dispositional availability of the pattern has taken on a further dimension of availability and usefulness.

When experience patterns, whether previously dispositionally available or not, come to the fore in experience, they are not always either actually experienced or recognized, they are often scarcely more than intimated in experience or experientially adumbrated. An experience pattern is adumbrated in an experience if and only if in that experience only a trace or fragment of that experience pattern is experienced and the agent involved is immediately ready to produce or to recognize an experience exemplifying that experience pattern. Such adumbrating of experience patterns can occur with reference either to separate patterns or to combinations of patterns that must be relatively new to the agent. Characteristically, it occurs with reference to dispositionally available experience patterns called to mind by present events. The experience of a man whose hand has just been cut will adumbrate certain patterns of pain felt in connection with other similar cuts in that he will be already mindful of certain aspects of pain patterns and be ready to recall them even in this moment when temporary shock has prevented his actually as yet experiencing pain. A primitive who sees a certain tribal token image with which he has long been familiar will not at each moment of looking at the image think all the thoughts or feel all the emotions he has been taught to think and feel in the presence of the image, but he will experience some traces of these thoughts and feelings and be imminently readied for the rest. Similarly, when someone hears a word or a statement, while his experience need involve no such full consciousness of the patterns of thoughts and feelings that might be associated with a full savoring of the whole import of the expression, his experience is likely to involve at least some traces of those patterns, and his disposition to produce or recognize them is likely to be so activated as to make him immediately ready to produce or recognize experiences exemplifying the relevant thoughts and feelings.

If experience patterns can be experienced, recognized, dispositionally available and adumbrated in experiences, they can also be "instantiated" in objects, events, and situations. An experience pattern is instantiated in an object, event, or situation if and only if the object, event, or situation is such that, if it were to be encountered under certain conditions, it would yield experiences having that pattern. Thus many experience patterns and sets of experience patterns are instantiated in everyday events. For example, the experience pattern commonly connected with the term "redness" may be instantiated in a red box or a section of a rainbow, in that such a box or rainbow would in suitable circumstances yield the experience pattern in question. Similarly the set of experience patterns indicated by the expression "small yellow patch" may be exemplified in any of the many small yellow surfaces.

Once the concept of experience patterns is introduced, some ontologically oriented philosophers will wish to claim for experience patterns the ontological status of platonic subsistents. Others will want to say that they are classes of objects, and still others that they are resemblances to samples or something else. Some physiologically oriented philosophers will want to say that they are correlated products of brain functions and others that they are basically modes of behavior. In so far as possible, I wish to avoid such ontological and aetiological questions as these and to claim only that our experiences have in fact such repeatable and sharable patterns as have been discussed and that these patterns can be exemplified, dispositionally available, adumbrated, and instantiated in the ways indicated.

3. Meanings as Experience Patterns Satisfying Major Meaning Functions

In the first section of this chapter, it was suggested, on the basis of earlier inquiry, that while no single conjunctive set of sufficient and necessary conditions could be discerned for the concept of meaning or the application of the noun "meaning," a disjunctive set of such conditions could be pointed out by saying that a meaning always satisfies one or more of four major meaning functions and that whatever satisfies one of these functions is a meaning. It was further suggested that a more illuminating set of necessary and sufficient conditions for the concept of meaning might be achieved if to this disjunctive set of conditions could be added some account of factors that satisfied the various functions referred to in the disjuncts or even of a factor common to whatever satisfied each of these meaning functions.

I wish now to suggest that there is a discernable factor in meaning situations that does in fact satisfy each of the functions in question; and that, since the functions in question have been defined independently of the concept of meaning, the requisite necessary and sufficient conditions for the concept of meaning can be significantly formulated by adding the concept of this factor to the previously indicated disjunctive set of conditions. The factor in question consists, I now suggest, of experience patterns as defined by the concept delineated in the preceding section. Thus, the requisite necessary and sufficient conditions may, I suggest, be formulated by saying that anything is a meaning if and only if it is an experience pattern either as intended by an agent in using a bearer to be apprehended by a respondent, as disposed to be so intended by one or more agents, as causally inferable from a bearer, or as implied by a bearer.

To make this suggestion is not to imply that all experience patterns are meanings or that there are any meanings in general. Experience patterns as such are not meanings; only experience patterns *as* satisfying specified functions are meanings, and these are never meanings in general but always meanings of the kinds indicated by the determining meaning functions. Thus meanings are always either intentional meanings consisting of experience patterns as intended by agents in using bearers to lead respondents to apprehend what they intend, or dispositional meanings consisting of experience patterns as disposed to be so intended by agents in using bearers, or experience patterns as inferable through causal connections from bearers, or experience patterns as implied by bearers.

If this account of meaning can be developed and defended, it will not, of course, have supplied a set of conjunctive or operational conditions of meaning; but it will have supplied the sort of conditions that presumably the concept of meaning itself initially permits, namely, a limited set of meaning functions satisfiable by a single factor in such fashion as to illuminate the quest for meaning and perhaps eventually to provide foundations for operational accounts. The account has not, however, as yet been either applied to instances or defended. In the next chapter I shall attempt to indicate how it can be worked out with respect to various kinds of meaning situations and in so doing offer some considerations in its defense.

CHAPTER X

EXPERIENCE PATTERNS AND VARIETIES OF MEANING

Since it has presumably been shown that anything can correctly be said to be a meaning as and only as it satisfies one of the major meaning functions, what is required in order to show that meanings are always experience patterns as satisfying one or more of these functions, and never anything else, is to show, with respect to each major meaning function that experience patterns as satisfying that function, and they only, constitute meanings of the variety determined by that function. Accordingly, in the endeavor at the same time to work out more fully than has so far been done the impact of the experience-pattern account of meaning and to support the essential soundness of that account, I shall attempt to show how each of the major meaning functions is satisfied by experience patterns, and by these only, and why each of the corresponding varieties of meaning should be regarded as experience patterns as satisfying the relevant meaning function. More specifically, I shall endeavor to support the following claims: that an intentional meaning is to be thought of as an experience pattern which an agent, in producing a bearer of meaning, intends a respondent to apprehend as what he intends him to apprehend; that a dispositional meaning is an experience pattern which one or more agents is disposed, in certain types of circumstances, to intend his respondent to apprehend as what he intends him to apprehend; that a causal meaning is an experience pattern correctly inferable from a bearer of meaning by way of a casual connection, and that an implicative meaning is an experience pattern logically implied by a bearer of meaning. Since what is possible and wanted in matters of the kind in hand is not proof but reasons and examples supporting the plausibility of the indicated conceptual scheme, I shall, in the pages that follow, attempt with reference to each variety of meaning, not indeed to prove that it must consist of experience patterns satisfying the relevant func-

275

tion, but to give some reasons for thinking that it does and to consider as examples some meanings of some representative bearers of meaning.

1. Intentional Meanings as Intended Experience Patterns

a. Intentional meanings have thus far been characterized by saying that they are whatever satisfies the following function: "X is a meaning of a given bearer in the intentional way if and only if someone, in producing that bearer, intends to lead a respondent to apprehend X as what he intends that respondent to apprehend." If the concept of intentional meaning is to be rendered more revealing than this rather general function suggests, this must be done by determining specific characteristics of that which can satisfy this function. By examination of the actual modes of operation of this function, a number of such characteristics can be readily brought to light.

Although an agent may occasionally, in producing a bearer of meaning, intend to refer to, or focus attention upon, what he intends his respondent to apprehend, what he characteristically intends is rather to elicit, or alert his respondent to, structural meaning factors functioning as parts of logically oriented systems, in order in the process to do certain other things. Among the other things an agent intends to do by alerting his respondent to what he intends him to apprehend are these: referring to, characterizing, and relating things other than what he intends his respondent to apprehend; describing things and events; raising questions and doubts expressing and arousing feelings; amusing people; getting people to believe various things and persuading people to do various things. If what agents intend their respondents to apprehend is, when apprehended, to contribute to these ends, it must not only consist of factors involving their own structures and belonging to logically oriented systems, but also be capable of being instantiated in objects and events. It must in addition be capable of being represented by things, other than either the bearer which lead to its apprehension or the things which instantiate it, that are more or less isomorphic with it, e.g. images, drawings, diagrams, pantomimes, paintings, recordings, symbolic notations, electronic memories, etc. It must also be capable of being elicited by bearers of meaning other than those by which a given agent leads a respondent to apprehend it; for speakers can often put their meanings in other words of their own language or translate what they have said into another language. Since agents intend their respondents to apprehend the same things over and over again by the bearers of meaning that they repeatedly produce, that which a respondent is intended to apprehend must be repeatable. What an agent intends a respondent to apprehend as intended must be in principle such that it can be apprehended in the sense in which meanings can be apprehended and what can be thus apprehended is always a context of actual or possible awareness. Since the agent intends the respondent to apprehend the same meaning that he intends, and since presumably this often occurs, meanings are also sharable and sometimes shared. Finally, since communication is presumably sometimes fully successful, a respondent sometimes fully comprehends what an agent intends him to apprehend.

Of what sort now can that be which can meet the foregoing requirements of whatever satisfies the function by which intentional meanings are defined? Without attempting to review fully all of the answers considered in previous chapters, I wish to consider four kinds of answers that may initially seem plausible: that what agents intend to lead their respondents to apprehend consists of physical objects or events, that it consists of neural traces, that it consists of dispositions, and that it consists of actual experiences.

Can what meets the requirement of what agents intend their respondents to apprehend as intended consist of physical objects? The answer seems plainly negative. Although physical objects and events often stimulate, or are referred to by, bearers of meaning, they are not what people intend in using bearers of meaning to lead their respondents to apprehend. One does not intend, in using bearers of meaning, to elicit physical objects functioning as parts of logically oriented systems, in order to refer to, characterize, or describe other things or to question or express doubts or fears. Physical objects do not belong to logical systems, are not repeatable, and cannot be instantiated. They cannot become contents of awareness or be shared as meanings can. And even under the most favorable circumstances, they are never fully comprehended.

Is it possible then that that which meets the conditions of

being intended to be apprehended as intended is not just any sort of physical object or event but a special kind consisting of neural traces? Again the answer must be negative. Neural traces, however refined, are as much physical objects or events as anything else and hence, as little capable of belonging to logical systems, referring, characterizing, being instantiated, being contents of awareness, or being shared or completely comprehended as any other physical objects or events. To be sure the intending and apprehending of meanings rests upon neural traces, and some of our expressions specifically refer to neural traces. But that our intendings and apprehendings rest upon, and sometimes refer to, neural traces in no way implies that such traces are what they intend or apprehend. Indeed, in most instances, neural traces are far from the thoughts of intending and apprehending respondents; and for most of the centuries through which men have intended and apprehended meanings, neural traces were not known to exist. Even in those relatively rare instances in which we refer to neural traces, the meanings through which we refer to them are not, for reasons already given, these traces themselves but their repeatable forms.

Is what is intended to be apprehended in the production of intentional bearers of meaning some sort of disposition? If dispositions are taken to be physical structures that give rise to certain reliable behavior, the identification of these dispositions is open to the same objections that apply to identification of intentional meanings with any physical objects or events. But if dispositions are interpreted, as they more properly should be, as readinesses to respond in certain ways under favorable circumstances, they still cannot, for fairly obvious reasons most of which have been dealt with in discussing meanings of responses, be what is intended in the manner in question. To be sure, the dispositions that make up their language capacities are involved in the intentions of speakers and in the apprehensions of hearers, and we sometimes specifically refer to these dispositions. But, in speaking, an agent does not ordinarily intend a respondent to apprehend his own or anyone else's dispositions; and, in apprehending a speaker's meaning, a hearer does not ordinarily apprehend his own or anyone else's dispositions. Even when one refers to someone's dispositions, what he intends his respondent to apprehend is not those dispositions as such but patterns by way of which those dispositions are referred to. Particular dispositions are, moreover, not inbedded in logical systems, repeatable, sharable or instantiatable. They are never objects of immediate awareness and are never fully comprehended in any experience.

Are the actual experiences of the agent in producing bearers of meaning what he intends his respondent to apprehend? The answer must again be negative. For one thing, the experience of the agent in producing a bearer of meaning is likely to contain a great deal of detail which is irrelevant to what he intends his respondent to apprehend. Moreover, this experience may, in cases in which the agent attempts to deceive the respondent or to conceal aspects of his experience from the respondent, contain elements that the agent specifically does not intend his respondent to apprehend. However, in addition to these special difficulties, the actual experiences of the agent fail to meet most of the previously indicated requirements of what agents intend respondents to apprehend as so intended. Belonging uniquely to the agent, they cannot be elicited in another to refer, characterize, or do anything else. They do not as such belong to logical systems, are not repeatable or sharable, cannot be instantiated, and cannot be objects of direct or fully comprehending awareness on the part of respondents.

If the most promising alternative candidates for the role of that which agents intend their respondents to apprehend all fail to meet the requirements for this role, to what extent do the experience patterns characterized in the preceding section meet these requirements? I want to suggest that they seem to meet all these requirements and that since the most promising alternatives fail to do so, these experience patterns may be taken to be the only factors that do. The claim that they do meet the requirements in question has substantial backing in what has already been said about them. Experience patterns are repeatable, sharable, and belong to logically oriented systems. They can be objects of direct awareness fully comprehended. They can also be instantiated in physical objects and events. Experience patterns can be represented in diagrams, drawings, paintings, musical scores, and many other things that, without being identical with them, are isomorphic with them in important respects. Agents can, and often do intend to elicit experience patterns, or alert respondents to them, in order to refer to, characterize, or describe things or to question, doubt, or express feelings.

An account of the concept of intentional meanings as experience patterns seems, moreover, to be in accord with the kinds of things we commonly say about intentional meanings. Thus, one speaks of an agent's intended meaning as the idea the agent intended his respondent to grasp or the thought he meant his respondent to apprehend. When a respondent correctly apprehends an agent's meaning, one is likely to say that the respondent gets the agent's idea, grasps his thought, senses the sort of impression he intends; and when a respondent misapprehends an agent's meaning, one is ready to say that while the respondent gets an idea, thought, impressions, etc., which he takes to be intended, it isn't the idea, thought, etc. intended. When communication is successful, one is likely to say that the speaker's idea came through, that the audience was able to get the pattern of feeling that the composer intended, or that the reader was able to get just what the writer was trying to convey. And when communication fails, one is likely to complain that the speaker's idea failed to come through or that what he said failed to convey the pattern of thought he intended. In all such instances attention is focused upon logical content rather than psychological process, and the suggestion of transporting something remains figurative; but the notion of eliciting a pattern intended seems to be basic and, indeed, to represent a constant aim of the whole communicative process.

b. Now that some general reasons have been given for thinking that the concept of intentional meaning is best construed as a concept of experience patterns as intended to be apprehended as so intended, what remains to be done in further elucidation and support of this account of intentional meaning is to consider some examples of meanings of representative bearers of meaning in the intentional way. For this purpose I consider three kinds of bearers of intentional meaning, namely, elemental signals, uttered and written sentences, and works of art. In referring to and describing the experience pattern that seem to constitute the meaning of these and other bearers, I shall need to use words, for words are the most readily available vehicles for reference and description; but the fact that experience patterns are described in words no more reduces them to words than the fact that one speaks of physical objects in words turns such objects into words.

(1) Consider the case of a well-understood elemental signal such as a low whistle which a watcher gives for a group of primitive hunters to signify the approach of a deer. In view of the practical purpose of this signal, one might be tempted to think of the intentional meaning as being the deer itself; but in fact the meaning of the signal would remain the same even if the watcher were mistaken in thinking that a deer was approaching or if he wished to deceive the hunters. Hence, the deer as such can scarcely be any part of the meaning of the whistle. Is the intentional meaning of the whistle then the watcher's experience in the whistle? Scarcely so, for that experience as such remains irrevocably the watcher's own and, though representable to the others, is never actually shared as the intentional meaning is. What the meaning in fact seems to consist of appears rather to be the sort of pattern experientially adumbrated by the watcher and apprehended by the hunters when the whistle is produced. The pattern in question, though simply signalized, is itself complex. It is an assertive experience pattern intended by the watcher to be apprehended by the hunters in order to direct their attention to the approach of an animal having a complex set of specifiable characteristics. Only as the watcher's intending experience at least adumbrates some such patterns does his whistle take on the meaning that it has, and only as the hunters' apprehending experiences adumbrate some such pattern do they get his meaning. Since the case under consideration involves no peculiar features that relevantly distinguish it from other cases, the general character of the meaning involved may be taken as representative of most meanings of simple signals actually produced.

(2) The bearers of meaning through which by far the largest portion of human communication takes place are spoken and written sentences. Although the meanings of such sentences are fundamentally of the same kinds as the meanings of simple signals, the complexity and flexibility of sentences are far greater than those of simple signals. Instead of being, like simple signals, devoid of parts or structural features that have meanings of their own, sentences have both parts and significant structural

features. Most of the parts of sentences carry meanings, and each part and each structural feature contributes in its own way, according to specifiable rules, to the meaning of the whole though the meaning of the whole need be no mere sum of the meanings of the parts. A spoken or written sentence may of course have both intentional and cultural meaning, but it is with the former that I shall be primarily concerned here. With respect to each sentence spoken or written by an agent and each meaningful part or structural feature of each sentence, the intentional meaning as such is directly determined by the intention of the agent; but both the possibility of expressing any meaning by a sentence or by any part of one and the range of the meanings that can be expressed by such an expression are in turn dependent upon natural and cultural factors beyond the direct control of the agent.

According to a traditional doctrine of long standing the principal parts of any sentence are a subject and a predicate. Provided this doctrine is interpreted liberally enough to allow for suppressed subjects and relational predicates, it remains sufficiently sound to serve as a working basis for the remarks on meanings of expressions that are to follow.

The subject expression of a sentence consists nearly always either of some descriptive phrase such as "the man in the blue shirt," some proper name such as "John," some pronominal or demonstrative expression such as "he," "it," or "this," or some combination of these or similar expressions. Expressions actually used as subjects of sentences purport to refer or direct attention to something in order to characterize it. Since the primary function of subject terms is to refer in this sense, one may be inclined to think of the meanings of such expressions as that to which they refer. But such an account of meanings of subject terms has already been seen to be objectionable on a number of grounds. In case what a subject term of a spoken or written sentence purports to refer to does not exist, the attempted reference may indeed fail, and, as Strawson suggests, the sentence may be thought of as neither true nor false; but neither by the failure of the referent to exist nor by that of the sentence to be true or false, is the meaning of the subject expression either abolished or altered. The actual experiences of the intending agent are no better candidates for the roles of meanings of subject expressions in spoken and written sentences than are referents, for what the agent intends to have apprehended is only in exceptional cases his own actual experiences.

The most plausible account of the intentional meanings of subject expressions in actual use is, I suggest, that these meanings are to be found in designative experience patterns intended to refer or direct attention to something that is further characterized in the remainder of the sentence. That subject terms of spoken and written sentences are experience patterns intended to serve this referential purpose is clearer in cases of descriptive phrases than in cases of other kinds of subject terms; for each significant word of a descriptive subject expression is likely progressively to narrow the range of application of that expression in such fashion as to render it increasingly suitable for referential functions. Thus in the subject expression of "The man in the blue shirt is tall," the term "man" adumbrates a pattern of a male human being; the expression "in...shirt" restricts this pattern by way of that of wearing a shirt; the term "blue" narrows the pattern by specifying a color; and the term "the" narrows the pattern so as to make it applicable to a single individual and, taken with contexual factors, focuses the pattern upon the individual referred to.

The manner in which intentional meanings of subject pronouns and demonstrative expressions can be seen to consist of designative experience patterns intended to refer in the sense indicated is only a little less immediately apparent than that in which the meanings of descriptive terms can be seen to consist of experience patterns of this sort. In many instances, pronouns and demonstrative phrases are substitutes for previously occurring descriptive phrases and their meanings are to be found directly in experience patterns that point back to the expressions for which they are substitutes and, indirectly, in experience patterns meant by these prior expressions. In nearly all other instances, the contexts of the uses of pronouns and demonstrative phrases tend to indicate experience patterns more or less sufficient for the references they are designed to make. Thus, if having just now talked about my brother, I go on to say that "he is now living at . . .", though the term "he" in itself directly conveys a relatively uniformative experience pattern, in its actual speech situation the experience pattern constituting its initial meaning points back to expressions, such as "my brother," having as their meanings experience patterns sufficient to establish a reference to my brother. Similarly, if while looking at a certain clear piece of material, I say "This is quartz"; although this term "this" carries directly only a largely formal experience pattern content directing attention to whatever I am looking at, the context of my looking indicates a much richer content which is likely to suffice for the referential purpose in hand.

With regard to proper names, many writers are inclined to deny them any meaning at all; and if one is concerned with conventional meaning in a language, names have indeed very little meaning. However, the present concern is with names in actual use; and names actually used nearly always have a great deal of meaning to the user, else he would be without criteria for using them or expecting others to apprehend his references in using them. The meanings of proper names as actually used are complexes of experience patterns by which a speaker identifies the persons to whom he refers and which he expects his respondent to apprehend and, in so doing, to be able also to identify the persons so designated.

The bearers of meaning constituting the predicative expressions of spoken and written sentences are broadly of two kinds which linguists are learning to distinguish largely by their forms but which for present purposes may be roughly distinguished by their functions. On the one hand, there are predicative expressions, such as "is white," "is running," "is a man," in which an adjective or some other kind of expression is so linked with a subject term by way of an expressed or implied copula as to indicate an attributing of a property to what is referred to by the subject term. On the other hand, there are predicative expressions, such as "is on my right," "is on the floor," "is to the left of the man in the blue shirt," and "is John's brother," which link other expressions designed to refer to something further characterized in the sentence to which they belong by way of relational terms and copulas, with subject expressions. The intentional meanings of predicative expressions of the first kind in actual use are to be construed broadly as experience patterns of the sort that can be instantiated in properties of things or events. Thus, if someone says, "The book is red," the meaning of "is red" is here a pattern of possible experience of the sort that can be instantiated in red things. Similarly, if someone says "John is a man," the meaning of the expression "is a man" is best construed as a pattern of possible experiences such as can be instantiated in human beings.

The intentional meanings of the second kind of predicative bearers of meaning, the relational ones, consist of experience patterns of the sort instantiated in the relations of one thing to another. For example, the meaning of the expression "strikes John," in the sentence "James strikes John," is a complex experience pattern including both an experience pattern instantiated by John and an experience pattern of the sort instantiated when one person is struck by another. The experience patterns constituting meanings of both varieties of predicate expressions differ from those constituting meanings of subject expressions in that, although they may happen to be applicable to single individuals and sometimes contain designative experience patterns, they are not themselves designative and they function, not to pick out or refer to something for further characterization, but rather to characterize what is already picked out or referred to by subject term experience patterns.

Subject and predicate expressions are made up of particular words, many of which may be said to have meanings of their own, but all of which contribute in their own ways to the meanings of whole sentences. However, although the intentional meaning of a particular word in a spoken or written sentence is in the end determined by the intention of the speaker or writer, what the speaker or writer can normally intend by a word is always in considerable measure controlled by the syntactical rules and the vocabulary of his language together with the character of the context of use. I shall, accordingly, defer discussion both of the meanings of various types of meaningful words and of the contributions of syncategorematic words to meanings of sentences until dispositional meanings are under consideration.

Subjects and predicates may contain complex phrases and even subsentences as parts of themselves; and in such cases, the eventuating meanings are complex experience patterns in which the experience patterns of the component phrases or subsentence are components of experience patterns constituting the meanings of the whole sentences. Thus, if someone says "The woman is brave but the man is cowardly," the meaning of the sentence as a whole is a conjunctive experience pattern in which the experience pattern constituting the meaning of the one sentence is added to that constituting the meaning of the other. If someone says, "If John is brave Mary will marry John," the sentence constituting the consequent is linked with the one constituting the meaning of the antecedent to form a complex experience pattern of a sort readily recognizable as conditional. For the meanings of conjunctive and conditional sentences, as well as for other such meanings, one would like to have, and should search for, criteria that are more objective than recognizable experience patterns as such can be; but the fact seems to remain that that for which such criteria are sought consists of experience patterns that have first to be recognized in experience before they can be linked with objective criteria.

Neither sentences nor any of their component parts could possibly have anything like the flexibility they do have nor their meanings anything like the variety, richness, and precision they have if they were merely collections of words. Actually they are collections of words ordered by means of highly complex systems of rules that are mastered by competent users of the language to which they belong and that determine, in large measure, both what orders of words are acceptable and what effects on the meanings of sentences each possible order has. Thus, while the order of the words of a sentence does not by itself have a meaning, it has a very substantial bearing on the character of the experience patterns constituting the meaning of the sentence and the various parts of the sentence. The experience pattern constituting the meaning of "James strikes John" is very different from the one constituting the meaning of "John strikes James," and the one constituting the meaning of "If something is a man, it is an animal" is very different from the one constituting the meaning of "If something is an animal, it is a man."

The focal factors in the intentional meanings of uttered or inscribed sentences may, initially at any rate, best be thought of as what I called in the preceding chapter propositional experience patterns. Such patterns are not propositions construed as sentences or even as ideal sentences or classes of synonymous sentences. They are rather to be construed as the sorts of experience patterns that can be instantiated in facts, in "something's having some property or standing in some specified relation to something else. They are the kind of experience patterns that are exemplified in the contents of someone's thinking, believing, supposing, or pretending that something has some property or stands in some relation. Although their apprehension, formulation, and recognition are facilitated by language and although they become verbally expressible by virtue of the designative, predicative, and syntactical conventions of languages, recognition of them need not depend on language and may contribute as much to language as it gains from language.

That the intentional meanings of sentences are propositional experience patterns by no means implies that propositional experience patterns exhaust the meanings of sentences. Actually, many sentences are questions, commands, requests, or other non-declarative sentences; and while the meanings of all of these can be said to include propositional experience patterns, none of them can be said to be such patterns. For the meanings of sentences to be propositional experience patterns all that is required is that they link predicative experience patterns with designative ones to form complex experience patterns such as may be referred to as thoughts. Such linking of predicative with designative experience patterns occurs in the meanings of suppositions, questions, requests, and the like as well as in those of declarative sentences. This becomes plain when, for example, taking a cue from C. I. Lewis, one formulates the thoughts constituting propositional experience patterns in participial form. Thus the underlying propositional experience pattern common to the meanings of a certain group of related statements, suppositions, questions, commands, requests, etc. is that expressed by "John eating apples." The group in question includes the following: "Suppose John is eating apples," "Is John eating apples?" and "John eating apples, please!"

Since propositional experience patterns thus construed are obviously incomplete in that they are neither assertive nor inquisitive nor imperative, etc. whereas the meanings of uttered and inscribed sentences usually are, it seems clear that there is more to the intentional meanings of uttered and inscribed sentences than has thus far been discussed. The major additional feature indicated by this consideration would seem to consist of experience-pattern frames of assertive, suppositional, inquisitive, and other related kinds, within which propositional experience patterns are to be found. The characters of the required frames, with reference to meanings of particular sentences, are suggested by such factors as word forms, word orders, punctuation, and voice inflection. Sometimes they are indicated by non-verbal contexts and sometimes they can be only guessed at. Many contemporary writers, to be sure, regard the differences between assertions, questions, commands and the like as belonging to speech acts only and not to meanings. But while these differences are in fact differences among speech acts, they are also rooted in differences among the experience patterns constituting the meanings of sentences. Indeed, if they were not to be found here, speech acts themselves could not differ from one another as they do. To perform different speech acts is, among other things, to express different meanings. Thus it seems plausible to say, for example, that the meaning of "John is eating apples" is an assertive propositional experience pattern in which an individual referred to by "John" is represented as eating apples, and that the meaning of "Is John eating apples?" is an otherwise similar propositional experience pattern set within an experience pattern of an inquisitive kind.

Recognition that the core of the meaning of an uttered or inscribed sentence is a propositional experience pattern expressed by the sentence by way of conventions of a language helps to render intelligible the notion of the truth of an assertive sentence, i.e, a statement. A statement is true if and only if the propositional experience pattern constituting its core meaning is instantiated in a fact. More specifically, a statement is true if and only if the experience pattern expressed by the combination of its designative and predicative terms, in its context and in the light of the conventions of the language in which it occurs, is exemplified in a state of affairs in which what is designated by way of the experience patterns expressed by its subject term has properties, or stands in relations, instantiating the experience patterns expressed by its predicate term. The statement that this is square is true if and only if, in the context of the utterance, what is designated by "this" has the property of being equal-sided and rectangular; and that the grass is wet is true if and only if what is designated by the expression "the grass" in the context has the property of having upon its blades droplets of water.

To describe intentional meanings of sentences as experience patterns intended by agents, guided by ordinary meanings of words and principles of grammar, and often instantiated in facts is by no means to say all that needs to be said about such meanings. By way of literal meaning patterns produced in the manner already indicated, figurative meanings that greatly enrich the initial literal ones can be developed. For many utterances and inscriptions, these meanings are quite as important as the more basic literal meanings. Figurative meanings occur in different ways with reference to various sorts of expressions. Not infrequently single words carry as aspects of their cultural meanings suggestions over and above their literal meanings and these as well as the literal meanings are likely to be included in the experience patterns intended by agents. Thus, often when one speaks of something as "dead," or "alive," or "white" or "black," or "smooth" or "rough," he intends to be understood to suggest a good deal more than the basic meanings of these words would signify; and when he speaks of his own or another's "head" or "heart" or "eyes" or "ears," he may well be suggesting much more than is normally intended in the fundamental anatomical meanings of these words. The expression of meanings by way of intentions grounded in conventions but reaching beyond basic conventions is even more evident when one considers certain combinations of words in sentences than when one considers separate words. Such expansion is evident, for example, when one speaks of a "dead metaphor," a "live wire," a "hot potato," a "rotten tomato," a "good egg," or an "egg-head." More to the point for present purposes, however, is the fact that, quite apart from meanings of words or phrases as such, two (or more) objects, events or situations are often so connected by similarity, causality or custom that when one speaks of one such object, event, or situation, experience patterns likely to be instantiated in the other come readily to mind and are intended as one speaks. Thus, for example, many references to doves and palm branches are intended to carry meanings involving the notion of peace. Many references to harps are intended to convey meanings concerning heaven; some references to ripe fruit have sexual import; some references to pens are concerned with literary activity; and some references to swords, with warfare. More extensive narratives relating literally to specific events may, by way of similarities with broader aspects of life, be intended to convey meanings in terms of experience patterns relevant to these broader aspects of life. For example, a celebrated poem about a man lost in a snowstorm appears to be intended to convey a meaning concerning the bewilderment of man; and a play about a woman's search for her long lost dog seems to be intended to signify a hopeless human longing to recapture a lost love. Extensions of meanings usually referred to as metaphorical occur when the meaning of a spoken or written expression unites experience patterns meant by one word or set of words with others meant by another word or set of words in such fashion as to create new meanings. Many combinations of words now commonly in use involving such blended meanings first came into use as live metaphors in this way. Language is constantly being enriched in this manner with new meanings, and the opportunities for saying things never said before are greatly enlarged. The first teacher who referred to a student as a "donkey" was creating a new meaning blended of the meanings of "student" and "donkey"; and the first student who referred to his teacher as a "monster" was creating a new meaning blended of the experience patterns constituting the meaning of "teacher" and those constituting the meaning of "monster." When a poet tells us that "The snow fell as a while veil over the brow of the mountain," his readers are expected not only to apprehend the experience patterns commonly intended to be apprehended by "brow" and "mountain" on the one hand, and by "white veil" and "snow," on the other, but more especially to apprehend in the conjunctions of the established experience patterns newly formed experience patterns constituting the full import of the new expression.

Although the experience patterns constituting intentional meanings of utterances and inscriptions are characteristically mainly cognitive, they frequently include patterns of feelings and volitions. To be sure it is commonly recognized that utterances and inscriptions sometimes refer by way of their meanings to emotions and volitions; but what is not commonly seen, and must now be noted, is that the patterns of emotions belong in a more intimate way to meanings; i.e. they are often important components of the experience patterns that constitute these meanings. To say this is not by any means to say that emotions or volitions themselves enter into meanings. Any such possibility is excluded by the consideration that emotions and volitions themselves are particulars that cannot be shared as meanings are. The meaning of an utterance or inscription is likely to consist of the cognitive experience patterns making up the propositional content that its producer intends to convey; but the patterns of feelings and volition that the producer intends to convey by what he says often prove even more interesting than those of the propositional content, and they are just as much a part of the meaning. Thus ordinary folk, as well as poets, often speak or write about common objects with no mention of any feeling and yet clearly intend to lead their respondents to apprehend certain patterns of feeling. Similarly, writers of personal letters and intimate journals often write of common occurrences with no mention of their own feelings yet all the while intending to convey patterns of their feelings. Again, lovers in speaking of the sights and sounds around them often do so in such fashion as eloquently to convey a sense of the love that prompts them. Indeed, a large part of literature and much of daily conversation is grounded in intent to convey not merely patterns of thought but also patterns of feeling and impulse that people seek to share with their fellows.

(3) Meanings of non-literary works of arts even more than meanings of verbal expressions are likely to be closely connected with feelings, either feelings that artists have in creating their works and intend to stir in their respondents or feelings that respondents have in enjoying works of art. Moreover, there can be little doubt that, on the one hand, artists sometimes do produce their works under the impact of feelings the like of which they hope to stir in respondents or that, on the other hand, respondents often come to have similar feelings. Indeed, an artist may insist that only what he creates under the impact of feeling is worth creating and that only what deeply moves his

respondents has satisfied his purpose. Respondents may also be inclined to say that works of art that leave them unmoved are superficial and fall short of the ends of genuine art.

Nevertheless, it is by no means the case that artists always do their work under the impact of feeling or always intend to create feelings in their respondents even when their subject matter is deeply concerned with feelings. Nor is it true that persons who respond suitably to significant works of art, even when such works are concerned with strong feelings, always respond by having feelings. To be sure significant art involves creativity and often concerns feelings, and both artists and those who fully appreciate art need to have had feelings akin to those with which works of art are concerned. But the creativity required in the artist and the sensitivity, in his respondents do not themselves consist of feeling. Feeling is by no means always present in creation or sensitivity and when it is, it is accompaniment rather than essence. Indeed, feeling sometimes hinders rather than helps the creative and appreciative processes. Both artist and appreciator of art may need to cultivate a certain coolness in order to achieve fully an intended artistic import. Ferruccio Busoni put it perhaps too strongly but with some justification when he writes: "Just as an artist, if he is to move his audience, must never be moved himself—lest he lose, at that moment, his mastery over the material—so the auditor who wants to get the full operatic effect must never regard it as real, if his artistic appreciation is not to be degraded to mere human sympathy."[1]

What needs emphasizing, however, in the present connection, is that whether or not the feelings of an artist or an appreciator of art are aroused and whether or not the artist intends to arouse feelings, the feelings involved are as such no part of the artist's intended meaning. Feelings of artists are as such particular occurrences which can never be directly apprehended by observers nor intended for such apprehension by artists nor shared by artists and observers in the manner in which meanings are. The closet approximation to the sharing of

---

[1] Ferruccio Busoni, *Entwurf Einer neuen Aesthetik der Tonkunst,* quoted from Susanne K. Langer, *Philosophy in a New Key* (New York: New American Library, Second edition, 1948), p. 189.

intends observers to have feelings similar to the ones he has in creating the work of art and succeeds in producing such feelings in an observer. But when this occurs two sets of feelings are feelings that can be achieved through art occurs when the artist involved, those of the artist and those of the observer; each is quite distinct from the other, and each belongs uniquely to the person who has it and is not sharable by the other. What, in the realm of feeling, is intended by the artist, apprehended by the sensitive observer, and shared in the experience of the two is a pattern of feeling. But while the intentional meanings of works of art include patterns of feelings, they include other factors as well.

What seem to constitute the intentional meanings of a work of art are patterns of experience including congitive, affective, and volitional elements intended by the artist to be apprehensible to sensitive observers. Thus a painter in painting sees a vision and seeks to lead others to see it too. A composer in composing apprehends a pattern in the flow of the feeling of men, or perhaps even creates some new pattern never felt before, and intends, in the music he composes, to enable others to apprehend this pattern also. An architect in planning grasps certain satisfying patterns of tension and repose present in some place in nature, or perhaps in part invented by himself, and seeks to make these patterns available to those who see and use his work. If the painter, composer, or architect, having himself been deeply moved in his own experience, seeks by its embodiment, not only to lead others to grasp the pattern that he grasps, but also to be moved as he is moved, this too may be an important part of what he intends; but his intentional meaning lies, not in the emotion that he wishes to produce, but in the patterns he intends to make apprehensible and through which he wishes his respondents to be moved.

2. *Dispositional Meanings as Experience Patterns Disposed to Be Intended*

In discussing dispositional meanings, I shall adopt the same general procedure as in discussing intentional ones. I shall begin by explaining the view of dispositional meanings proposed and

offering some general reasons in support of this view. I shall
then go on to examine the meanings of some representative
bearers of dispositional meaning to determine the extent to
which they conform to the view proposed.

a. In accord with the over-all view of meaning thus far
indicated, I suggest that dispositional meanings are, neither
physical objects or events, nor actual experiences, nor mere
dictionary entries, but experience patterns as satisfying the
function by which the dispositional way of meaning is defined.
Thus, a dispositional meaning of a given bearer of meaning is an
experience pattern such that if someone were to produce that
bearer to lead a respondent to apprehend anything, he would in
all probability intend his respondent to apprehend that
experience pattern. More briefly a dispositional meaning is an
experience pattern that someone is disposed, in using a bearer of
meaning, to intend to lead a respondent to apprehend.

The essential correctness of this account of dispositional
meanings seems to be indicated from the outset by the character
of the initial account of the dispositional way of meaning in
conjunction with the character of intentional meanings as
experience patterns that agents intend to lead respondents to
apprehend. If dispositional meanings are, as they have all along
been said to be, meanings that agents are disposed in producing
bearers to intend to lead respondents to apprehend, and if
intentional meanings are experience patterns that agents intend
in using bearers to lead respondents to apprehend, then
dispositional meanings must be experience patterns that agents
are disposed in using bearers to intend to lead respondents to
apprehend. Moreover, if the view that dispositional meanings are
experience patterns that people are disposed in using bearers to
lead respondents to apprehend follows in the manner indicated
from the character of the dispositional way of meaning and the
character of intentional meanings, then every argument directly
supporting the view that intentional meanings are experience
patterns as intended by agents becomes an argument indirectly
supporting the view that dispositional meanings are experience
patterns as agents are disposed to intend them. If experience
patterns only are such that they can be elicited to refer,
characterize, describe, etc., and if they only are repeatable,
sharable, systematic, representable and suited to direct and

complete apprehension in the manner in which what can be intended to be apprehended as intended must be, then they only can be disposed to be apprehended in the manner in which dispositional meanings must be.

A further general consideration in favor of the interpretation of dispositional meanings as experience patterns as agents are disposed in using bearers to intend to lead respondents to apprehend them, in addition to the sort of considerations previously adduced in favor of the view that intentional meanings are experience patterns as intended to be apprehended, is that dispositions, being readinesses rather than intentional acts, are not likely to be directed to particulars and are even more easily thought of as directed toward repeatables than are intentions themselves. One reason that people are sometimes inclined to think of what is intentionally meant as a physical or psychological existent is that what is intentionally meant becomes a meaning through a particular intention; but since what is dispositionally meant becomes a meaning, not through a particular intention, but through a disposition to intend that is only occasionally exercised, much of the inclination to think of what is intentionally meant as a particular object or event disappears in the case of dispositional meanings, and the view that meanings are patterns of possible experiences becomes more obviously plausible. For example, the word "lavender," the phrase "this rose" and the imperative expression "Go away" are most of the time not in use and hence scarcely likely to have particulars as their meanings; but they remain ready for use when needed, and hence their meanings are even more plausibly regarded as patterns than are the meanings of particular utterances of these expressions.

A still further consideration tending to render an experience-pattern account of dispositional meanings even more plausible than a similar account of intentional meanings is not especially important in its own right but is worth noting in conjunction with the considerations already indicated. It is that, since the bearers of dispositional meanings are usually types rather than tokens, even they must be regarded, not as particular objects or events, but as instantiatable, non-particular forms whose character, not only poses no special difficulty about regarding their meanings as patterns of possible experiences, but actually suggests some such non-particular character for these meanings. Thus, for example, if the type words "red," "man," "cough," and "ugly" must themselves be regarded as patterns ready for suitable occasions, one should scarcely feel too uneasy about regarding their meanings as experience patterns.

Since none of the major considerations that support the account of dispositional meanings as experience patterns as disposed to be intended by agents for apprehension by respondents is dependent upon special features of any of the special modes of dispositional meanings, the claim that dispositional meanings are experience patterns dispositionally intended in the manner indicated may be applied equally to all modes of dispositional meaning. Accordingly, dispositional meanings in the natural mode are experience patterns as all, or nearly all, human beings are disposed to intend to make them apprehensible in using bearers. Dispositional meanings in the cultural mode are experience patterns as members of culture groups are, by virtue of cultural conditioning, disposed to intend to make them apprehensible in using bearers. And dispositional meanings in the personal mode are experience patterns as individuals are, by dispositions peculiar to themselves, disposed to intend to make them apprehensible in using bearers.

b. By way of illustration and in further support of the view that dispositional meanings are experience patterns disposed to be intended in the manner indicated, I shall consider some representative kinds of bearers of meaning having meanings in each of the major modes of dispositional meaning. As illustrative of bearers of meaning in the natural mode of dispositional meaning, I shall consider two simple kinds of gestures. As representative of bearers of meaning in the cultural mode of dispositional meaning, I shall consider words, selected sentences, and some works of art; and as representative of bearers of meaning in the personal mode, I shall consider words in the process of being learned as well as some selected kinds of images.

(1) Although there has been a great deal of speculation and some scientific and quasi scientific inquiry concerning signs and symbols supposedly employed by human beings of all cultures with essentially the same meanings, what is actually known concerning such signs and symbols is extremely limited. I am

accordingly restricting what I have to say to comments upon two very simple kinds of gestures though even here one can scarcely claim to be sure that the meanings in question are universal.

When someone extends his forearm and hand in a certain direction with his forefinger extended in line with his forearm and looks steadfastly in the same direction he seems very likely, regardless of his culture, to be attempting to direct a respondent's attention to some object or event before him. Although the intentional meaning of any instance of this sort of gesture will vary according to the circumstances, the dispositional meaning of the type, i.e. what people are disposed, subject to contextual variations, to mean by it, seems to be just the sort of experience pattern that tends to be depicted in it, namely, a pattern of looking at or attending to an object or event that is before the person who makes the gesture and is in line with his forearm and index finger. The objection may of course be raised that an agent could logically be intending the respondent to attend to something in a direction opposite to the one of his pointing, but in fact this seems rarely to be the case. The further objection may be raised that pointing is always ambiguous in that many things are in the line of pointing, but that a respondent may in a given case fail to select the proper referent does not affect the basic dispositional meaning of the type of gesture. The meaning of the gesture appears to be a pattern so depicted in the gesture itself that people all over the world are ready to come quickly to recognize it and to make use of it even when other avenues of communication are closed to them.

If someone voluntarily falls upon his knees before another person or an image, the likelihood is that he intends to acknowledge superior power of authority in that person or image in at least some respect relevant to the circumstances of his act. The dispositional meaning of this type of gesture seems to be an experience pattern varying somewhat according to the circumstances but in general instantiated in recognition of power or authority. Such an experience pattern seems to be so naturally depicted in the gesture that people in quite different cultures are likely to make use of the gesture apart from intercultural influences. The agent shortens his own stature by comparison with that of another, deprives himself in large part of his capacity for fight or flight, renders himself relatively helpless, and awaits the pleasure of the other. Even when the gesture becomes largely formalized, it does not entirely lose the primitive character of this depicted and readily recognizable experience pattern.

(2) The kinds of words that belong to any language may be many or few depending on what groupings are adopted, and the kinds of groupings suited for one language are not always altogether appropriate for another language. The words that I have chosen to illustrate the character of meanings of words fall within some important groups of which instances seem to be found in most languages, namely, common and abstract nouns, adjectives, transitive verbs, and connectives often characterized as "syncategorematic." With respect to instances of all these groups of words, the meanings will, of course, vary widely according to specifiable kinds of contexts.

The meaning of the common noun "man," in English, in one frequently encountered kind of context, is a schematic experience pattern which speakers of English tend, when they use the term in this kind of context, to intend to lead respondents to apprehend. This pattern excludes inorganic, subhuman, female, non-adult individuals, and applies to male and adult human beings. When speakers use the word in the relevant contexts they tend to experience or adumbrate this schematic pattern, and so do hearers when they hear the word. Similarly, the meaning of the abstract English noun "justice," in many contexts, is an experience pattern such as is instantiated in actions and situations in which one person accords to another what is due him and is such that speakers of English are disposed in using the word to intend their respondents to apprehend this pattern.

The meaning of the English adjective "red," when that word is used of a surface, is a schematic experience pattern exemplifiable in experiences of properties involving a considerable range of shades and hues, experienced or adumbrated in the experiences of agents who use the word in appropriate contexts and in those of respondents who apprehend the meaning of the word, noticed when someone becomes aware of the character of the range of experiences to which the word is applicable, and "instantiatable" in any one of multitudes of colored surfaces. The range of meaning of the word "scarlet" is a schematic experience pattern exemplifiable in some, but by no means all, of the experiences exemplifying the pattern meant by red. The meaning of the adjective "rectangular," is a schematic experience pattern experienceable in experiences of figures bounded by four straight lines and all of the interior angles of which are right angles. It is "instantiatable" in four-sided, right-angled figures of all manner of sizes and varieties. The meaning of the adjective "square" is a schematic experience pattern instantiatable in those of the instantiations of the pattern involved in the meaning of rectangular in which all sides are equal. This schematic pattern also includes no specification concerning sizes.

A meaning of the transitive verb "loves" in English may be any one of many experience patterns depending upon whether its object is a person or a thing, one person or many, a child or an adult, a person of the same sex or one of the opposite sex, whether the context is religious or secular, erotic or non-erotic, personal or impersonal, and upon a variety of other contextual considerations. In a context, e.g., in which the word is applied to a parent's relation to his child, the meaning is a schematic experience pattern of tender feeling and solicitous concern such as is felt by many parents for their children, and adumbrated by other sensitive persons. The meaning of the relational word "above," in contexts in which it is used of spatial relations, is a schematic experience pattern that is experienceable in instances in which one thing is in a certain recognizable position relative to another within a broader spatial frame of reference; it is a pattern instantiated, for example, when one thing more or less in line with another relative to the center of the earth is farther from the center of the earth than that other thing.

In addition to substantives, adjectives, transitive verbs, and other varieties of terms to which experience-pattern meanings can be readily ascribed for various kinds of contexts, there are some words to which such meanings seem to be directly attachable only with considerable difficulty or not at all. Such words, often referred to as "syncategorematic," include, for example, some prepositions such as "of" and "by," the definite and indefinite articles, such quantificational words as "some," "all," "every," and "both," and such logical connectives as "if," "and," "not," and "or." Although it is difficult to specify experience patterns signified by these terms alone, one must not suppose that the break between them and the terms for which such patterns can be specified is altogether sharp or that these terms are in no way connected with such patterns. After all, some substantives, adjectives, and transitive verbs are such that their meanings are difficult to specify, and some words that fall outside these groups and are often classified as syncategorematic are such that experience patterns can without too great difficulty be pointed out as approximating meanings for them. For example, it has proved notoriously difficult to point out the precise experience patterns answering to such adjectives as "good," and it is scarcely likely to be very much more difficult to point out an experience pattern answering to "and." The possible contexts of syncategorematic words are in general much more varied than those for categorematic words, and this creates special problems. But even with reference to instances of words for which experience patterns can not be directly specified, their presence always modifies the meaning of the expressions in which they appear; and by comparing the experience patterns constituting meanings of expressions in which they appear with meanings of expressions in which they do not, one can indirectly arrive at some notions of their contributions to the meanings of the expressions in which they do appear and sometimes even of elemental experience patterns meant by them in certain types of contexts. For example, one meaning of "and" seems to be represented by an experience pattern instantiated in one thing's happening after another. One meaning of "or" seems to be represented in an experience pattern exemplified in one's hesitating between two courses of action. And one meaning of "not" seems to be represented in experience patterns exemplified in one's being prevented from doing or saying something he starts out to do or say.

With regard to all the types of words here considered I have thus far spoken only of those aspects of the experience patterns constituting their meanings that can be experienced as primarily cognitive experiences. However, the experience patterns constituting meanings of many words for nearly all contexts and of some words for selected contexts include also experience patterns that can be experienced in affective and conative experiences. To say this is not to say that either feelings or conations themselves enter into these meanings any more than cognitions themselves enter into these meanings. It is to say that patterns of actual or possible feelings and conations enter, along with patterns of possible cognitions, into meanings of some words, and accordingly that meanings of some words consist of complex experience patterns including both patterns of cognitive experiences and patterns of affective and/or conative ones.

That patterns of non-cognitive experiences sometimes enter into meanings of words is obvious in cases of words mainly used in designating or ascribing feelings and conations; for, otherwise, such words could scarcely perform any such functions. Thus, for example, one can scarcely use or hear such terms as "fear," "afraid," "sadness," "sad," "eagerness," "eager" and the like without experiencing, adumbrating, or apprehending experience patterns that are non-cognitive. But even words not used primarily either to refer to affective or conative attitudes or to ascribe them to anyone nevertheless often include, as part of their meanings, non-cognitive experience patterns. For example, whereas such terms as "jewel," "junk," "fragrant," "stench," "statesman," "rogue," and "rascal" make no reference to, and involve no ascription of, non-cognitive experience patterns; they are neither properly used nor correctly understood unless, in using them and apprehending their meanings, people experience, adumbrate, or apprehend certain non-cognitive attitude patterns dispositionally linked with them in their usual roles in the English language.

As has been repeatedly noted, the meanings of words in a language are always relative to specific kinds of contexts. Among the most crucial kinds of contexts are grammatical ones. Although grammatical contexts do not as such constitute separate bearers of meaning, so crucial are they for the production and understanding of linguistic bearers of meaning that, apart from them, these bearers would be capable of only a fraction of their actual achievements in yielding meanings. Every word in a language carries with it some syntactical principles of its own, having important bearings upon the experience patterns constituting its meaning. Thus, for example, whereas "man" as the initial word in a sentence is very likely to have as its meaning an experience pattern of the sort that we intend in speaking of human beings, the same word preceded by "the" is very likely to have as its meaning the sort of pattern we intend in speaking of a particular male human being. In addition to the special grammar of particular words, every language includes general syntactical principles linked with substantial variations in possible meanings of expressions according to their structures and positions in larger contexts. Indeed so vital is the bearing of grammatical principles upon the shaping of the experience patterns constituting the meanings of most words in any language that every dictionary that discriminates between various meanings of words must indicate both parts of speech and other grammatical features of the uses of words in the course of describing these meanings of words.

Although where cultural meanings of linguistic expressions are concerned interest tends to center upon words, people often want to ascertain the cultural meanings of sentences. This is especially true when the sentences in question have some special political or social significance. But even with respect to less important sentences, one may often wish to know what cultural meaning they have; and it is ultimately in the light of what he takes to be the cultural meaning of his sentences that a speaker tries to express his intended meaning.

In the last analysis, the cultural meaning of any sentence depends on what experience patterns users of the language in which the sentence occurs would be likely to intend, in using it, to lead respondents to apprehend. However, since the number of possible sentences in any language is very great and the number of sentences that may be considered standard is relatively small, the usual approach to the cultural meanings of sentences is not directly by consideration of how whole sentences would be likely to be used but rather constructively by consideration of the vocabulary of the language together with the syntactical principles of the language. Apparently, it is by bringing together learned vocabulary and mastered rules of grammar that competent users of a language produce meaningful spoken and written sentences and respondents understand them; and it is by careful analyses and syntheses of these same factors that students of language interpret sentences. Indeed, by such procedures, it seems to become increasingly possible for students of language to construct meanings for whole sentences in terms of patterns of possible experiences that conform to the patterns that competent users of these sentences can be shown to be disposed to intend in using these sentences.[2]

(3) Although the intentional meanings of works of art are always of special interest, they are by no means the only interesting meanings of works of art. Partly because non-literary works of art do not fully articulate the meanings intended in them and partly because they often endure long after their creators are no longer available to indicate their own intentions, intentional meanings of these works of art are often difficult to ascertain; and, in any case, because artists often express more than they specifically intend, other meanings of these works of art are often even more interesting than intentional ones. Prominent among the non-intentional meanings of works of art are natural meanings, for no work of art is likely deeply to affect human beings without relying directly or indirectly upon links between materials and meanings that are in some degree natural to human beings. But more to the point for present purposes are cultural meanings of works of art which, however grounded in such natural links, are shaped by culturally conditioned dispositions.

Every artist expresses experience patterns that are experienced and adumbrated not only in his own experience but also in that of other participants in his culture. Cultural meanings of non-literary works of art, with respect to a given culture, consist of those experience patterns that gifted persons of that culture would be likely to intend in producing such works and that sensitive persons of that culture would be likely to apprehend in appreciating these works. Special interest always attaches to the cultural meaning of works of art relative to the artist's own age; for that meaning is likely to approximate his own intended meaning and also to disclose the spirit of his age. But because the artist's production may arise from depths which neither he nor his age fully comprehends, succeeding cultures may find in it more than he or his culture fully knew; and the whole import of a work of art may come to light only after

---

[2]Cf. Noam Chomsky, *Aspects of the Theory of Syntax* (Cambridge, Mass.: M.I.T. Press, 1965), Chapters 1 and 3; and Jerrald J. Katz, *The Philosophy of Language* (New York: Harper and Row, 1966), Chapter 4.

many generations have passed. Thus, while a part of the cultural meaning of the Mona Lisa is no doubt disclosed in a Renaissance sense of the mystery of woman, other parts may be disclosed only in growing insights concerning the character of her motives and the power of her intelligence that were at first but dimly felt. Similarly, while some aspects of the cultural meaning of Beethoven's Fifth Symphony are disclosed in patterns of Romantic awareness of man's struggle with his destiny, further aspects of this meaning may be disclosed in new patterns of understanding of man's place in nature that were only vaguely foreshadowed in Beethoven's time.

The manner in which the cultural meaning of a work of art emerges from the component ingredients is very different from the manner in which the cultural meaning of a sentence arises from its parts. In the case of the sentence, the experience patterns that emerge as meanings are largely determined by the grammatical principles involved together with the experience patterns constituting the meanings of the words. However, while the work of art involves principles of technique as ingredient factors having meanings of their own, the experience patterns constituting the meaning of the work are more presented than constructed and they are non-discursive rather than discursive. Each element contributes in its own way to the meaning of the whole, but the elements are put together, not so much by rules, as by creative insight into the nature of the materials and their potentialities for the meaning of the whole. Moreover, the basic materials themselves are richer in natural meaning potential than are the elements from which sentences are built. They are, accordingly, less likely to be fully subordinated to completely foreseen sets of experience patterns, and each makes its own unique, and never completely predictable, contribution to the shaping of the experience patterns constituting meanings of works of art.

(4) Such are the differences in the natures and experiences of different individuals that the meaning which one individual is disposed to intend in producing an utterance, a work of art, or any other kinds of bearer of intentional meaning is often different from the meaning which another individual is disposed to intend in producing a bearer of the same type. For this reason dispositional meanings are often encountered in the

personal mode. The personal dispositional meaning of a bearer of meaning, relative to a given agent, is, as has been previously indicated, a meaning different from the usual cultural meaning of that bearer and such that if that agent were to use that bearer to lead a respondent to apprehend a meaning, he would in all probability use that bearer to lead his respondent to apprehend that meaning.

Meanings in the personal mode of the dispositional way cannot be either physical objects or events or actual experiences for the same reasons that dispositional meanings in the natural and cultural reasons cannot be. They are rather experience patterns which individuals, in partial ignorance or neglect of their cultures, are disposed to intend in using bearers of meaning to lead their respondents to apprehend. The grounds for holding that meanings in the personal mode are experience patterns include all of the grounds for holding that the intentional meanings, from which they are derivative, are experience patterns and most of the grounds for holding that cultural meanings, which are built upon them, are experience patterns. There are, moreover, further considerations giving to the claim that personal meanings are experience patterns some special advantages by comparison with the claims that intentional and cultural meanings are such patterns. Whereas intentions involve actual experiences of a kind with which the experience patterns constituting intentional meanings are often confused, personal dispositions to intend are obviously not actual experiences and so are more readily identified with possible experiences. In like manner, whereas cultural meanings may have considerable stability and can be delineated in dictionaries by the use of synonymous words, with which they are all too readily confused, no such delineations exist for meanings in the personal mode; and these meanings remain the more readily regarded as purely patterns of possible experience which individual persons are disposed to intend in using them.

The most evident examples of dispositional meanings in the personal mode are to be found in meanings which learners of a language are erroneously disposed to attach to words whose cultural meanings they have not yet mastered. These latter meanings are most plausibly regarded as experience patterns, deviating from cultural norms, that learners are disposed in using words to intend to lead their respondents to apprehend. Thus, for a given child, the personal meaning of "man" may consist of experience patterns identical with those involved for him when the word "father" is used; and the personal meaning of the word "cat" may be the same experience patterns that for most people constitute the meaning of the word "animal." Various signs, symbols, and works of art, as well as words, may have personal meanings. Their personal meanings also seem clearly to consist of experience patterns which individuals are disposed, in their own peculiar ways, to intend in using bearers of meaning. Thus an individual may regularly use such a symbol as the World-War II V-for-victory sign intending to indicate an experience pattern of being undecided. Or he may make a sign of the cross to display a pattern of personal annoyance. The dispositional meaning of a certain song for a person may be the set of experience patterns that were present to his experience when first he heard the song, and the meaning that a child is disposed to intend in pointing to a piece of sculpture may be just an experience pattern of the joy of being barefooted.

3. Causal Meanings as Experience Patterns

a. In the chapter on the ways of meaning, a bearer of meaning was said to have a certain causal meaning if and only if that meaning could be correctly inferred by way of a relevant causal connection. A causal meaning of a bearer was accordingly taken to be a meaning that could be correctly derived from that bearer by way of one of its causal connections.

Thinking of such common examples as that clouds mean rain or that thunder means lightning, one may feel inclined to regard causal meanings as things such as raindrops or events such as lightning. Such an account of causal meanings must, however, for at least two reasons, be regarded as mistaken. One such reason hinges directly on the manner in which we use the word "meaning." Although we say that clouds mean rain and that thunder means lightning, we should not ordinarily want to point to the raindrops and say, "There's the meaning of those clouds," or to refer to the lightning and say, "There's the meaning of that thunder." Nor would we, for that matter, point to any other physical object or event caused by, or causing, any other object or event, and say without qualification that the one was the meaning of the other. The most we would want to say in this vein of an object or event whose existence could be causally inferred from another object or event would be that the first object or event was something that disclosed or illustrated a meaning of the second object or event. The other main reason for rejecting the notion that causal meanings are particular things and events causing, or caused by, bearers of causal meaning depends upon the fact that causal meanings are, as has already been shown, not just causes or effects, but rather what can be correctly inferred by way of causes or effects. Raindrops are effects of clouds, and lightning is a cause of thunder; but raindrops themselves are not what is causally inferred from clouds, and lightning is not itself what is causally inferred from thunder. Nor, indeed, is any causing or effected physical object, itself, what is causally inferred from anything.

Useful clues to the character of meanings in the causal way are to be found in the manner in which we actually use the word "meaning" in causal settings and in what we in fact arrive at by causal inference. While we are not ready to say that the meaning of the clouds is the rain itself, we are quite ready to say that the meaning of the clouds is that it will rain; and while we can scarcely say that the meaning of the thunder is the lightning, we are quite ready to say that a meaning of the thunder is that there has been lightning. In like manner, what we causally infer from the clouds is not rain but that it will rain; and what we causally infer from the thunder is not lightning but that there was lightning. Indeed, it seems to be the case quite generally that what we are willing to recognize as a causal meaning and what we claim to infer causally is always expressible in a *that* clause to the effect that something happens, has happened, or will happen. But what all such *that* clauses express is, in accord with the previous account of experience patterns, to be construed as propositional experience patterns in which designative subject experience patterns are linked with relational predicative ones in assertive propositional frames. The conclusion would accordingly seem to be indicated that causal meanings are assertive propositional experience patterns that can be causally inferred from things or events.

b. (1) The most prominent bearers of causal meanings are

natural events, and the meanings of such events appear to be assertive propositional patterns characterizing events causing or caused by them. The clouds mean that it will rain, the thunder means that there has been lightning. The return of the robins means that warmer weather is coming. The continuous sunshine means that the thermometer will rise. The rapid rise of the river means that the town will be flooded. The bearers of causal meaning may be either particular objects or events, or types of objects or events. The corresponding meanings are accordingly either particular propositions descriptive of particular causes or effects or general propositions descriptive of types of causes or effects. Thus, this cloud means that it will rain, and such clouds generally mean that it is likely to rain whenever they appear. Since any event may have many causes and many effects, there is of course no one propositional experience pattern that constitutes the causal meaning of a natural event. Thus, that it will rain may be one meaning of a certain cloud, and that there will be lightning may be another. Effects caused by natural events may of course be psychological as well as physical. Hence, a meaning of the flood may be that the people are in terror, as well as that the town will be flooded; and the return of the robins may mean that the hearts of the people rejoice, as well as that warmer weather is coming. Although causal infererences from events to causal meanings by way of causing or effected events depend on people's actually making these inferences, the inferability of such meanings does not depend upon people's either actually making the inferences or even being ready to make them. To this extent causal meaning may be said to be independent of human activity in a manner in which intentional dispositional ones are not.

(2) Bearers of meanings in the causal way include, in addition to natural objects and events, utterances and inscriptions whose primary meanings are of other sorts. The causal inferences on which the causal meanings of utterances and inscriptions depend often proceed from these utterances and inscriptions, through their causes, to experience patterns instantiated in these causes. Thus, although the primary meaning of the utterance "Here is a red book" is its intentional meaning, the utterance may also have causal meanings at several different levels. At one level, the utterance may mean that certain of the brain cells of the speaker

are activated in a certain way. At another level, a causal meaning of the utterance may be that a red book is visually before the speaker. And at still another level, a causal meaning of the utterance may be that the speaker, knowing his respondent's partiality for red books, wishes the respondent to purchase the book. The inference on which a causal meaning of an utterance or inscription depends may, however, proceed in the opposite direction, from the utterance or inscription, through the effect on the hearer or reader, to an experience pattern characterizing that effect. Thus a causal meaning of one's saying that the book is red may be, on one level, that a hearer's brain cells are affected in a certain manner; on another level, that he will see the red book; and on still another level, that he will purchase the book.

(3) Bearers of meaning in the causal way are often biographical or historical events that combine utterances and overt actions. In such cases meanings may be either experience patterns characterizing causes of these events or experience patterns characterizing effects of these events. Thus Jones's outburst of violence against his wife may either be said to mean that his wife had been nagging him for a long time or be said to mean that the marriage is headed for divorce. Similarly President Kennedy's sending ships of the United States Atlantic fleet to surround Cuba at the time of the missile crisis may be said to have meant either that the United States was determined to keep Russian weapons out of Cuba or be said to have meant that the Russians would abandon their project of supplying Cuba with nuclear weapons.

(4) Bearers of meaning in the casual way may include substantial collections of events such as the life of an individual, an historical epoch, or even the life of man as a whole. Presumably convinced theists take life as a whole to have an intentional meaning which consists in experience patterns characterizing what God intended men to apprehend in his creating the life of man. Even for non-theists, life may have a dispositional meaning which consists in what a reasonable man would intend to make apprehensible if he brought the life of man into being. However, when life is a bearer of meaning, it is with causal meanings that one is likely to be most concerned. Thus, calling attention to experience patterns instantiated in causes of man's life, one may say that a meaning of the life of

man is that a remarkable coincidence of chemical events long ago has made possible the appearance of protein molecules, whose further development has led to the emergence of highly complex organisms, awareness, and rational activity. Or, looking to experience patterns characterizing effects of the present life of man, one may say that man's life means that man has an opportunity to achieve phenomenal mastery over nature and perhaps over himself in the centuries before he either destroys himself or is destroyed by forces of nature.

A feature common to many ascriptions of causal meanings comes to focus in connection with ascriptions of meaning to life, namely, that statements making such ascriptions often have the effect of saying, not merely that life has characterizable causes or consequences, but that these causes are important or good. Recently a well known popular philosopher declared that the state of Israel must survive if life is to have a meaning, and that life must have a meaning. Often people commend life as full of meaning and sometimes they complain that life is without meaning, has lost its meaning, or is "full of sound and fury signifying nothing." Such talk as this is sometimes taken to indicate a new dimension of causal meaning that embraces value in meaning. However, it is more plausibly thought of as adding to ascriptions of causal meanings distinguishable qualifications concerning the importance or value of the causes or effects in which causal meanings are grounded. Its ascriptions of causal meaning are recognitions of intelligible causes or effects, and its added but separable factors are evaluations of those causes and effects. When one says that life, or something else, must have a meaning, what he usually seems basically to be saying is that there are intelligible causes or consequences of life as it now exists and that, moreover, these causes or consequences are of considerable importance or value. And when one complains that life, or something else, is without meaning, what he seems often to be saying is in effect, not just that life is without intelligible causes or consequences, but that life lacks causes or consequences that are of any considerable importance or value. That the valuations thus associated with ascriptions of causal meaning to life and other things and events remain distinct from the underlying ascriptions of causal meaning may readily be seen in the sorts of replies that one would make to questions about his ascriptions of causal meaning to life and other things. For example, if, on the one hand, it were pointed out to a man who praised life for its wealth of meaning that the discernable causes of life were purely mechanical and that the consequences of life were without value, he might still be prepared to say that, though life neither was grounded in nor promised to yield anything of value, it nevertheless had meanings which he would be obliged to reject only if he could be shown that life had no intelligible causes and yielded no intelligible consequences at all. If, on the other hand, it were pointed out to a man who condemned life as being without meaning that life had intelligible causes and consequences, he might be led to acknowledge that, though life had no meaning that was worth commenting upon, it nevertheless had meaning that he could justifiably reject only if he were able to show that life had no intelligible causes or consequences at all. Moreover, the fact that valuations alone, apart from associated ascriptions of causes and effects, do not by themselves constitute ascriptions of meaning is evident in the fact that while we often say that the occurrence of a valued effect that has resulted from an event is the meaning of that event, we never want to say just that the value of any event alone is the meaning of the event.

(5) Works of art may have causal meanings; and these meanings are always basically different from, even when they are similar in content to, intentional and dispositional meanings of the same works. These causal meanings consist of experience patterns characterizing the causes, or effects, at various levels, of works of art. For example, looking, on the one hand, to causes, one may say that the meaning of a gargoyle on a medieval church is that in the Middle Ages the pagan gods of Europe were not quite dead. In the same vein, one may say that a meaning of the brilliant colors and tortuous lines of a Van Gogh painting is that Van Gogh was a man of intense feeling. Picasso finds the meaning of paintings not in isolated canvases, but in "the inner life of the men who painted them."[3] Similarly, Roger Sessions reminds us that great music is rooted in "certain

---

[3]Christian Zervos, "Conversation with Picasso," by Brewster Ghiselin, in Brewster Ghiselin, The Creative Process (New York: New York Library, 1955), pp. 58 and 60.

gestures of the spirit . . ., the energies which animate the psychic life."[4] On the other hand, looking to effects, one may say that a meaning of Watteau's "Clown" is that viewers are likely to feel something of both the joy and the pathos of life and that a meaning of Rodin's "Thinker" is that viewers are likely to feel something of the strength and depth of the spirit of man.

4. Implicative Meanings as Experience Patterns

In the characterization of the ways of meaning in Chapter II, a bearer of meaning was said to have a certain meaning in the implicative way if and only if that bearer implied that meaning, and an implicative meaning was accordingly said to be a meaning implied by a bearer of meaning. Although many things were seen to be sometimes properly said to have implicative meaning, the basic bearers of implicative meaning were said to be assertive propositions; and everything properly said to have an implicative meaning was said either to be itself such a proposition or to have its implicative meaning by way of such a proposition applicable to it. The implication giving implicative meaning to a bearer of meaning was said to be, not mere suggestion, not a "strict implication" by virtue of which a self-contradictory proposition implies any proposition whatever and a necessary proposition is implied by any proposition, and not merely logical implication, but a relation of following or entailment that includes logical connections and other necessary connections as well.

a. I wish now to suggest that implicative meanings are propositional experience patterns as implied in the manner indicated by the propositional factors which are their basic bearers. Three main kinds of general considerations seem to lend support to this suggestion. One has to do with the bearers of implicative meaning; another with the implicative relation; and a third, with the kinds of things we say about implicative meanings.

(1) While objects, events, facts, and situations of many kinds may appropriately be said to mean this or that, the bearers of implicative meanings are, as has been seen, basically always propositional. More specifically, they are propositional experience

---

[4]Roger Sessions, "The Composer and His Message" in *op. cit.,* p. 46.

patterns, for what carries the weight of entailment is not sentences, or even classes of synonymous sentences, but experienceable or thinkable patterns. This in itself does not of course prove that implicative meanings are experience patterns; but it does render that suggestion highly plausible; for from propositional experience patterns, nothing other than propositional experience patterns can plausibly be seen to follow. Moreover, this propositional-experience-pattern character of the bearers of implicative meanings further suggests that implicative meanings have even stronger claims to be regarded as propositional experience patterns than have intentional ones; for if the meanings of intentional bearers of meaning, which bearers may be material objects or events, can be nothing other than propositional experience patterns, then surely meanings of bearers of intentional meaning, which are themselves propositional experience patterns, can scarcely be plausibly thought of as anything other than experience patterns.

(2) That only propositional experience patterns can be implicative meanings would seem to follow from the character of the sort of implicative or entailment relation that links propositional experience patterns with that which is entailed in them. Whatever else entailment may be, it seems to be a logical relation that justifies the ascription of a concept to something on the basis of the applicability of related concepts in entailing propositional patterns. That entailment is properly spoken of as rule-governed in no way alters this fact; for while one may, by selecting the concepts to be considered, vary the rules he wishes to apply, rules of entailment are applicable only insofar as the relation of the concepts involved are as the rules represent them to be. But the ascribability of a concept to something is always, in accord with what has been previously said, a pattern of possible experience of a propositional kind. Hence, what is meant by way of being entailed must presumably always be a propositional experience pattern. By virtue of the character of entailment and the concepts involved, that here is a square means that here is a rectangle, that all men are mortal and Socrates is a man means that Socrates is mortal, that here is a man means that here is an animal. Moreover, that here is a rectangle, that Socrates is mortal, and that here is an animal are all basically propositional experience patterns.

(3) The suggestion that implicative meanings are implied or entailed propositional experience patterns receives additional support when one considers the manner in which one thinks and talks about implicative meanings. One would scarcely ever want to say that some particular tree, book, storm, war, or other such physical object or event as such, or any sadness, sense of well-being, process of thinking or planning, or any other particular mental state or event as such was an implicative meaning of anything. What one would want to say by way of linking such factors with implicative meanings would rather be to the effect that the meaning of . . . . was, for example, that that tree or that book would be seen, or that there would be a storm or a war, or that Jones would be sad or happy, etc.; and all such "that" clauses as these can scarcely be construed in any other way than as expressing propositional experience patterns. When one does mention something other than a propositional experience pattern as though it were an implicative meaning, as when someone says that the meaning of these two couples of apples is four apples or that the meaning of these grapes is food, his manner of speaking seems plainly to be elliptical for statements fully expressed by saying that the meaning of there being twice two apples is that four apples are here and that the meaning of there being grapes here is that there is food here.

b. In order to illustrate and give further support to the suggestion that implicative meanings are to be construed as entailed propositional experience patterns, I shall call attention to examples in which implicative meanings are entailed in a variety of ways. In the first examples implicative meanings follow from given propositions by way of laws of logic.

(1) Although such expressions as "(A and B) implies A," and "[(either A or B) and not A] implies B" are sound formulas for drawing out implications, and although a strong case can be made for saying that their soundness is rooted in their accurate reflection of relations of conceptual experience patterns that can be formulated by them, these expressions are not as such propositional and are to be regarded rather as formulas for arriving at implicative meanings than as themselves ascribing such meanings. However, exemplifications of these formulas may ascribe implicative meanings to certain bearers of meaning, and these meanings are propositional experience patterns as the

following examples suggest. "The Kremlin's being both powerful and severe means that the Kremlin is powerful." "That if the Kremlin is powerful it will suppress revolt, and that it is in fact powerful means that the Kremlin will suppress revolt." "And, that either Smith is unable to do his work or Smith is neglecting his work and that Smith is not unable to do his work, together mean that Smith is neglecting his work."

(2) Whether or not the postulates and principles of inference of mathematics can be reduced to laws of logic, it is just as true of implications based on mathmatics as of those based directly on logic that they are often rightly said to be meant by their premises. These implications also are propositional experience patterns instantiatable in situations involving innumberable effects and events. That here are two couples means that here are four things, and that here are five apples and seven apples means that here are twelve apples. Similarly, that of the flock of 100 sheep, all are safe but the three that were stolen and the seven that were lost in the storm means that ninety are safe; and that the gun fired at an even rate of 1000 rounds per minute means that in a half of a minute the gun had fired 500 rounds.

(3) When certain definitions and laws in science become sufficiently established to be, at least for certain contexts, subject to no further empirical testing, they give rise to meaning connections that can be regarded as implicative, and the meanings to which they give rise have the character of propositional experience patterns. Thus, that the distance traveled by a body is established means that its average velocity depends upon the time. That a given body has a certain mass means that the force required to alter its motion is proportional to that mass. That an action of a certain magnitude occurs means that a reaction of precisely the same magnitude also occurs.

(4) Apart from the implicative meanings of logical, mathematical, and scientific bearers of meaning, all of which depend on more or less formal systems, many commonly expressed propositions have implicative meanings by virtue of conceptual relations that are likely to be deeply embedded in ordinary language. Some of these meanings are closely connected with cultural meanings of key words used in expressing the relevant propositions. For example, that John is a bachelor

means that he has no wife, and that Bess is a mule means that Bess is a hybrid. Some of the connections in question are not contingent solely upon dispositional meanings of key terms but involve other assumptions. Thus that John is a bachelor means that he has no legitimate children and that Bess is a mule means that Fred's mule is not descended from Bess. Other connections yielding implicative meanings depend on relations alleged to be grounded in synthetic *a priori* insights but in any case involving informal entailments of the sort now under consideration. Thus, that here is something colored means that here is something extended, and that this has tone quality means that this has pitch. Still others of the relevant connections are rooted in accepted classifications. Thus, one properly says that Fido's being a dog means that Fido is a mammal, and that this fuselage is aluminum means that this fuselage is metal. Whatever the differences between such cases as the foregoing, all are instances in which a proposition entails a propositional experience pattern; for that John is unmarried, that he has no legitimate children, that Bess is a hybrid, that Fred's mule is not descended from Bess, that here is an extended surface, that this fuselage is metal, and that Fido is a mammal, all constitute propositional experience patterns entailed by the propositions that were said above to entail them.

5. Experience Patterns and Other Factors in Meaning Situations

If the foregoing lines of thought are essentially sound, then, on the one hand, while stimuli, responses, referents, confirmatory conditions, and uses can under favorable circumstances provide empirically operational tests for meanings, they are as such neither equatable with nor capable of adequately disclosing meanings; and, on the other hand, while experience patterns as satisfying meaning functions are equatable with meanings, they provide no operational tests for meanings. The outlook for a quasi objective approach to meanings may not, however, be as gloomy as this situation may suggest. It may well be that the experience patterns in which meanings seem to consist and the other indicated factors in meaning situations are so related to one another that initial insights concerning the former contribute to the selection of those instances of the latter that are most relevant to meanings, and that these instances of the latter, once selected, contribute to the objective confirmation of hypotheses concerning meanings. Much that has already been said about the relations of other factors and meanings indicates that this is so. In the pages that follow I wish to indicate somewhat more explicitly how it is so. That is to say, I wish to indicate briefly how, on the one hand, informal search for meanings construed as experience patterns satisfying the previously indicated meaning functions contributes to the selection of observable stimuli, responses, referents, confirmatory conditions, and uses that are especially pertinent to the disclosure of meanings, and how, on the other hand, once such selections have been made, consideration of these observable factors contributes to the objective confirmation of hypotheses concerning meanings. Since the relevance of the observable factors in question is mainly to intentional and cultural meanings, I shall be primarily concerned here with meanings of these varieties.

a. Although stimuli to utterances and inscriptions can, under favorable conditions, be revealing with regard to the meanings of these utterances and inscriptions, they often contain, as has been previously noted, a great deal that is only remotely relevant to these meanings. So long as no definition of meaning or any independent method of recognition of meaning is available, it is quite impossible to determine what in a stimulus to the production of a bearer of meaning is relevant to the meaning of that bearer and what is not. If, however, intentional meanings of utterances and inscriptions are recognized to be experience patterns that agents intend in producing these utterances and inscriptions to lead respondents to apprehend as intended, it becomes at once evident that a stimulus is, under favorable circumstances, very likely to instantiate an experience pattern intended. When, for example, a person staring intently at a fox says, "Fox," the experience pattern intended is in all probability instantiated in the fox before him. Moreover, by correlating experience patterns intended, and reliably reported to be intended, in the production of certain utterances and inscriptions with observed stimuli to the production of these utterances and inscriptions, very significant principles governing the relations of the experience patterns constituting the meanings of certain utterances and inscriptions can be discerned. Once such principles are firmly established, then, for the limited ranges of instances to which they apply, inquiries concerning stimuli to utterances and inscriptions can yield excellent clues, by way of experience patterns instantiated in them, to meanings of these utterances and inscriptions. Indeed, they may often enable one to predict, without further recourse to introspection or to any parallel line of evidence, just what experience pattern is likely to constitute the intentional meaning of a given utterance, though any such prediction remains subject to confirmation by other tests for the experience pattern actually intended by the producer of the utterance.

By repeated revisions of hypotheses concerning principles of correlations of stimuli and intended experience patterns, it may well be possible to develop a fairly substantial machinery for predicting intentional meanings, and the extent to which such machinery can be developed is well worth exploring. Furthermore, since dispositional meanings are defined by reference to intentional ones, essentially the same considerations that apply to the relations of stimuli and experience patterns constituting intentional meanings can be shown to apply, with appropriate modifications, to the relations of types of stimuli and experience patterns constituting dispositional meanings.

b. The relations between meanings of and responses to bearers of meaning are like those between meanings of and stimuli to bearers of meaning in that while responses are sometimes revealing with reference to meanings, they are sometimes only remotely relevant to meanings. Indeed, responses, even when they are quite relevant to meanings, are a step farther removed from meanings than are stimuli; for between bearers of meaning and responses to them intervene perceptions and interpretations by a respondent. If we knew no more about meanings than that responses, which cannot be identical with them, were sometimes relevant to them, we should have learned little about how to identify meanings; for we should know neither when nor how responses were relevant. However, if meanings to which responses are relevant are experience patterns as intended or disposed to be intended in the ways previously indicated, then it is possible to see of how, and to what extent, responses are relevant to meanings. Since when agents produce utterances, inscriptions, and other bearers of intentional meaning to lead respondents to apprehend certain experience patterns, they do so in the light of considerable experience concerning what is likely to be apprehended, the experience patterns that respondents apprehend may, in many circumstances, be presumed to be those intended by agents. Responses are in turn in substantial measure determined by experience patterns that respondents apprehend, and the responses that respondents make in the light of these experience patterns are likely to be made in accord with ascertainable regularities of human behavior. Hence, within limits, one may reliably infer apprehended experience patterns from total responses, and intended experience patterns from apprehended ones. Moreover, if the intentional meanings of utterances and inscriptions are experience patterns that are all experienceable, experientially adumbratable, and manifestable in other ways than by responses, it becomes possible to establish significant correlations between responses to utterances and inscriptions and experience patterns intended in the production of these utterances and inscriptions.

Substantial inquiry may very profitably be devoted to the establishment of such correlations, and from it considerable advances may be made toward the objective determination of some meanings. When such correlations have been either explicitly established or implicitly recognized, considerable use can be made of responses in determining intentional meanings of utterances or inscriptions or any other kinds of bearers of intentional meaning. Thus, for example, when a plane watcher calls out, "Enemy aircraft approaching from north-northwest," the response of the members of the air squadron, who do not yet see or hear the plane, is much as though planes instantiating the experience patterns intended by the watcher and apprehended by them were already perceived in the distance; and even bystanders unacquainted with English may grasp from these responses the meaning of what has been said. Similarly, when a parent says to a worrisome child, "Go away," and the child goes, the child's instantiation of a significant part of the experience pattern intended in the utterance is often sufficient to disclose that experience pattern even to a person who does not distinctly hear, or could not directly understand, the command.

The relation between dispositional meanings and responses

is such as to render an experience-pattern account of such
meanings quite as useful in identifying responses that are relevant
to these meanings as an experience-pattern account of intentional
meaning is in identifying responses relevant to these meanings;
and the former is even more useful in showing how responses
help to disclose dispositional meanings than an experience pattern
account of intentional meanings is in showing how responses
help to disclose intentional meanings. There are two main reasons
why responses can be even more useful in disclosing experience
patterns dispositionally meant than in disclosing experience
patterns intentionally meant. The first is that the repeated
occurrences by which experience patterns dispositionally meant
gain their dispositional status involve repeated interaction
between agent and respondent that tends to adjust experience
patterns intended to those of associated responses and conversely.
The second reason is that, whereas errors of interpretation based
on responses to bearers of intentional meaning involve relatively
little opportunity for correction, interpretation based on responses
to bearers of dispositional meaning can be repeatedly corrected
owing to the occurrence of repeated responses to repeated
manifestations of the relevant dispositions. If the child or the
linguist is led by someone's response to misjudge the meaning of
a particular statement, his error is likely to go uncorrected; but
if he makes a mistake about the meaning of a word by way of a
response to it, he may well still have many opportunities to correct
his mistake.

  c. One may, as has been earlier shown, know what an
expression refers to without knowing what its intentional meaning
is. But if intentional meanings are experience patterns intended
by agents in producing expressions to be apprehended by
respondents, then it is surely to be expected that experience
patterns so intended by agents in producing referring expressions
will be instantiated in the referents of these expressions. Moreover,
if these experience patterns can in many instances be identified
in other ways, it becomes possible to establish guidelines
concerning the sorts of experience patterns instantiated in referents
of expressions that are likely also to constitute meanings of these
expressions. Through such guidelines, referents of expressions may
become as useful in the disclosure of the experience patterns
meant by expressions as experience patterns are initially in

identifying referents. Thus, when a senator says that the President's procrastination is inexcusable, if one can know what the senator is referring to, he has already gone a long way toward apprehending the experience patterns intended by the senator, even if he did not previously know what "procrastination" meant. Similarly, when a teacher tells a child that the notebook is brown, the child is already on the way toward grasping the experience pattern intended by the teacher's word "notebook" as soon as he knows what the teacher is referring to.

Word types and other expressions constituting bearers of dispositional meaning do not as such refer or have referents; but, being types whose tokens are often used to refer, they may in many instances, as has previously been explained, be appropriately spoken of as in a broad sense "referring expressions." Because the principal function of expressions as referring expressions is to direct attention to referents, the more the experience patterns constituting the dispositional meanings of expressions are equatable with experience patterns prominently instantiated in referents, the more successful they are as referring expressions, and the more useful their referents are for the disclosure of their meanings. Indeed, for this latter purpose, the referents commonly referred to by tokens of type words have an advantage over the particular referents of token expressions as such in that, being repeatedly referred to in various circumstances, they afford ample opportunities for the elimination of mistaken interpretations such as those to which derivations of meanings from single instances are always subject. Because of the frequent equivalence of experience patterns constituting meanings of type expressions and experience patterns prominently instantiated in things and events that these type expressions are commonly used to refer to, it is in very considerable part by way of indicating common referents of words that children are taught meanings of words, that linguists discover them, that dictionary makers define them, and that philosophers seek to analyze them.

d. In discussing in an earlier chapter the role of confirmatory conditions in meaning situations, I pointed out that while such conditions, because of their failure to include certain cognitive, affective, and valuational features of meanings of indicative sentences not reducible to sensible experiences, could not be fully equated with meanings even of these expressions, such confirmatory conditions, nevertheless, constituted experienceable patterns identifiable with certain aspects of the meanings of these expressions. Now that meanings are themselves being interpreted as experience patterns, it becomes clear how such identity can be possible. Since, as has been shown, any meaningful statement concerning a matter of fact involves some indication of experienceable conditions that tend to show it to be true, if it is true, the propositional experience patterns constituting meanings of sentences formulating matters of fact will always include experience patterns which may be expected to be instantiated in situations to which these sentences refer in case these sentences are true; and these latter experience patterns are precisely those that constitute the confirmatory conditions of the sentences in question. Moreover, since any meaningful predicative term must, for reasons previously considered, involve at least some indication of experienceable conditions that would tend to show it to be true of something, in case it is, the experience patterns constituting the meaning of any predicate term will include experience patterns instantiated in anything of which that term is true.

If the range of confirmatory conditions is broadly conceived, as was earlier suggested it should be, to include patterns of some experiences not strictly sensible, the range of the use of confirmatory conditions for testing meanings and even the range of identity of such conditions with important aspects of intentional and dispositional meanings becomes enormous. Thus, not only do the experience-pattern conditions that tend to confirm "My logic book is on my desk," and "Water flows downhill" come to be identical with important aspects of their meanings, but confirmatory experience patterns even for "Mary's hair is lovely," and "That book is worth reading" come to be identical with important aspects of their meanings. Moreover, because confirmatory conditions are identical with certain aspects of meanings of words included in sentences that are not indicative, confirmatory conditions become indirectly relevant to meanings even of these sentences. Thus they become relevant not only to "This is red" but also to "Is this red?" and even "Would that this were red!"

e. Whether uses are thought of as regularities of circumstances, rules, or functions, many features of these uses of the bearers of intentional and dispositional meanings are, as has been seen, only minimally relevant to the meanings of these bearers. When one speaks or writes of times and places, of men and morals, of things and events, only certain selected groups of the circumstances that accompany his speaking tend to be revealing with reference to what he says; all the rest of the vast array of physical and mental features present when he speaks is only remotely relevant. Most rules of rhetoric reveal little of the meanings of the expressions to which they apply, and many rules of syntax are concerned with structures that are largely uninformative concerning meanings. That to place a word at the beginning of a sentence emphasizes it tells us almost nothing about the meaning of a word so placed, and that infinitives are not to be split is little help in disclosing what any infinitive expression means. Even functions of expressions may be unhelpful with respect to their meanings. One does not learn much about the meaning of "detest" by learning that its utterance often serves to relieve pent-up feeling, and one learns little about the meaning of "twelve" by learning that its employment often leads to the satisfaction of curiosity.

However, once intentional meanings are thought of as experience patterns as intended to be apprehended and dispositional meanings as experience patterns as disposed to be intended, then both at the level of ordinary experience and at that of philosophical inquiry, features of use that are largely irrelevant to intentional and dispositional meanings tend to recede into the background, and those that are especially pertinent to meanings tend to come into focus. With reference to Mary's utterance that "the iron is hot," the patterns of all the accompanying circumstances concerning the temperature, arrangement and condition of the room, and concerning Mary's own thoughts and feelings are excluded from primary consideration, and the experience pattern concerning the temperature of the iron that she intends to convey is seen to be directly pertinent to her meaning. Similarly, all the merely rhetorical and formal rules that guided Mary's statement sink into the background and only those indicating experience patterns answering to her words in the given order remain focal. The functions of the statement in relieving Mary's feelings of anxiety, leading her husband to be patient, or warning her children to keep clear of the iron are seen to be only indirectly relevant to the meaning of her utterance, and the relevant function may be seen to be that of leading her listeners to apprehend an experience pattern concerning the condition of the iron.

Moreover, such is the relationship of experience patterns as intended or disposed to be intended in the requisite ways to uses that, once one has learned—as men of common sense and many advocates of use accounts of meaning have learned—which aspects of uses to look for, uses can be more revealing than any of the other factors previously considered, with respect to the experience patterns in which intentional and dispositional meanings consist. A basic reason for the superiority of uses in disclosing the experience patterns constituting intentional and dispositional meanings is that the uses of bearers of such meanings often include that which, with respect to each of the other factors, has proved helpful to this end. Stimuli to the production of utterances are circumstances the patterns of which these utterances are often used to lead respondents to apprehend as intended. Responses to expressions often involve experience patterns that expressions are used to lead respondents to apprehend. Referents of expressions are what expressions are used to refer to by way of patterns that these expressions are used to lead respondents to apprehend. And verifying conditions are conditions the patterns of which expressions are frequently used to lead respondents to expect to find exemplified under suitable conditions.

Among readers who are ready in some sense to link experience patterns with meanings, some will be inclined to say that experience patterns are nevertheless relatively uninformative with reference to meanings; others may be disposed to substitute inquiry into experience patterns for investigation of other avenues of approach to meanings. However, if the foregoing considerations concerning experience patterns and other factors in meaning situations are at all sound, on the one hand, experience patterns, far from being uninformatively added to meaning situations adequately described by way of other factors, are themselves important aspects of meaning situations by way of which what in the other factors is pertinent to meanings is identified. Hence accounts of meaning in terms of experience patterns, instead of being unnecessary, are required for the apprehension of what is focal in meanings as well as for adequate recognition of that which in other accounts is revealing regarding meanings. On the other hand, experience patterns, far from being adequate substitutes for other factors in meaning situations, bring to focus the crucial roles of these other factors including the usefulness of these other factors for identification of many meanings themselves. Hence the experience-pattern approach to meaning, instead of disparaging other approaches, shows how essential such other approaches are in linking inquiry concerning meaning with more objectively oriented scientific investigations.

INDEX